W9-CTW-113

DATE DUE

PITT SERIES IN POLICY AND INSTITUTIONAL STUDIES

THE

HIGHER CIVIL SERVICE

IN

THE UNITED STATES

Quest for Reform

Mark W. Huddleston
AND
William W. Boyer

University of Pittsburgh Press
PITTSBURGH & LONDON

TO OUR STUDENTS

Published by the University of Pittsburgh Press, Pittsburgh, Pa. 15260
Copyright © 1996, University of Pittsburgh Press
All rights reserved
Manufactured in the United States of America
Printed on acid-free paper

Library of Congress Cataloging-in-Publication Data
Huddleston, Mark W.
   The higher civil service in the United States : quest for reform / Mark W. Huddleston
and William W. Boyer.
        p.   cm.
     Includes bibliographical references (p.   ) and index.
     ISBN 0-8229-3906-1 (cl). — ISBN 0-8229-5574-1 (pb)
        1. Civil service reform—United States—History.   2. Civil
   service—United States—Personnel management.   3. Government
   executives—United States.   I. Boyer, William W.   II. Title.
   JK681.H83   1995
   353.006—dc20   95-32780

A CIP catalogue record for this book is available from the Library of Congress and the
British Library.
Eurospan, London

Contents

List of Tables

Preface

In a sense, this book was begun in 1971 when one of us served in the Summer Faculty Program of the Bureau of Executive Manpower of the U.S. Civil Service Commission to study career patterns of federal executives in connection with the bureau's formulation of President Nixon's proposal for a Federal Executive Service.

After President Carter's proposal for the Senior Executive Service became law in 1978, we became faculty colleagues at the Univeristy of Delaware, where each has taught courses and written on public personnel administration. We spent the summer of 1981 together in the nation's capital researching the evolution of the U.S. higher civil service, particularly the genesis of the Senior Executive Service. Since then, the other of us served as a consultant on that service to the U.S. General Accounting Office and Office of Personnel Management and wrote the comprehensive background paper on the development of the U.S. civil service for the published report of the 1987 Twentieth Century Fund Task Force on the Senior Executive Service, entitled *The Government's Managers.*

For permission to draw in part on the substance of the published contributions that one or the other of us has written over the years, we wish to thank the publishers of: the fund's report (Priority Press); *The Civil Service Reform Act of 1978* (University of Pittsburgh Press, 1992); *Public Personnel Management* (Longmans, 1991); *Principles of Public Personnel Administration* (University of Delaware, 1976); *Bureaucracy on Trial* (Bobbs-Merrill, 1964); *Policy Studies Journal* (Winter 1989); *Review of Public Personnel Administration* (Spring 1982); *Political Science Quarterly* (Winter 1982); *Public Personnel Management Journal* (1981); and *Personnel Administration* (November-December 1959).

Many individuals have assisted us in one way or another. Particularly, we wish to acknowledge the late Washington luminary Roger

W. Jones; Edward Schroer, Sally Greenberg, John Howland, and A. J. Mackelprang, former staff members of the Bureau of Executive Manpower; Rosslyn Kleeman and Rachel Hathcock of the General Accounting Office; Bede Bender and Kirke Harper of the Office of Personnel Management; Thomas McFee of the Department of Health and Human Services; and Ron Chernow, formerly of the Twentieth Century Fund.

We should like to add that, despite all the assistance we have received, we alone are responsible for the contents of this study.

THE HIGHER CIVIL SERVICE IN THE UNITED STATES

Introduction

On January 20, 1993, Bill Clinton was inaugurated as the forty-second president of the United States, the first Democrat to hold the office in twelve years. Indeed, with the exception of Jimmy Carter's brief interregnum in the 1970s, Republicans had held the presidency for almost a quarter of a century.

By the rules of America's political game, this was a problem for Clinton. For virtually an entire generation, Republicans had been the party of government, creating a deep pool of talent and experience. While Democrats gazed wistfully at the parapets of executive power from their desks in law firms and think tanks, the men and women who actually managed the federal government on a day-to-day basis—the agency directors, bureau chiefs, assistant secretaries, and other top political leaders—had been Republicans or at least had been designated by and presumably loyal to Republicans. It was not surprising, then, that the new president was slow in finding candidates to fill the nearly three thousand positions deemed political appointments. Nor was it surprising that so many of his early, most serious gaffes—finding an acceptable attorney general and handling the flap over Lani Guinier, his initial designee for head of the Justice Department's Civil Rights Division—turned on personnel questions. Not only was the president himself an outsider, but in addition, his staff was young, inexperienced, and by necessity drawn from beyond the corridors of government.

We say "by the rules of America's political game" because that is how the system works: Every four years, or at least every time the control of the presidency is passed from one party to another, far more than a president or vice president changes. Far more, indeed, than a dozen or so cabinet members and a few score advisors change. In fact, the entire top layer of the executive branch changes. Thousands of men and women take down their pictures, empty their desks, and move back to private life, just as others dust off their pictures and move in, in a rite of passage almost as old as the Republic.

In one sense the reason for this mass migration is clear. Democracy demands it. When the people speak at the ballot box, they expect their elected officials to respond. How better for a president to act on his mandate than by appointing *his* people to key positions of authority in the executive branch?

How better, indeed. The fact is that the United States is virtually alone in the world in operating by these rules. In almost every other country, certainly in every other advanced democracy, transitions from one party to another are painless experiences, at least in terms of the functioning of government. There are no mass migrations. The reason is that except for the elected officials themselves and a handful of top aides in each department, government is managed by permanent professionals—by, that is to say, higher civil servants.

This book is the story of America's efforts—largely frustrated—to develop a higher civil service. It is, if you will, the story behind the story of Bill Clinton's difficult first months as president. We discuss, in turn, the post–World War II creation of the supergrades, the Eisenhower administration's proposed Senior Civil Service, the Executive Assignment System of the Kennedy-Johnson years, and President Nixon's effort to build a Federal Executive Service. And we devote three chapters to an analysis of the Senior Executive Service, which is the system now in place for managing senior career executives.

We conclude that the highly politicized U.S. system of higher administration has not worked. It has failed presidents. And more important, it has failed the American people.

Before we begin this story, however, we need to set the stage. To understand U.S. administration, it helps to have a broader context, to gain some historical and comparative perspective. Such is the purpose of our first chapter.

CHAPTER I

Bureaucratic Elites in History

Those who hold top career administrative posts in most governments throughout the world are selected through highly competitive examinations. They form a prestigious cadre to which a nation's highest achievers aspire. Indeed, at the core of most developed—and many developing—political systems is a bureaucracy headed by a "higher civil service," which we define as *an elite corps of career public officials who fill key positions in governmental administration.* Even militarily dominated polities often depend on a higher civil service at the apex of their administrative structures. Most of the highest civil servants are generalists, but technological developments have speeded their decline and the rise of specialists among them.

In the United States, even a nominal higher civil service was not authorized until the Senior Executive Service was created by the Civil Service Reform Act of 1978, long after most countries formed such a system. In this chapter, we trace the historical evolution elsewhere of higher civil service systems both to determine their influence on the United States and to understand better the peculiarities of the U.S. system.

A WESTERN PHENOMENON?

The emergence of public administration and its higher civil service systems, according to prominent students, is almost completely a Western phenomenon.

After castigating political scientists as giving "very slight attention to the history and development of governmental institutions," Dwight Waldo ascribes influences on the development of public administration to Rome and to the industrial revolution "centered in the United States and Western Europe."[1] Similarly, Brian Chapman begins with the "Roman State."[2] And Joseph LaPalombara flatly states that "the system of public administration we denominate bureaucracy is in fact an invention of the West and that reasonably pure examples of it are not to be found before the seventeenth century."[3] Although Ferrel Heady, in his comparative study of higher civil bureaucracies, cursorily acknowledges that imperial China's civil service "exercised great influence on the development of modern civil service systems in the West," he fails to explain any historical connections; and he asserts that the Mediterranean basin areas most influenced Western Europe.[4] Similarly, although Lawrence Herson advised that "administrative theory might do well to examine the administrative system of Imperial China," he did not mention any Chinese influence on Western bureaucracies.[5]

It is no accident that Mattei Dogan in the title of his book on top civil servants in Europe refers to them as the "Western Mandarins," and characterizes them as follows: "The top civil servant who plays an important political role has a hybrid personality: half-political, half-administrative. Like Janus the Roman god, he has two faces. He is a kin to the mandarins of old Imperial China."[6] But there the linkage ends, as no other reference to China is made by Dogan.

John Armstrong's book on Europe's administrative elite makes no mention of Chinese influence.[7] Rupert Wilkinson's comparative study of Britain's and imperial China's elites draws many parallels between Confucian China's educational and examination systems, and its emphasis on an administrative class of generalists (mandarins), and those of Victorian England and its "gentleman-amateur ideal." But Wilkinson stops short of attributing such similarities to Chinese influence.[8]

IMPERIAL CHINESE ROOTS

It is our contention that, with few exceptions, Western scholars have given inadequate attention to evidence of Chinese roots of most of the extant higher civil service systems in the world. There is abundant evidence of such Chinese influence which has been generally neglected by Western scholars. We contend that knowledge of imperial China's mandarin system was diffused over time by foreigners to form a basis for adaptation and development of administrative elite systems elsewhere in the world.

It is true that the feature of competitive examinations in the civil service system of the United States was influenced mostly by Britain, but the British civil service was rooted in China. In a lecture delivered in 1921, Dr. Sun Yat-sen stated:

> Regarding the history of the examination system, England instituted the civil service examination system . . . early. In America, civil service examination is only about twenty to thirty years old. At present, the civil service examinations in the [Western] nations are copied largely from England. *But when we trace the history further, we find that the civil service system of England was copied from China.* We have very good reason to believe that the Chinese examination system was the earliest and the most elaborate system in the world.[9]

The Chinese bureaucracy was far more developed than that of the Roman Empire or any comparable state (e.g., ancient Egypt or Byzantium) before modern times. There is no certain answer to the question of why the Chinese Empire perdured, but not the Roman Empire. One reason may have been that China's bureaucratic ideal, institutionalized through the civil service examinations designed to produce moral and scholarly men trained in the classics and good government, may have provided a more enduring cohesion than did the Roman ideal of rule through impersonal law.[10] In any event, Max Weber's description of Chinese bureaucracy as "patrimonial" or "prebendal" is contradicted by the fact that Weber's stated characteristics of modern bureaucracy were already fully developed in China by the time of the Han rulers (202 B.C.–A.D. 221). Indeed, China was "an outstanding example of the managerial state in practice. . . . Confucian China evolved much that has entered the common heritage of personnel administration in the modern state."[11]

In fact, China was the first country to open competitive examinations for the public service, which date as early as 2200 B.C., as witness this passage from the Canon of Shun: "Every three years there was an examination of merits, and after three examinations the undeserving were degraded, and the deserving promoted. By this arrangement the duties of all departments were fully discharged."[12] Harry Krantz has described this development:

> Four thousand years before the French named it, Max Weber defined it, or the British refined it, the Chinese invented bureaucracy and elaborate competitive examinations to select government personnel. . . . As early as 2200 B.C., the Chinese emperor examined his officials every third year to determine their fitness for continuing in office. After three such oral exams, officials were either promoted or dismissed.
>
> By 1115 B.C., there were both oral and performance entrance exams. During the Han dynasty (202 B.C.–A.D. 221), a Chinese invented paper, and written examinations were developed to test candidates. Although the "merit principle" was established during the Han dynasty, it was not until the Teng dynasty (A.D. 690) that the selection system was fully developed. By A.D. 1370, the system took final form, and after that year the mandarins achieved a monopoly of public office. Not only were all Chinese civil servants recruited from their midst, but even their rank depended on the number of examinations they had successfully passed.[13]

Descriptions by foreigners of imperial China's higher bureaucracy and examination system are well documented and were widely read in the Western nations, from the establishment of Macao by the Portuguese about 1585 and thereafter.[14]

In his definitive 1943 article about the Chinese influence on the Western examination system, which should be read by all Western scholars of public administration, Ssu-yu Teng researched more than seventy works or articles describing the Chinese examination system, mostly available in English and published in the West between 1570 and 1870. "In the light of all this contemporary evidence," he concluded, "there can remain no doubt that the Chinese system of examinations for government positions was responsible for the introduction of similar systems into Western Europe . . . adapted by each individual government to fit national characteristics."[15] At about the same time, Y. Z. Chang independently arrived at the same conclusion:

> The evidence, summarized, indicates (1) that the Chinese examination system was well known in England; (2) that in the periodical

literature and the parliamentary debates of the times the idea of the competitive examination was linked with China; (3) that both in and out of parliament the assertion was made that the examination system was a Chinese institution and no denial was ever made; and (4) that no country other than China had previously made use of a system of competitive civil service examinations.... Surely, a measure of Chinese influence must be admitted upon the basis of this evidence.[16]

THE BRITISH ADMINISTRATIVE CLASS

The British East India Company, chartered in 1600, became active in India from 1623 and in China from 1699. The company introduced civil service examinations on a limited basis for India in 1829, and in time it was responsible for the "full development in India of this Chinese invention,"[17] which was then applied to the Home Service in Britain and the establishment of its elite "administrative class" of generalists.

The salient officials in the Indian colonial administration of the nineteenth century were the district officers, described by Woodruff as "Platonic guardians,"[18] whose virtuous exercise of their generalist responsibilities, reminiscent of the Chinese mandarins, served as the " 'all-rounder' role definition to be inculcated in the British educational system" and in the administrative class of Britain's Home Service.[19] Indeed, the term *civil service* originated in the East India Company, whose officers were called civil servants to differentiate them from military and ecclesiastical employees.[20]

The most persistent advocate of British adoption of the Chinese examination system was Britain's consul in Canton, China, Thomas Taylor Meadows, whose 1847 book warned that "England will certainly lose every colony she possesses unless she adopts some system of impartial elevation of colonists to the posts and honors at the disposal of the crown."[21]

Although many district officers and other East India Company officers in India had attended the company's college established in 1806 at Haileybury, near London, the company did not introduce civil service examinations for India until 1829, and then only for those who had not attended Haileybury. Meanwhile, admission into the

9

civil service in Britain was purely a matter of patronage. Adam Smith and Jeremy Bentham, among others, called for open competitive examinations.

In 1853, Sir Charles Trevelyan and Sir Stafford Northcote issued their famous report on the civil service which laid the foundation of Britain's civil service examinations. Trevelyan had attended Haileybury and had served in the East India Company in India, as had Northcote's grandfather. Moreover, Trevelyan's brother-in-law was Lord Macauley, and the two were known to have discussed in India the efficacy of competitive examinations for the Indian Civil Service. The Macauley Report of 1854 advocated examinations for the civil servants of the East India Company "to be confined to those branches of knowledge to which it is desirable that English gentlemen . . . should pay some attention"—history, jurisprudence, finance and commerce, and languages—a considerable number of whom "should be men who have taken the first degree in arts at Oxford or Cambridge."[22]

These proposals were clearly similar to the principles of the examinations in the classics by which imperial China's mandarins were selected. The parliamentary debates included many references to the influence of the Chinese mandarin system on the civil service examinations proposed by the Northcote-Trevelyan Report and the Macauley Report.[23] The two reports in retrospect are often considered together, for they laid the foundation for Britain's administrative class and the diffusion of a model of a higher civil service throughout the world.

The Macauley Report was implemented almost immediately, with the closing of Haileybury College and the recruitment and examination of mainly Oxford and Cambridge graduates for service in India. After the Sepoy Mutiny of 1857–58 led to the replacement in India of company rule with Crown rule, "Oxbridge" recruits were to dominate British civil service "probationers" in India and later in the Home Service. The substance of the Northcote-Trevelyan Report was implemented by the Order in Council of June 4, 1870, which made open competition the normal mode of entry into the Home

Service, with compulsory examinations for admission to all departments.[24]

During most of its history since 1870, the British civil service was divided into three major classes—administrative, executive, and clerical—in descending order of responsibilities and qualifications. In 1968 the elite administrative class comprised fewer than 3,000 members, or less than 0.5 percent of the total civil service. They were directly responsible to political officials for policy initiation and implementation. Although these three classes were unified in 1971 into a new administrative category as part of a system of occupational groupings, as recommended earlier by the Fulton Committee Report of 1968, the essential features and structure of the elite higher civil service nevertheless remain. A small select cadre continues to dominate policy, although it is no longer identified as a separate administrative class.[25]

It is true that the Fulton Committee strenuously attacked "the cult of the generalist" that was based on the Northcote-Trevelyan and Macauley reports. The British generalist tradition remains intact, however, to the extent that a "disproportionate number of entrants to the higher civil service come from . . . public schools and 'Oxbridge,' " who "despite Fulton . . . continue to be drawn from a narrow social and educational stratum."[26] It is uncertain to what extent they remain a group of gentlemen selected on the basis of the philosophy of the "amateur," "all-rounder," or gifted layman who, allegedly, "moving from job to job . . . can take a practical view of any problem, irrespective of the subject-matter."[27] It is certain, however, that the top civil servant is still much more a generalist than a specialist, for "if the new administrator turns out not quite to fit the old model of the 'talented amateur,' it is even less likely that he will fit the model of the 'narrow specialist.' "[28]

DIFFUSION TO COMMONWEALTH ELITES

The Macauley Report predicted that "the examinations for situations in the civil service of the East India Company will produce an effect which will be felt . . . throughout the realm."[29] As a result, vestiges of imperial China's mandarin system became institutionalized not only in India and Britain itself, but also among the colonies of the British Empire. Within the contemporary Commonwealth of Nations, spanning six continents, the essence of higher civil service systems still exists: in Asia (e.g., Malaysia, Singapore, Bangladesh, Pakistan, Sri Lanka); in Africa (e.g., Nigeria, Kenya, Botswana); and in the Western Hemisphere (e.g., Jamaica, Barbados, Trinidad, Guyana). Each nation has adapted, modified, or recast its British-inherited administrative system according to its own peculiar circumstances. Although British-type parliamentary control of administration with ministerial responsibility is typical in Commonwealth nations, the elitist elements of British administration have been diluted or rejected in Australia, New Zealand, and Canada, "where there was a premium on specialists and professionals in administration and no particular need for the gentleman-amateur."[30]

The image of the colonial administrator as a high and haughty Platonic guardian or mandarin, keeping order and performing routine services by deploying instruments of authority toward a passive and compliant public, from which he maintains an appropriate social distance, appeared archaic and antithetical to development administration. Nevertheless, "many administration similarities do exist between Britain and those nations once under British rule,"[31] and paramount among these is the perdurance of a higher civil service system, generally comprised of a cadre of administrators, to which admission is gained through competitive examinations, marked by rank in the person rather than rank in the job.

Another similarity is the struggle for power between the professional or specialist and the generalist within the Commonwealth nations. The British tradition of placing the generalist on top was based in part on the assumption of the gentleman ethic. Although the importance of generalist skills in multivalued policy making are still recognized, the role of the specialist as in post-Fulton Britain is accorded greater balance in Commonwealth administrative systems.[32]

DIFFUSION TO THE PACIFIC RIM

Higher civil service systems in many Asian countries owe much to the influence of Western colonialism (e.g., British, French), which in turn was influenced by imperial China's examination and mandarin system. That system's influence was more direct on so-called Pacific Rim countries.

The People's Republic of China

It is a paradox of sorts that China should have rejected so completely the mandarin system it had founded,[33] for Mao Zedong was committed to erasing elitism in the People's Republic of China by destroying the traditional social system and political hierarchy and replacing it with an egalitarian socialist system. Accordingly, as in other communist-ruled countries, two bureaucratic hierarchies were created: one for the party and the other for the government, with the party bureaucracy ("reds") controlling the government bureaucracy ("experts"). However, at the top of the two hierarchies of party and state there was a complete overlap of personnel; all of the members of the State Council—responsible for both policy making and implementation—were also high-level party members.[34]

Since its inception, the People's Republic of China has wrestled with the issue of the authority of reds versus that of experts, the Cultural Revolution (1966–1976) representing the zenith of red power. If the ideological component is subtracted, then red versus expert becomes in essence an issue of generalists versus specialists not wholly unlike that vexing other political systems. In Mao's China, reds (generalists) sought to dominate and control experts (specialists).

> Party intervention in the administrative process had been a recurring tendency in China. In theory, the Party should avoid becoming bogged down in administrative tasks and should instead maintain itself as a distinct elite of dedicated generalists in government administration. But, in practice, the Party had been repeatedly unable to resist the temptation to intervene in government administration and take over the responsibility of running things itself.[35]

By assuring party control over the bureaucracy, Mao in a sense had created a new class of generalists to replace the mandarins of old China. But after Mao's death in 1976, China's new leader, Deng Xiaopeng, advocated in a 1980 speech the professionalization of the bureaucracy. "From now on, in the selection of cadres we should pay special attention to expert knowledge. . . . Unless we do so, we cannot proceed with modernization."[36]

South Korea

The Chinese examination and mandarin system was replicated in Korea during the Yi dynasty (A.D. 1392–1910).[37] Although favor has tended to replace merit since World War II in the recruitment of many South Korean administrators,[38] an elite corps of higher civil servants continues to exist and is marked prominently by graduates of Seoul National University, especially law graduates.[39] The higher civil service comprises "the relatively permanent top group of civil servants" between the political appointees and the rank-and-file civilian bureaucracy.[40] Between 1960 and 1980, only 2.5 percent of those examined passed the higher civil service examination, and only about half of that percentage passed in 1981–1982.[41]

Japan

Similarly, Japan's bureaucratic elite (*kanryo*) comprises some twenty-five hundred senior administrators plus seventy-five hundred future successors in lower positions, described in 1988 as follows:

> The "kanryo" has occupied most key administrative positions and has been reinforced by as many as 400-odd new recruits every year through the highly competitive open entrance examination at the senior level. Most of these recruits have graduated in law from recognized universities, Tokyo University in particular, and have been recruited and trained primarily by the ministry or agency to which they belonged at the start of their career. They are called the "career class," a core group among the national civil service, and are given a combination of training and development programs, including a wide range of job rotations, interministerial off-the-job training and study abroad. The work they are given usually relates to policy formulation and subsequent coordination. The objective has been to develop administrative generalists.[42]

In Japan, too, the dominance of the generalist (*jimukan*) and the subservience of the specialist (*gikan*) is stirring controversy. "Indeed, the *jimukan* view of his *gikan* colleague is reminiscent of the attitudes held by the Confucian official in traditional China towards 'mere specialists.' "[43]

DIFFUSION TO WESTERN EUROPE

Most higher civil service systems in Continental Western Europe are variants of those of unitary France or federated Germany, which Ferrel Heady labels as classic administrative systems because they conform most closely to Max Weber's classic bureaucratic theory.[44]

France

The influence of imperial China's civil service examinations on France is also well documented in the research of Ssu-yu Teng. Teng cited Voltaire and others. "If there has ever been a state in which the life, honor, and the welfare of the people have been protected by law, it is the empire of China," wrote Voltaire. And he added: "The human mind certainly cannot imagine a government better than this one . . . of which the members are received only after several severe examinations." Similarly, Teng relied on the works of Montesquieu, Diderot, Quesnay, Brunetière, and others in concluding "that the French civil service examination system came from China." For example,

> Brunetière . . . wrote that the physiocrats were united in the attempt to introduce "l'esprit chinois" into France. Brunetière believed that French education was really based on the Chinese principle of competitive literary examinations, and the idea of a civil service recruited by competitive examinations undoubtedly owed its origin to the Chinese system which was popularized in France by the philosophers, especially Voltaire.[45]

Among the distinguishing features of the higher civil service system of modern France is its highly institutionalized recruitment based on class and merit and its training marked by the existence of *grandes écoles*, principally the École Nationale d'Administration, created in 1945 to serve as a bulwark against political instability by assuring the continuity of the state. "In no other country does a set of institutions exist for the purpose of creating a higher civil service elite in quite the same way as in France,"—institutions that shape "the entire world of the civil servant."[46]

The French higher civil service comprises two complementary elites, the *grand corps* on the administrative side and the *polytechniciens*, the top technical corps. Each is rigorously selected and highly trained, and because the latter's training includes economics and management, the two elites have common ground on which to meet. Accordingly, generalist/specialist conflicts are avoided.[47]

Some variant of France's prefectoral system is observable in many parts of the world. In its pure form this system commonly means, according to James Fesler, "a single set of administrative areas each headed by a single national official—prefect, provincial governor, or district commissioner—with authority and responsibility for all national functions in his area." Concerning the diffusion of this generalist model of higher civil servants, Fesler adds:

> The Napoleonic system of prefects has been widely copied, partly because it was imposed by Napoleon on conquered countries which, once free of the yoke, simply retained the prefectoral system, partly because France later introduced the system in new colonies, and partly because France has long exercised considerable intellectual influence on countries of the Middle East and Latin America. Copying of the Napoleonic system has also, of course, been attractive to rulers of countries having the characteristic predisposition to authoritarian patterns.[48]

The German Federal Republic

Given the historical background of the German bureaucracy, with its Prussian antecedents, one would expect that higher civil servants in Germany would conform closely to the model of the classical Weberian bureaucrat, which accurately describes many but not all German bureaucrats. Most are law graduates and are legalistic in orientation. Although not as elitist as their French counterparts, most are generalists and comprise a corps of top administrators whose status and prestige as members of the *Beamte* set them apart. Heady describes them:

> The *Beamte* in the higher civil service continue to characterize the West German bureaucracy, but they no longer receive the special deference and respect accorded to them in the past. . . . Recruitment to the higher civil service is on a career basis, with a high proportion of the recruits coming from families of former civil ser-

vants. During their careers, these recruits are expected to be prepared for assignment to positions covering a wide variety of duties, particularly in the functional category of general administration.[49]

THE UNITED STATES OF AMERICA

We now address the initial civil service experience of the United States and the influence on it of other countries. Van Riper found no indication that foreign civil service experience made any impression in the United States prior to 1860.[50] In 1862, U.S. Consul John Bigelow recommended from Paris the U.S. adoption of the French method for examining tax collectors. Bigelow's statement was reprinted in the 1868 Congressional report on the civil service systems of China, Prussia, France, and Britain.[51]

Under an act of 1871, President Ulysses Grant appointed a seven-member civil service commission to initiate reform that helped prepare the ground for what later was to be accomplished under the Pendleton Act of 1883. In its 1874 report to President Grant, the short-lived (1871–1875) Grant Commission took special note of China's experience, including the observation that "Confucius had taught political morality, and the people of China had read books, used the compass, gunpowder, and the multiplication table, during centuries when this continent was a wilderness." But most important, "the most enlightened and enduring government of the Eastern world had required an examination as to the merits of candidates for office," a benefit that should not be denied the American people. The Commission added that it "looked especially into the political history of England, which had profited by these methods."[52]

Although Ssu-yu Teng found other "fragmentary material indicative of direct Chinese influence on the United States civil service,"[53] most contemporary references in the United States to foreign experience, especially after 1870, were to British documents—including the Northcote-Trevelyan and Macauley reports—and to British experience.

In the Pendleton Act of 1883, which launched the U.S. civil service system, the central concept adapted from the British was that of competitive examinations. Other concepts adapted from the British were relative security of tenure and political neutrality.

On the other hand, as President Arthur commented, "there are certain features of the British system which have not generally been received with favor in this country, even among the foremost advocates of civil service reform."[54] One of these rejected features was tests consisting of academic essays; instead, the Pendleton Act explicitly directed that tests be "practical in character." Another significant British feature rejected by the United States was the system's closed character—it was normally closed to outsiders except at the bottom; from the start the U.S. system was to permit lateral entry at almost any level.

The rejection of these two features was to have fundamentally systemic consequences for the U.S. civil service, because "practical" tests were to assure a system dominated by specialists rather than generalists, and an open system was to ordain a permeable civil service devoid of a separate administrative elite—a far more representative bureaucracy than one closed to outsiders.

THE U.S. SYSTEM COMPARED

The essential characteristics of the federal career executive system in the United States, therefore, are radically different from the generalist/elite tradition of Great Britain and many other countries.

Frederick Mosher has distinguished three main types of higher public services in principal European countries: the British, with its "Oxbridge" and public school allegiances and its "professional-amateur" administrative class; the Continental (excluding the French), with its predominance of lawyers; and the French with its *grand corps* tradition. Through colonialism each model was exported and, therefore, currently conditions bureaucracies throughout the world.[55]

The U.S. system differs more from each of these three types than the three differ from one another. Although the higher civil service systems of Great Britain, Western Europe, the Commonwealth, and the Pacific Rim are becoming more representative as opportunities for higher education broaden and as specialists are accorded higher status, still common to most is the dominance of the generalist, with its elitist corollaries, and the subservience of the specialist. A major theme of this study is that the exact opposite is true of the U.S. model. In this respect, the civil service system of imperial China, with its mandarin tradition of the "virtuous man," had more in common with the European models than with the U.S. model.

Whereas all modern civil service systems—including that of the United States—may be said to have accepted the Chinese-imparted concept of competitive examinations, the United States has rejected the unrepresentative generalist/elitist model—also diffused from China—common to most major systems in favor of the specialist/egalitarian and more representative model.

In comparing administrative systems, two factors therefore appear of major importance: the degree of specialization characteristic of top administrators; and the extent to which the bureaucracy is representative. These factors are so central to any administrative system that other differences are largely encompassed within them.

The generalist/specialist theme is pervasive in the literature.[56] In the broadest sense, this dimension indicates the extent to which public programs are staffed and directed by professional administrators as opposed to administrative professionals. The generalist/specialist factor has implications for the type of individual recruited into the system, the type of education requisite for selection, the type of training given during the administrator's career, and the degree of interorganizational mobility within the system.

The representativeness of an administrative system has many sides.[57] We call attention to two dimensions: the presence or absence of an administrative elite; and the composition of the civil service in terms of ethnic, gender, socioeconomic, educational, and geographical distribution of the population. The more stratified and closed the system, the less representative it will be.

These two major defining parameters of administrative systems (generalist/specialist, representative/unrepresentative) are closely linked; hence we draw, in turn, two postulates. First, the more generalist top administrators are, the more they comprise an unrepresentative bureaucracy. Second, the more specialists dominate a civil service, the more representative is the system.

Among the systems we have considered, the United States stands apart—through most of the history of its civil service—as having been devoid of a bureaucratic elite while drawing its administrators from different walks of life.

CONCLUSION

The following conclusions may be reached from the foregoing analysis: (1) Western scholars by and large have ignored the influence of imperial China on modern public administration; (2) competitive civil service examinations and the institution of a higher civil service system originated in and were well developed by imperial China; (3) the Chinese experience, directly and/or indirectly, influenced the institutionalization of civil service examinations and elite higher civil service systems throughout the world; (4) most of these systems have been marked by the dominance of generalists and unrepresentative bureaucracies; whereas (5) comparatively, the United States is characterized by a specialist-dominated civil service generally more representative of its society at large.

CHAPTER II

Background to the Supergrades

Political appointees among executives of the U.S. government have been the subject of considerable scholarly attention.[1] As a whole, the highest civil servants of the federal bureaucracy also have been given increasing attention because of the awesome and manifold responsibilities thrust on them since World War II.[2]

From our discussion in chapter 1 of bureaucratic elites in history, it is apparent that the top U.S. civil servants do not constitute an elite corps, nor do they—as a group—have most other attributes usually associated with career services in the United States or elsewhere. Does this mean, then, that the concept of a civil service executive system is alien to the United States and beyond the reach of future developments?

Actually, establishment of the Senior Executive Service by the Civil Service Reform Act of 1978 marked the culmination of a long-time effort toward institutionalizing in the federal government an executive system marked by the nurturing of several major attributes associated with other career services. Much of the remainder of this study is devoted to the unfolding and direction of this development, which is so portentous for the U.S. political system.

This chapter first analyzes major characteristics of the U.S. civil service with special reference to its executive level and then considers developments relevant to them from the passage of the Classification Act of 1923 through 1954.

CHARACTERISTICS OF TOP CIVIL SERVANTS

Several characteristics of high-level civil servants in the national government of the United States stand out. First, they are important politically, especially in terms of their influence on policy. Second, they are predominantly career civil servants, despite the prevalence of lateral entry and the permeability of the service. Third, most of them are immobile specialists and professionals rather than generalists who move from job to job. And fourth, they are classified according to their positions rather than as members of a corps. Each of these characteristics merits elaboration.

Political Actors

Although they are so-called merit rather than political appointees, it is a grievous error to underestimate the political importance of top civil servants of the federal government. To be political is to exercise power, which means to make policy decisions that allocate resources. Opportunities for bureaucratic policy making increase by level from lower to middle to higher echelons in the civil service.

One of the outstanding legal developments of the twentieth century has been the growth of government policies made by high federal career administrators. They—not political appointees or legislators—initiate most major legislation and issue most policies, rules, and regulations that impact on practically every human endeavor. Their actions prescribe and proscribe individual, group, and institutional behavior. Their regulations have the force of law. Violations of their policy decisions incur loss or withholding of government services or benefits or the imposition of sanctions. Within parameters set by political appointees and legislators, they manage more money, people, and material than do other officials in or out of government.[3] Where nongovernmental actors participate in "governance" (defined as the action of government plus its interaction with its nongovernmental partners in the process of governing)[4] through contracting out and other arrangements, it is the responsibility of higher civil servants to regulate such participation.

It is true that, unlike parliamentary systems elsewhere, the powers of lawmaking and law execution in the United States are constitutionally and institutionally separated between legislative and executive branches. But in practice the old dichotomy of politics and administration is gone. Substance has replaced form. And career administrators have indeed become political actors in the sense that as a group they form much of the political fabric of the nation. Within discretion delegated to them, they decide who gets what, when, and how. In other words, they make heavily weighted decisions that determine the allocation of resources, as well as the private rights, interests, and obligations of general classes of persons, and of particular individuals and organizations. In short, they exercise great power. It is time that political scientists move them to center stage of the U.S. political system.[5]

Because federal career executives are civil servants, they generally manage the daily affairs and provide the continuity of the national government. Presidents, political appointees, and legislators come and go, but—comparatively speaking career executives stay on. They have a controlling stake in the government, transcending by their tenure the intermittent program and policy thrusts of in-and-out politicians. "The effect of this tenure is that they enjoy an often unappreciated leverage on American public policy. They have simply dealt with the problem longer than most other people in government and control the administration (and thus the policy to a large extent) of whatever decisions are made in their respective substantive fields."[6] Top federal civil servants, then, are not only public administrators. In terms of the politics of program and policy (as distinguished from party politics), they are also political actors—though neglected as such—and this despite the political sterilization and the "keep-the-rascals-out" philosophy underpinning the civil service since its inception in 1883.

A Career System?

However important federal career executives are in the U.S. political firmament, they do not comprise a career system similar to the elite establishments of other bureaucracies, particularly European and Asian. According to Ferrel Heady, the most significant difference between the U.S. and European approaches to staffing for the public service is that the European emphasis has been on career staffing whereby individuals customarily enter the service at an early age and remain throughout their career, whereas the U.S. orientation has been toward shorter-term or "program" staffing. "The absence of a career system and the prevalence of movement in and out of the civil service have inhibited the emergence of a cohesive cadre of high-ranking bureaucrats comparable to the administrative class in Great Britain or members of the *grand corps* in France."[7] In this respect, therefore, it may be a misnomer to refer to the general civil service system of the federal government as a career service. But Heady was comparing U.S. with European systems. The career designation does serve to distinguish U.S. civil service executives from political appointees, which is doubtless the reason for its wide usage.[8]

Within the U.S. civil service, the average tenure of political appointees is about two years whereas the average top civil servant has more than twenty years' service and has thus made a much more substantial career commitment to government service. It is quite appropriate, therefore, to refer to top civil servants as federal career executives.

Immobile Specialists

Civil service executives of the United States are also distinguished from their counterparts of other bureaucracies by their identification with program and professional competencies, or specialist skills, rather than with general administrative capacities. "The American Civil Service emphasizes loyalty to one's profession, program, bureau, and department, probably in that order, and not to the Civil Service career system."[9]

The question of specialist versus generalist remains not only a lively issue elsewhere but has also refused to remain dormant in the United States, where, according to a 1965 observation, "the weight of contemporary opinion has decisively favored the generalist."[10] Nevertheless, as one British scholar has concluded:

> Any possibility of swift emergence in [the U.S.] government . . . of a self-confident, powerful, policy-determining group of career generalists should be cooly discounted. Americans still do not appreciate the virtues . . . of the highly intelligent talented amateur. A man should have a clearly recognizable and saleable skill and it is for the exercise of this expertise that he is paid at preferential rates.[11]

Although various meanings attach to the concept of the generalist, Michael Cohen has emphasized transferability as a central element for what he terms the "mobility generalist." His study of federal career employees in the highest grades concluded that interorganizational mobility is easiest for those who possess strong administrative skills and background and who are not closely allied with the interests of specific programs.[12] Thus Cohen's findings tend to confirm Frederick Mosher's suggestions that the administrative leadership of the federal government is increasingly professional in terms of educational and experiential backgrounds and that individual specialisms have come to dominate public agencies in the United States.[13] Because interorganizational mobility decreases as professionalism increases, federal career executives do not transfer freely between one department and another—a phenomenon to which the dominance of the rank-in-the-position approach contributes.

Position Classification

In U.S. public administration, "position classification" is considered not only the "most important" and "basic" personnel tool, but also "one of the marked successes in the development of the science and art of personnel management."[14]

The classical bureaucratic pattern of civil service elite systems elsewhere emphasizes rank-in-the-person (as against rank-in-the-position) and the sense of oneness, of loyalty to the service or to membership in the corps. These "closed systems" have been described as follows: "The corps systems are characterized by rank-in-man (Civil Service grades depend on job classification), entry at junior levels with a commitment to a career within the service, periodic rotation in job assignments, and, perhaps most important, selection and promotion based on the judgment of one's senior officers."[15]

In other words, the person is the main criterion in administering the personnel system. An individual is first recruited to a certain rank and then assigned to a position classified by rank, not the converse. Tenure is based upon the rank, not on the position, held by the individual. Ranked-based corps in the federal bureaucracy are limited to the Foreign Service, the military services, the Federal Bureau of Investigation, the U.S. Public Health Service, the Environmental Science Service, and, in a limited sense, the Senior Executive Service.

Position classification, on the other hand, "centers attention on the work assignment of the individual (the 'position') and the status of that assignment relative to other assignments in the organization."[16] Positions are arranged—not the personal factors of individuals filling them. A job description of the position is first made, and then an individual is selected who is considered qualified to perform the job. Tenure is based upon the position held by the individual.

Position classification has a close relation to the historical development of the federal civil service, and it evolved in the decades following establishment of the merit system by the Pendleton Act of 1883. The "immediate causes" for the passage of that act were the political scandals that rocked the 1870s and the assassination of President Garfield in 1881 by a disappointed office seeker.[17] Accordingly, civil service reform was viewed in the late 1800s as "a good beginning in reforming the patronage system of distributing offices," as "relief of officeholders from compulsory political assessments," and as "the making of subordinate official tenures coequal with efficiency and fidelity, instead of their depending on the politics of chief officials."[18]

The purpose of position classification, therefore, was to produce more equity in the treatment of employees, particularly by striving for "equal pay for equal work."[19] The civil service reformers, who pressed for competitive examinations and passage of the Pendleton Act, were motivated by a moralistic condemnation of the "evil" spoils system. By the classification of certain positions requiring competitive examinations under the act, they believed that "a new political morality would be generated which would be the salvation of the country."[20]

In 1884, a year after the act was passed, only about 10 percent of the government's positions were classified. All presidents from Cleveland to Hoover expanded the classified list. At the conclusion of the Coolidge administration in 1928, the classified service included three-fourths of all federal employees.[21] No provision was made for the separate treatment of federal career executives.

SALARY CEILINGS AND SUPERGRADES,
1923–1954

The basic purpose of a position classification system, which involves the grouping of individual positions into homogeneous classes, is to establish in personnel management the principle of equal pay for equal work. Accordingly, integral with position classification is the salary or pay plan that provides a flat rate or a graduated scale of pay for each class of position.[22] Despite the power of the president as chief executive under the Constitution, Congress considered these matters within its jurisdiction. Its refusal to give the Civil Service Commission authority to operate as an arm of the president was "typical of Congress's aversion to attempts to interfere with historic legislative prerogatives in personnel matters."[23]

Position Classification Act of 1923

The major significance of the Position Classification Act of 1923 is that it set the trend of the structure of pay and position classification for the next fifty-five years. It fixed exact salary ranges and distinctly limited pay raises that could be made within them. The law's additional features were summarized, in part, as follows:

1. Very broad occupational divisions, called "services," were established. These services were defined in the act and designated as the Professional and Scientific Service; the Subprofessional Service; the Clerical, Administrative and Fiscal Service; the Custodial Service; and the Clerical-Mechanical Service.

2. Each service was subdivided into a number of "grades" or levels of importance, difficulty, responsibility, and value of work.

3. Uniform compensation schedules consisting of these services and grades were enacted into the law, each grade having a salary fixed by Congress, and a short, very general description of the kind of work falling in each grade.

4. The pay of individual positions was to be determined through a process known as "allocation," i.e., a determina-

tion of which grade covered the duties and responsibilities of the position to be allocated; or, in other words, an appraisal of the duties and responsibilities of an individual position according to general standards of appraisal (grades) set by Congress. When a decision was reached that a position was of such difficulty, responsibility, and importance as to bring it within a particular grade, the salary range stated in the statute for that grade would mandatorily attach to the position.

5. As a mandate for the uniform interpretation and application of the compensation schedules and as a guiding principle for the process of "allocation," the policy that equal pay for equal work, irrespective of sex, should be observed, was expressly written into the statute.

6. "Classes" of positions were authorized to be established within grades, each class covering positions substantially alike as to character, difficulty, importance, responsibility, and value of work; and descriptions of those classes, known as "class specifications" were authorized to be written, to serve as administrative guides.[24]

No provision was made in the law for an "executive service," nor was there any reference to rank in the person. Rather, the new law "followed the American custom of placing 'rank in the job.' "

> Further, in the large number of different categories of positions . . . provided, the law reflected the extensive specialization and emphasis on personal skills acquired before individual employees entered the public service, which had long been typical of American employment practices in private industry as well as the government service. The Classification Act of 1923 merely systematized rather than modified some of the fundamental characteristics of American public management.[25]

Salary Ceilings, 1924–1949

The act of 1923, effective July 1, 1924, provided a single rate of $7,500 a year for the highest grade. This was increased in 1928 to a minimum rate of $8,000 and a maximum of $9,000. No further change in the ceiling rate was authorized until 1945—notwithstanding a number of studies recommending increases—first because of the emphasis on economy during the Great Depression, and second because of the intervention of World War II.

In its 1931 report to Congress, the Personnel Classification Board recommended a top salary range of $9,000–10,000 and observed: "The salaries paid by private concerns to their major executives exceed those paid by the Federal Government to positions of similar responsibility anywhere from 100 to 500 percent."[26] The President's Committee on Administrative Management recommended a $15,000 ceiling in 1937. Nevertheless, Congress raised the ceiling by only $800 (to $9,800) in 1945, to which it added $200 in 1946 and $330 in 1948, to fix a new salary ceiling of $10,330.[27]

A precedent-setting exception was made in 1947, however, when Congress authorized the then secretary of war (now defense) to establish and fix compensation for thirty positions in his department within the range of $10,000–15,000, which was over the $10,000 ceiling allowed at the time. Hence recognition was given to the need to establish a pay level for civil service positions for scientific and research professionals above the existing ceiling. In retrospect this was to be viewed as a very significant action because it was the first example of the isolation and special treatment of higher-level positions in the civil service.[28]

While Congress authorized increases to the highest-grade civil servants totaling only 15 percent after the war, the lowest pay grades received increases of 43–56 percent, a change that resulted in severe pay compression. This was cause for grave concern to the First Hoover Commission in 1949. Thus one of its task forces lamented that inadequate pay prevented recruitment of desirable top staff. "We are certain that few men today are attracted by the standard salary of $10,000."[29] The commission agreed and recommended that "immediate consideration should be given to providing adequate salaries for top civil-service employees," because such action "is imperative in the interest of sound management of the Federal Government."[30]

The Classification Act of 1949 ("Supergrades")

In response to the first Hoover Commission, Congress passed the Classification Act of 1949, which made sweeping changes in the structure of personnel management.[31] Replacing the Classification Act of 1923, the new law consolidated the separate occupational services in the General Schedule (GS). Although the 1949 law made no attempt to create a higher civil service with distinctive responsibilities, it added three new grades at the top of the schedule—GS-16, GS-17, and GS-18—comprising a total of 400 new positions: 300 for GS-16, 75 for GS-17, and 25 for GS-18. The original 400 positions and those to be added later became known as the government-wide quota. A new salary ceiling of $14,000 was established, which was $4,000 higher than the previous one. Table 1 sets forth the salary schedule for these grades fixed by the 1949 act.

The 1949 act also provided that only the Civil Service Commission, not the individual agencies, could approve the placement of a position in grade GS-16 and GS-17, whereas positions could be placed in or removed from GS-18 only by the president on the recommendation of the commission. An amendment in 1955, however, gave the commission the same authority to place positions in GS-18 as the 1949 act had given it with respect to GS-16 and GS-17 positions. The commission's authority over these positions was expanded even more by the 1955 amendment, which also assigned it responsibility for approval of the qualifications of individuals proposed for those positions, including positions excepted from competitive civil service requirements.[32]

TABLE 1. TOP PAY RATES IN THE CLASSIFICATION ACT OF 1949

GRADE	STEP 1	STEP 2	STEP 3	STEP 4	STEP 5
GS-16	$11,200	$11,400	$11,600	$11,800	$12,000
GS-17	12,200	12,400	12,600	12,800	13,000
GS-18	14,000				

Allocating and Increasing Supergrades

Immediately the new jobs became known as supergrades and, as Donald R. Harvey noted, "therein may have been the beginning of difficulty. They continued to be looked upon as something unique, requiring special controls."[33]

On October 31, 1949, the Civil Service Commission issued Departmental Circular no. 620 requesting departments and agencies to recommend positions for allocation to grades GS-16, GS-17, and GS-18. The commission asked that recommendations be supported by descriptions of the positions; functional or organizational charts; analyses and evaluations of duties, responsibilities, and qualifications required; and statements of the reasons for the allocations.

Obviously, the many agencies coveted this limited number of positions. For the existing 400 spaces, 47 agencies recommended a total of 1,008 positions, most of which—708—were then in GS-15. Of the remainder, 34 were in GS-14, 122 were new positions not allocated before, and 141 were being brought under the Classification Act for the first time.[34] It took the commission almost six months after the 1949 act was passed to perform the thankless task of determining which positions merited supergrade status and hence to break the logjam in promotions.[35] In the final list of 400 supergrade positions approved by the commission, 38 departments and agencies were represented.

It was not long afterward, however, that Congress added to the 400 government-wide quota—in a piecemeal, hit-or-miss fashion—by allocating to specific agencies certain numbers of "nonquota" supergrade positions—thus complicating the task of the Civil Service Commission. For example, soon after the onset of the Korean War, 250 supergrade positions were authorized by the Defense Production Act of 1950; 22 for the Federal Civilian Defense Administration; and 26 for the Defense Department—all within a year of the commission's allocation of the original 400 positions.[36]

This practice of spot authorizations by Congress in response to pressure from specific agencies was to continue through the years. As of December 1, 1953, a total of 835 supergrade positions had been authorized for 45 departments and agencies. Of these, 400 were authorized by the Classification Act, 160 remained under the Defense Production Act, and 305 were specially authorized by appropriation acts, other statutes, and reorganization plans. Requests for additional supergrade authorizations totaled 692 positions, of which the Civil Service Commission found, on preliminary evaluation only 287 to be warranted. As of September 1954, authorization for 1,133 supergrade positions had been granted. Meanwhile, the commission recommended to Congress that the total limitation on Classification Act supergrades be increased from 400 to 700, with no fixed grade distributions.[37]

The overall ceiling on the number of supergrade positions was to remain despite repeated commission efforts to have this constraint removed, with the result that agencies increasingly transferred their pressure from Congress to the commission. Moreover, the commission had to approve not only supergrade positions but also the persons who filled them, and this approval was to extend to those supergrade positions not subject to the requirement of competitive examinations—positions at the so-called policy-making level, where more overt political considerations might enter into the selection.

The Civil Service Commission's role of establishing supergrade positions and approving appointments to them was an acutely sensitive political responsibility, for it placed the commission squarely between the agencies and the administration, on the one hand, and within the separation-of-powers conflict between the executive branch and Congress on the other. While the commission had to apply congressional constraints, it was also required to be responsive to the needs of the president and executive branch.[38]

Promotion from Within

Meanwhile, supergrade positions were made more attractive by virtue of Congress's action increasing the ceiling salary in 1951 from $14,000 to $14,800, only $200 below the $15,000 salary fixed for assistant secretaries, members of Congress, and federal district judges. Thus Congress continued its policy since the Classification

Act of 1923 of establishing the ceiling rate under the act close to but not in excess of the rate paid members of Congress. As the latters' rate was to soar years later, Congress was to establish a pay cap for supergrades not in excess of the rate paid to top congressional staff.

Despite the justification for creating the supergrades in 1949 of attracting "desirable" top staff from outside the government, only 12 of the original 400 positions were filled by persons from outside the government.[39]

When Congress in 1950 was considering authorizing additional supergrade positions in the Department of Defense, the department emphasized the necessity of recruiting "men with the unique qualifications of technical competence, leadership, and resourcefulness" from outside the government.[40] During the House debate on this matter, the chairman of the Appropriations Subcommittee stated flatly, "It is not the purpose of the committee in agreeing to this amendment to permit the Department of Defense to make promotions from within Government employees to fill these grades."[41] Notwithstanding these congressional admonitions, the Defense Department nevertheless filled many of its supergrade positions from within the department. Thus the House Appropriations Committee found in 1954 that "records of the Department show that of a total of 69 supergrade positions filled since January 1, 1953, a total of 43 or over 62% were filled by departmental promotion."[42]

Not all members of Congress agreed that supergrades should be filled by recruiting from outside. For example, when considering proposed supergrade positions in 1954 for the State and Commerce Departments, Senator Monroney observed: "I think the only purpose of the provision affecting high salary classifications was to give hope to the career Government workers that if they remained with the Government, if they developed their talents and their understanding of the job they can have a future to which to look forward. I should not like to weaken the whole idea of supergrades by driving a wedge into that very noble purpose."[43] According to a senior political advisor to President Truman: "There wasn't much room to play politics with these jobs. If there had been room, we might have tried it, but the fact is we were creating a system in the midst of people already in their jobs. . . . Few jobs fell vacant, and mostly we were promoting from within."[44]

CONCLUSION

The transformation of top civil servants, after years of deprivation, into supergrades with salaries almost equivalent to those of political executives and members of Congress did not change the dominant characteristics of the higher civil servants as a whole. Their policy influence was not diminished, and by and large they were still immobile specialists locked into the agencies rather than mobile generalists. Promotion to more highly paid supergrade positions from within was a practice that could only enhance the career dimension of the civil service. On the other hand, supergrade positions afforded greater opportunity for lateral entry at higher levels.

Whether because of the exigencies of the Korean War or massive technological change wrought by the arms and space programs after World War II, the early 1950s witnessed an influx of "outsiders" through lateral entry into supergrade positions that were made available to specific agencies through Congressional spot authorizations.[45] Opportunities for lateral entry were expanded in 1953 with the establishment of Schedule C positions under President Eisenhower for positions at any grade level of a so-called confidential or policy-determining character. Although utilization of lateral entry might have been conducive to or necessary for representative bureaucracy, it challenged the concept of career within the service, including higher-level positions. And resort to "excepted" positions presented a challenge to the examining system and the concept of merit implicit within it, because this practice "made it difficult . . . to delineate precisely the boundaries between the spoils system and the merit system."[46] If anythiing, the higher civil service was made more permeable both to outsiders and to centers of power and influence outside of the civil service.

The conclusion is inescapable, therefore, that the onset of the supergrades was not a step forward toward the institutionalization of a higher civil service system in the United States.

CHAPTER III

The Second Hoover Commission's Proposal

When Republican Dwight Eisenhower was inaugurated as
president in January 1953, twenty years of control of the
White House by Democrats came to an end. During
that period, Democrats had controlled both houses of Congress
except for 1947–1949. Now that the Republicans also regained majority control of the Congress in 1953, they were anxious to rid the
government of the influence of Truman Democrats.[1]

A HOSTILE ENVIRONMENT

Dwight Eisenhower had waged an antigovernment campaign for the
presidency in 1952, pledging to lead a crusade with the purpose "to
clean out every vestige of crookedness from every nook and cranny
of the Federal Government."[2] A year after he took office, in his State
of the Union Address, President Eisenhower had added a "small government" pledge—to reduce federal employment and expenditures.[3]
On August 23, 1954, he told a nationwide radio and television audi-
ence of his administration's commitment to decentralization.[4]

During his first two years in office, President Eisenhower's only
public references to higher civil servants had been his requests for
more supergrade positions. Indeed, the first Republican administration in twenty years had exhibited a built-in bias against top civil
servants, especially "idea men" or intellectuals, termed egg heads. It
proceeded to undertake a series of actions and policies adversely affecting the morale of incumbent civil servants, thus creating a "general environment of repression, suspicion, and contempt for the civil
servant."[5] During his first six months, the Eisenhower loyalty-

security program had been launched, and no less than ten reorganization plans had been put into effect, including establishment of the Department of Health, Education, and Welfare and, more threatening, the institutionalization of presidential control over the civil service.

The environment of personnel policy in the first two years of the Eisenhower administration was deeply sullied by the anticommunist antics of Republican Senator Joseph McCarthy of Wisconsin, until his censure by the Senate on December 2, 1954. In response to the congressional feeling that the Truman loyalty and security program had been too "soft," President Eisenhower issued Executive Order 10450 on April 27, 1953—applicable to 2,300,000 employees—which abolished the Truman Loyalty Review Board and fixed complete responsibility on the head of each agency to determine whether the employment of an individual was "clearly consistent with the interests of the national security"—a far more rigid standard, by which agency heads could dismiss employees summarily. Clearly, McCarthyism was in its heyday. "For two years almost no influential member of the administration had effectively supported the federal service against vitriolic attacks. All evidence indicates that by the fall of 1954, the morale of federal civilian employees had hit a new low."[6]

On May 1, 1953, President Eisenhower issued Executive Order 10452, which replaced his White House Liaison Office for Personnel Management with the chairman of the Civil Service Commission. By this bold move, Philip Young became the president's personnel advisor, attended cabinet meetings, and simultaneously chaired the commission. Critics alleged not only that the independence of the Civil Service Commission was thereby eroded and presidential control extended but also that the very concepts of neutral competence of the civil service and traditional congressional suzerainty over it were put in jeopardy. Another reorganization quickly followed whereby Philip Young's control over the commission (and hence presidential control by extension) was tightened by the creation of the position of executive director and the restructuring of staff and line units within the commission.[7]

Other personnel measures taken by the Republican administration that created an adverse personnel policy environment were: severe cuts in the number of federal employees; removal of civil service protection to make way for more high-level patronage appointments; and a secret effort to mandate political clearance of all high-level federal appointments—including those to the civil service.

In the aftermath of the Korean War, the total number of federal civilian employees was reduced by almost 10 percent—by 212,700—during the administration's first year alone, with more cuts in 1954. These reductions-in-force (RIFs) created tension and uneasiness among civil servants.[8]

On March 31, 1953, Eisenhower announced by Executive Order 10440 the establishment of a new category of "policy-determining or confidential," positions to be excepted from civil service protection and known as Schedule C, as we mentioned in chapter 2, in response to "patronage clamors" as well as an "immediate desire to have some freedom in choosing the incumbents of top-management positions." At the same time, Eisenhower rescinded procedural safeguards against removal of incumbents in Schedule A, an existing excepted category.[9] These actions, too, evoked considerable controversy and criticism.[10]

Nothing fanned more controversy, however, than the public disclosure of an audacious move to require political clearance of all federal appointees, under the direction of Charles Willis Jr., assistant to the White House chief of staff, Sherman Adams. The so-called Willis Plan appeared on May 17, 1954, among agency heads in the form of two mimeographed booklets marked confidential and entitled "Operation People's Mandate."

In the booklets, Willis complained that the new administration faced a shortage of political appointment positions, for which the new Schedule C appointments were inadequate. A new plan was thus necessary to make more appointments to bolster the Republican party for the 1954 congressional elections, a plan whereby for each appointment an incumbent Republican senator or congressman could take credit. Accordingly, a position was established in each agency for a special assistant to control appointments to all higher career and political positions by clearance of candidates with the Republican National Committee. Disclosures of the substance, if not the wording, of the Willis Plan were made during the summer and fall of 1954 in a series of articles in the *Washington Post* and *Times Herald* and the *Evening Star*. These articles initiated a heated public debate and became an important campaign issue.

Despite implementation of the plan, the Democrats gained control of Congress in 1954 and hence majority control of the Senate Post Office and Civil Service Committee, which undertook an investigation of the civil service under the Eisenhower administration. James Watson, then director of the National Civil Service League, was retained as a consultant for the study. The resulting Watson Report of 1957 retrospectively revealed details of the still unrescinded Willis Plan.

1. The special assistant would be in control of appointments to all key grades from GS-14 through GS-18 in the agency, superseding its regular personnel director.

2. The special assistant would report vacancies in these career grades to the Republican National Committee.

3. All candidates would be screened for political acceptability with the emphasis on attaining maximum political returns.

4. The Republican National Committee would handle publicity on appointments.[11]

There is no question that the Willis Plan and the consequent public controversy contributed to low morale within the higher levels of the federal civil service.[12]

THE PROPOSAL FOR A SENIOR CIVIL SERVICE

The first attempt to establish a distinct higher civil service in the federal government was made by the bipartisan Second Hoover Commission (The Commission on Organization of the Executive Branch of the Government) chaired by former President Herbert Hoover, which proposed in 1955 the creation of a Senior Civil Service (SCS). The proposal originated with the commission's Task Force on Personnel and Civil Service, under the chairmanship of Princeton University President Harold W. Dodds and comprised of ten highly placed personnel professionals, including the former chair-

man of the Civil Service Commission, Robert Ramspeck, and Professor Leonard White of the University of Chicago, a former U.S. civil
service commissioner.

Charging that the civil service system emphasized positions, not
people, and that jobs were classified, ranked, rated, and paid "on the
bland assumption that they can always be filled like so many jugs,
merely by turning the tap," the task force lamented that there was
no positive government-wide program to recognize competence or
supply managerial talent at any level, especially the highest. The existing concepts and procedures were designed for the many standard-
ized positions at lower levels and "disregard so completely both the
personalities and the careers of individual men." To meet these needs,
the task force recommended establishment of the SCS.

> The Senior Civil Service should consist of a group of professional
> administrators carefully selected from all parts of the civil
> service. . . . They . . . all would have status, rank, and salary as
> individuals, and could be employed flexibly in a number of author-
> ized positions calling for high administrative talents. The rules . . .
> should require them to keep clear of all "political" activity. . . .
>
> The primary objective is to have always at hand in the Govern-
> ment a designated group of highly qualified administrators whose
> competence, integrity, and faithfulness cannot reasonably be ques-
> tioned; who will make it easier for political executives to discharge
> their responsibilities; and who will add to the smoothness, the ef-
> fectiveness, and the economy of government operations. A second-
> ary but related purpose is to make the civil service more attractive
> as a career to able men and women.[13]

The principal features of the proposed SCS were: personal-rank
status; flexibility in job assignment; obligation to serve where needed;
political neutrality; and adequate compensation.

According to the task force, personal-rank status—in contrast to
the traditional practice of vesting rank and salary in the job—would
attach rank and salary to the person, who would in a sense be a commissioned officer of the United States. SCS members would be trans-
ferrable from one job assignment to another without loss of pay or
status, thus assuring flexibility unattainable within the civil service
system of classification by position. As the corollary of personal-rank

status, moreover, the senior civil servant would have an obligation to serve in Washington, in the field, or abroad, as needed. To preserve their political neutrality, senior civil servants as a group would be expected to serve each administration faithfully and avoid political party identification and public statements, speeches, or testimony of a political character. And finally, the task force recommended that their compensation be adjusted to range from a minimum of $10,800 to a salary equivalent to that of an undersecretary.[14]

Authority to establish and administer the SCS would be vested in a bipartisan Senior Civil Service Board comprised of five members appointed by the president, two of whom would be the chairman of the Civil Service Commission and the director of the Bureau of the Budget. Nominations for SCS membership would be made to the board, which would appoint or commission senior civil servants who had a minimum of five years' federal service, according to procedures and qualifications determined by the board. Appointments to and promotions within the SCS would be effective upon approval by the president.

Although assignment to a particular position would be the function of the head of a department or agency, approval of positions suitable for senior civil servants would be a function of the SCS Board, a procedure that would, in effect, amount to assignment of quotas of such positions for each agency. The board would also have authority to "retire" or "select out" unassigned or adversely evaluated senior civil servants.[15]

The task force anticipated an initial appointment of 1,500 persons in the SCS, with a possible ultimate strength of 3,000—the size dependent on the number of positions in which it would be determined senior civil servants could be used appropriately. These positions would include: "administrative assistant secretaries and equivalent posts; bureau chiefs; assistant bureau chiefs; some division chiefs; heads of regional or district offices, heads of budget, personnel and other organic staff offices; deputy heads of policy staff offices, and professional aides and assistants to important political executives."

The task force advised that the SCS Board, in examining nominees to fill such positions, should look for generalists ("they should be more than narrow specialists") with qualities of "leadership, judgment, adaptability, skill in working with people, and capacity for continued growth." Other desirable qualities to be added later would be: "experience in more than one agency, experience in both staff and line (operating) work, and experience in both the departmental and field services."[17]

The Second Hoover Commission approved the task force's proposal in all particulars and recommended establishment of an SCS "composed of politically-neutral, well-paid career administrators of exceptional skill and experience for continuing service in all departments and agencies."[18]

THE REACTIONS OF CONGRESS, THE BUREAUCRACY, AND ACADEMIA

Opposition to the proposal to establish a higher civil service surfaced quickly. The SCS concept "received a generally cool reception from Congress."[19] Indeed, the two members appointed to the Second Hoover Commission from the House of Representatives, Congressmen Clarence J. Brown and Chet Holifield, strenuously dissented in their minority reports from the recommendation that an SCS be established. Representative Holifield argued that the proposal was incompatible with the U.S. political system. Pointing to the 1,100 positions already created in supergrades GS-16–GS-18, Representative Brown observed: "The incumbents of supergrade positions can be assigned in the normal manner. . . . they serve when they are most needed. . . . Except for one additional element, . . . 'commissioned rank' and salary, they are a senior civil service. . . . I am fearful that the addition of lifetime security and tenure to these positions will strengthen and further entrench the bureaucracy."[20] Although Representative Stuyvesant Wainwright introduced, on June 27, 1957, H.R. 8207 to establish an SCS as recommended by the Second Hoover Commission, the bill died in the House Committee on Post Office and Civil Service.[21]

Within the bureaucracy, high-level civil servants were reported to be fearful that they would not be admitted to the SCS or that, if admitted, they would be assigned to unwanted jobs.[22] Public employee unions, moreover, were fearful of the advent of partisan politics through the proposed SCS Board because of its projected independence from the Civil Service Commission and because of their distrust of the motives of the Eisenhower administration, "dating back to some of the manipulations of 1953–54," to politicize the civil service.[23]

At a meeting of the Civil Service Commission's Interagency Advisory Group of March 31, 1955, of a total of 19 agency representatives, only 4 expressed approval of the SCS proposal, whereas 10 were opposed and 5 were unclear. Opposition from the agencies focused on the presumed centralization of personnel administration manifest in the proposed SCS Board, as against their preference for decentralization to the agencies and improvement of the existing system. Results of a June 1955 survey by the Bureau of the Budget were similar; of 39 agency responses on the SCS proposal, only 8 approved, 22 had reservations, and 9 had no comment.[24]

Among academic critics of the proposed SCS was Herman P. Somers, who thought the rank-in-person feature was contrary to the American value of egalitarianism and that the SCS selection requirement of five years' federal experience would discourage lateral entry.[25] Expressing similar views, Paul P. Van Riper, then of Cornell University, claimed that the SCS proposal conflicted with "representative bureaucracy" by virtue of its personal rank feature, elitist character, and emphasis on promotion from within. "In a pluralist democracy such as ours, emphasizing both liberty and equality, we must at all costs maintain a civil (and military) establishment which is as close to our grass roots as possible. The representative character of our bureaucracy is just as important as Congress."[26]

In the concluding chapter, entitled "Personnel Is Power—A Theory of Governmental Reform," of his definitive history of the U.S. Civil Service, Van Riper elaborated the theme of the representativeness of the U.S. bureaucracy by suggesting that: "to be representative a bureaucracy must (1) consist of a reasonable cross-section of the body politic in terms of occupation, class, geography, and the like, and (2) must be in general tune with the ethos and attitudes of the society of which it is a part. Both of these criteria the American federal service meets more completely than most civil bureaucracies."[27] As distinguished from the closed system under the Federalists and the spoils under the Jacksonians and the early Republicans, our civil service system from 1883 had been an "equal opportunity" system, which, of the three—according to Van Riper—was the kind that is "most likely to produce a fully representative civil establishment and an intelligent one." The SCS proposal, on the other hand, aimed in the direction of a career system of "recruitment from the bottom, promotion from within, and the planned movement of personnel both vertically and horizontally," which, he concluded, verged on a closed unrepresentative system.[28]

Still others opposed the SCS proposal because they believed it was not feasible in the U.S. political environment, however desirable it otherwise might be in terms of the public interest. The rank-in-person feature, according to this argument, would cause complex problems because it would create a "dual personnel system."[29]

REACTIONS OF THE ADMINISTRATION

Not all reactions to the SCS proposal were negative; the proposal also had its advocates.[30] The policy context in the government, however, was not very propitious for its favorable reception.

The Second Hoover Commission's SCS proposal surfaced in 1955. Two years of the Eisenhower administration had produced an atmosphere of distrust and hostility toward the higher levels of the bureaucracy together with extraordinary efforts to politicize the civil service. Rationalizations that tended to equate a desired increase in "responsiveness" with an increase of "merit" could not counter a general impression that the civil service had fallen to the lowest level of morale it had ever experienced.

Although the Eisenhower administration certainly had not created an environment conducive to a positive response to the proposal, there were nevertheless SCS supporters in the White House who felt that the situation was recoverable. After all, the Eisenhower administration had made significant progress on other personnel fronts. For example, Congress had enacted in 1954 "the most significant fringe benefits legislation in the history of the federal civil service,"[31] whereby the civil service gained parity with private industry.[32]

When asked which of the commission's 314 recommendations he most favored, former President Hoover picked "the recommendation for the setting up of a senior civil service." And he added: "That is why our Report on Personnel and Civil Service is the nearest to my heart."[33] Echoing Hoover, President Eisenhower in a January 26, 1956 letter to the chairman of the Civil Service Commission referred to the SCS proposal as "one of the most far-reaching and imaginative proposals made by the Commission. . . . I am fully in accordance with the principles upon which this highly constructive proposal is based. . . . I suggest that the Civil Service Commission submit promptly its analysis and recommendations."[34]

The Civil Service Commission's staff had spent much of 1955 deliberating about the SCS proposal and eliciting reactions to it from agencies and other actors. The commission was confronted with a dilemma. On the one hand, agencies reactions were preponderantly negative. On the other, the proposal was receiving its main support from high-level political executives in the White House. The president's letter now required the commission to make its recommendations. The result was a compromise.

The Civil Service Commission proposed the incremental approach of a "pilot program" to test elements of the SCS proposal in certain agencies and functional areas only, to be administered by a nonpartisan SCS planning committee, which thereby would establish "the frame-work for a permanent Senior Civil Service."[35] On April 6, 1956, the commission presented its proposal for a pilot program to the cabinet. Instead of reaching a decision, the president suggested that the agencies react to the proposal. At best, agency reactions were passive which, in effect, caused the commission to shelve its compromise proposal for a pilot program.[36]

The Career Executive Program

A stalemate lasting seven months ensued. There was general agreement on some sort of prescription for the top level of the civil service, but there were wide differences as to what ought to be done. To break this deadlock, the White House convened a meeting on December 5, 1956, of twenty concerned career and noncareer executives to "resolve the Executive Branch position regarding the Hoover Commission proposal for a Senior Civil Service" and—more specifically—to develop "a definite recommendation to the President as to the disposition of this . . . recommendation."[37]

Chaired by Meyer Kestnbaum, the group decided at the outset to scrap the SCS label. Kestnbaum later explained: "One of the fortunate things which came out of the discussion was, we found, that the connotation of the title 'Senior Civil Service' placed the wrong emphasis on the kind of a program that it was agreed is really needed. This then led to the development of the term 'Career Executive Program' which is a more accurate description of what is contemplated."[38] The group also decided that all supergrade positions, "except for specialists," should be filled through the proposed Career Executive Program according to authorized standards, that the SCS's proposed rank-in-person classification should be scrapped, and that a "Career Executive Board" should administer the program under the primary responsibility of the Civil Service Commission.[39]

Within a month of this meeting, on January 3, 1957, the staff of the Civil Service Commission issued a draft of an executive order to establish a Career Executive Program within the commission, with the Career Executive Board reporting directly to the commission.[40]

Meanwhile, the chairman of the commission, Philip Young, was coming under increasing criticism for wearing two hats—as commission chairman and simultaneously as the president's personnel advisor. As Hugh Heclo commented:

> This plan was adopted at the outset of the Eisenhower administration, but the "two-hat" arrangement for the Civil Service chairman did not work satisfactorily. By 1956 the top presidential advisers on civil service personnel were themselves dissatisfied with existing arrangements. As both White House aide and Civil Service Commission head, the chairman was strained between diverse part-time roles as an advocate for what the commission staff wanted, as a personal adviser trying to look at matters strictly from the President's point of view, and as a nonpartisan commissioner appearing before a Democratic Congress suspicious of Republican raids on the civil service.[41]

In February 1957, President Eisenhower replaced Philip Young, a chief advocate of the Career Executive Program, with former Congressman Harris Ellsworth. Although Ellsworth had no previous experience with civil service matters, he was named the new chairman of the commission.[42]

Young's departure ended the close cooperation between the commission and the White House. Accordingly, while the staff plan was being reviewed within the reconstituted commission, the White House came up with its own plan for a career executive program. The administration's plan called for an executive order to establish a Career Executive Board, independent of the Civil Service Commission, to develop a Career Executive Program prior to establishment of such a program itself. This draft executive order was sent to the Civil Service Commission for comment on March 27, 1957.[43]

At a meeting of the Interagency Advisory Group of April 18, 1957, representatives of the agencies uniformly expressed the view that the intended purpose and role of the Career Executive Board proposed in the administration's draft were too vague and unclear.[44]

The staff and commissioners of the Civil Service Commission were more obdurate against the "bureaucratic imperialism"[45] implicit in the White House proposal for a Career Executive Board independent of the commission. In a letter to Roger W. Jones of the Bureau of the Budget, Ellsworth, the new chairman of the commission, opposed the idea of establishing a Career Executive Board prior to creation of the Career Executive Program. He also felt that the proposed executive order was much too vague, especially in terms of the board's relationship to the commission. And he added: "We recommend, therefore, that Section 1 be changed to read: 'There is hereby established in the Civil Service Commission a Career Executive Board to be known hereafter in this order as the Board." Another paragraph should be added to Section 1 which states: "The Board will report to the Chairman of the Civil Service Commission.' " Ellsworth ended his letter by suggesting that, before the president signed the executive order, Congress be informed of "the purpose of the proposed Executive Order and the program it will initiate."[46]

Despite these objections by the agencies and commission, the

White House in July 1957 floated another draft executive order that differed from the previous draft in only one particular, namely, that a Career Executive Committee would be established instead of a Career Executive Board.[47] There was no question now that the administration fully intended to control development of the Career Executive Program by excluding the Civil Service Commission. Commission staff who had worked on this project for almost two years were abject. As one staff member lamented: "It seems to me that we have stepped back into history a full two years with this draft. . . . It is now eighteen months since the President urged some action on the Commission!"[48] All that remained for the commission to do was to terminate its work on the proposed Career Executive Program.

On August 12, 1957, the White House issued Executive Order 10742 to establish a five-member bipartisan Career Executive Committee "to develop specific recommendations with respect to establishment of a Career Executive Program within the Civil Service system."[49] This order was essentially the same as the draft order circulated the previous month. Named as committee chairman was Arthur Flemming, former member of both the Civil Service Commission and the Second Hoover Commission. The only relationship between the two bodies was the naming of Commissioner Frederick Lawton to the committee.

Recommendations of the Career Executive Committee were substantively retained in President Eisenhower's Executive Order 10758 of March 4, 1958, establishing the Career Executive Board and were incorporated into the board's regulations. These recommendations included:

1. The president, by executive order, should establish a presidential Career Executive Board whose members were: (a) appointed by the president; (b) of both major parties; and (c) from inside and outside the government.

2. The board should work with the Civil Service Commission in preparing:

    (a) regulations to be issued by the commission dealing with executive manpower;

       (b) legislative proposals for the president; and

       (c) an annual report to be sent to the president through the Civil Service Commission.

3. The nomination to the supergrades should be made by the agency.

4. The nominee should be recognized by the president. (The committee felt that this could be done by a letter or certificate from the commission.)

5. Replacements should be drawn from rosters but should not exclude outside searches.

6. The board should assist the agencies in filling positions.

7. The board should advise the agencies and the Civil Service Commission on training programs for the development of executives.

8. The board should establish broad standards in order to make the service more flexible.[50]

The Career Executive Board thereupon adopted policies, among others, that the Career Executive Service should initially include incumbents of supergrades (GS-16 and above) or equivalents. In addition to the Career Executive Board's regulations, which instituted recommendations of the Career Executive Committee, there were several concepts that were considered new and important, among which were:

1. The employee's rights.

    a. The employee could decline participation in the program.

    b. Career executive eligibles could have the designation discontinued.

    c. Career executives or eligibles could indicate restrictions on the referral of their names for other positions.

    d. Career executives or eligibles could accept or decline offers which came through referral.

2. The roster of career executive eligibles would contain:

    a. qualified personnel at grade 16 and above or the equivalent who were not designated as career executive;

    b. employees below grade 16 who had been nominated by the agencies.

3. The agencies could fill a position with anyone in the Career Executive Service, with a career executive eligible, or with anyone meeting SCS requirements for the position.

4. The CSC would maintain a central record of qualifications and keep it current.[51]

CONCLUSION

As we have observed, for its first two years, the Eisenhower administration created a hostile environment in the executive branch for consideration of the Second Hoover Commission's SCS proposal. When it sought to react to its critics, improve its personnel policy environment, and develop a more palatable prescription for the higher civil service, the Democrats gained control of the Congress. Accordingly, the White House undertook a cautious incrementalist approach that would bypass the Congress.

First, the administration worked closely with the Civil Service Commission. But after the departure of its co-opted chairman, Philip Young, the White House decided to take the lead in preparing the prescription.

In the entire process, major ingredients in the SCS proposal were lost, including its vital rank-in-person concept. In place of surgery through legislation, there was prolonged tinkering with the existing system, without resort to the Congress. As we shall see, these were not the last attempts to establish some semblance of a higher civil service system by circumventing Congress.

Meanwhile, the Second Hoover Commission's SCS proposal appeared to be in jeopardy. As Van Riper wrote in 1958:

The Senior Civil Service concept ran into trouble, not only because many high level civil servants saw themselves either as "whirling dirvishes" rotating from position to position at someone's whim, or as a selected group of "sitting ducks" all too clearly visible for congressional sniping, but also because of a long-standing American aversion to anything even suggesting a closed British-type administrative class.[52]

CHAPTER IV

Circumventing Congress

A distinguishing fundamental of the U.S. constitutional system, in contrast with the parliamentary systems of the United Kingdom and many other countries, is that members of the U.S. executive branch cannot serve at the same time as members of the legislative branch. In a parliamentary system, conflicts between the two branches are diminished or avoided because the leaders of the legislature serve at the same time in a dual capacity as ministers. The separation of powers system of the United States, however, is marked by separate memberships in the two branches. Indeed, in the U.S. system it was intended that power check power.[1]

SEPARATION MEANS CONFLICT

Much of the political history of the United States can be written in terms of the conflicts between Congress and the executive branch.[2] And when a majority of either or both houses of Congress are members of a political party other than that of the president, it is normal—if not requisite—that such conflicts become exacerbated.[3]

Still, the Constitution charges that the president "shall take care that the laws be faithfully executed."[4] By the Pendleton Act of 1883, moreover, Congress itself delegated authority to the president to exercise leadership in the development of the civil service through the Civil Service Commission.[5] Hence it is also normal—if not requisite—to expect the president to attempt to institutionalize the means by which an adequate number of the best-qualified top civil servants can be assured.

It is perhaps inevitable for the Congress, however, to attempt to insulate the apex of the civil service from what it may suspect to be politicization by the chief executive. And so a perduring conflict inheres in the separation of powers. This constitutional principle in action appears to ordain a continuing contest between the president and Congress for control of the higher civil service of the United States.

It should not have been surprising, therefore, that the Career Executive Service, as projected by the executive orders of President Eisenhower, a Republican, would be met with hostility by a Congress controlled by a majority of Democrats.

CONGRESSIONAL DISPLEASURE

Within two months of President Eisenhower's executive order creating the Career Executive Board, a House of Representatives subcommittee initiated hearings on the matter. That the hearings would be hostile was evident by the tone of the opening statement of James B. Davis, a Democrat and chairman of the Subcommittee on Manpower Utilization of the Committee on Post Office and Civil Service:

> Without prior advice to, or consultation with, the Congress, the President recently created, by Executive order, a new selection and placement program, which is over and beyond the authorities and normal procedures of the Civil Service Commission. . . . This subcommittee considers the proposed new personnel program, as promulgated by Executive action of the President, of sufficient importance to warrant an examination of the background, the need for, and proposed plans of operation of this so-called elite corps of career executives.[6]

President Eisenhower had appointed as the first chairman of the Career Executive Board Dr. Arthur Flemming, who had been chairman of its predecessor, the Career Executive Committee. The following exchange between Dr. Flemming and subcommittee members, during the six days of hearings on the matter, is illustrative of the major concerns of the subcommittee:

> *Mr. Dennison.* When the original Career Executive Committee was functioning under the Executive Order of August

1957, at any time was this particular committee or was Congress consulted with respect to the program . . . under consideration at that time?

Dr. Flemming. Not by the Career Executive Committee; no sir. . . .

Mr. Dennison. In your opinion, does this Career Executive Board in a sense set up a senior civil service?

Dr. Flemming. Well, it is a step in the direction of the kind of recommendations made by the Hoover Commission. Whether there should be a second step or a third step, I think, would depend upon the experience as we get with this Career Executive Board. . . .

Mr. Johansen. I do not know what functions this Board would perform that could not be performed by the Civil Service Commission.

Dr. Flemming. I agree with you on that but the President . . . chose to do it this way to get the program started.[7]

Subcommittee members disputed the anomalous role of the Civil Service Commission and President Eisenhower's motives. Thus Congressman Johansen charged that "this process . . . transfers to this johnny-come-lately super civil service board functions and responsibilities the Civil Service Commission can perform" and it reflected "a President who wants . . . to play politics . . . to use this Board as a 'Board of Admission' device to control the higher positions of government." And he added that the Career Executive Board's "potential of power and prestige . . . is potentially most dangerous."[8]

Representatives of five unions or associations of federal employees appreared before the subcommittee in opposition to the contemplated Career Executive Service. Typical of their testimony was that of James A. Campbell, president of the American Federation of Government Employees, who said that the proposed service "smacks of favoritism and special privilege," that it was fundamentally undemocratic, and that it would constitute "establishment of a caste system . . . peculiarly distasteful to the American people."[9]

DEMISE OF THE CAREER EXECUTIVE PROGRAM

After the hearings, Subcommittee Chairman Davis sent a letter to the White House quoting the subcommittee's resolution of July 23, 1958, which in part stated that it was the consensus of the subcommittee that no activity to further the creation or implementation of the Career Executive Program be taken until the subcommittee had had an opportunity to study the matter further. On April 28, 1959, a House Appropriations Subcommittee directed that no funds be used for support of the activities of the Career Executive Board. The full House then passed, and the Senate approved an appropriations bill stipulating that "no part of this appropriation shall be available for the Career Executive Board." This congressional action effectively scuttled the Career Executive Board. President Eisenhower had no recourse but to issue another executive order revoking its creation.[10]

There are several reasons for the demise of the Career Executive Board:

1. The egalitarian nature of Congress was offended. The idea of an elite corps was repugnant to the American tradition and ran against the grain of the Congress.

2. The unions felt it introduced a concept of control which was threatening to their role and relationship to Congress.

3. Heads of agencies felt threatened because they feared a diminution of their assignment authority.

4. Many executives who might be affected by the senior civil service concept were opposed to it because they thought it would force them to move against their will without regard to their desires, abilities, etc.

5. A segment of the academic world was opposed to it because they felt that people progressed in clearly defined professions or occupations and that there was really no room for this concept of broad generalists who were "just moved around from place to place."[11]

In its final report to President Eisenhower, the Career Executive Board stated:

The Board believes that no action program concerned with executive manpower has any reasonable prospect for success without two essentials: (1) the whole-hearted backing of the top executive level in each agency, and (2) the existence of a central point of leadership placed sufficiently high in the Executive branch to stimulate and give direction to service-wide activities to staff career manager positions with persons of the highest competence. . . . The Board therefore urges the Executive Branch give continued attention, including study of the need for possible new legislation.

And the board almost plaintively concluded that the discontinuance of its activities "should not be permitted to halt or impair constructive efforts to solve the problem of assuring a continuing supply of highly qualified managers to fill top career positions."[12]

A COMPLICATED SYSTEM

One of the first actions taken by Democrat John F. Kennedy after winning the presidential election in November 1960 was to ask James M. Landis to study, and recommend reforms of, the federal regulatory agencies. In his report the following month to President-Elect Kennedy, Landis claimed that there had been a significant deterioration in the quality of top-level administrative personnel since 1946. He identified two causes: appointment of unqualified high-level entrants and the use of Schedule C to pay off political debts.

Careful scrutiny of agency members, from the standpoint of their qualifications as well as their prejudices in behalf of administering the legislative goals to which they were to be committed, was during these years too often replaced by a consideration of what political obligations could be repaid through appointments. The area of so-called Schedule C appointments, free from Civil Service requirements, was increased affecting seriously the morale of those persons who looked upon government service as a career. Advancements to choice positions were also less rarely made from the staff. Instead outsiders not infrequently less qualified were appointed to these positions.[13]

Although there was evidence that the abuse of Schedule C was short-lived after its establishment in 1953, there is no question that during the Eisenhower administration agencies added many persons at supergrade levels without examination on temporary appointments and under a so-called rare bird provision.[14] But even if Landis's over-all assessment appeared too harsh, it was not incompatible with the Civil Service Commission's own assessment that the personnel system inherited by President Kennedy in 1961 for the management of upper-level positions worked poorly. This system was, according to the commission's Bureau of Executive Manpower, "complex and confusing, slow in responding to program changes, and erratic in the quality of the executives it could produce."[15]

Reasons for this adverse situation are discussed in chapter 2. It remains to be noted that when James Landis made his report at the end of 1960, there were authorizations for 1,553 supergrades (increased from the original 400) and 1,030 Public Law (PL) equivalent positions (increased from the original 30) over which the Civil Service Commission held stewardship.[16]

The 1950s were a decade of massive technological change in which the government's need for top-level executives, scientists, and professionals steadily increased. Congress, through its various committees, responded piecemeal to this need. It is a characteristic of the U.S. political system that agencies frequently interact with congressional committees and subcommittees in a manner that creates interdependencies, understandings, and even agreements between them.[17] As we discussed in chapter 2, spin-offs from such intimacy consisted of special congressional authorizations of supergrade or equivalent positions for specific agencies outside the established government-wide quota. Some of these special authorizations were placed under the control of the Civil Service Commission while others were not. In still other instances, only partial jurisdiction, such as classification only or approval of qualifications only, was granted the commission by Congress.

In the meantime, while munificent program or appropriation committees sporadically logrolled a largesse of executive positions by spot authorizations to their special client agencies, the remainder of the executive branch was dependent on allocations by the Civil Service Commission from its basic government-wide quota. Periodically, the administration, through the commission, would petition the congressional committees on Post Office and Civil Service to increase this quota.[18]

Even the existing organizational arrangements for handling executive positions within the Civil Service Commission reflected this segmented, incremental, and heterogeneous system. Within the commission, the Bureau of Inspections was responsible for the classification of jobs to the GS-16, -17, or -18 levels and for their allocation to agencies; the Bureau of Examining approved qualifications of individuals for these positions; and the Bureau of Programs and Standards considered whether positions should be in the career or noncareer service.[19]

Consequently, by the time President Kennedy took office in 1961, an extremely complicated arrangement with respect to managing executives had evolved, one so fragmented that no locus of responsibility for executive personnel existed anywhere in the federal government.

THE EXECUTIVE ROSTER

The circumstances that contributed to the disintegration of the executive quota system and the dispersion of authority within the Civil Service Commission also led to a diffusion of executive personnel policy within the federal government. The Kennedy administration responded in three ways. (1) President Kennedy appointed a former Federal career executive and executive director of the Civil Service Commission, John Macy, to the chairmanship of the commission. (2) Macy was also asked to serve the president as his chief personnel consultant (a role similar to Chairman Young's during Eisenhower's first term) to help him find the most qualified persons to fill noncareer and career executive posts in the government. (3) As commission chairman, Macy instructed his executive director to conduct a program review of the entire government-wide personnel program, including upper-level personnel management, in the context of a career continuum from entrance level to top executive positions.

Macy's dual role in the White House and Civil Service Commission brought some unity to the process of selection and assignment of executives insofar as the president sought to utilize his expertise—

and hence the commission's experience—in the search for and selection of cabinet-level and subcabinet-level federal executives, as well as those in the top career positions. But this development was not tantamount to constructing an executive personnel management program.

One of the potentially most significant steps toward creation of such a system was an early product of the task force conducting the commission's program review. This was the introduction of the Executive Roster by Chairman Macy at President Kennedy's cabinet meeting of March 2, 1961. Macy explained that the roster contained pertinent information on a selected group of over one thousand career executives at the GS-16, -17, and -18 levels.

The roster, he said, was being established to assist agency heads to fill key posts. All agencies would thus have an opportunity for the first time to consider government-wide executive resources for such positions. Moreover, the roster could be used by the agencies to locate highly qualified persons to fill short-term consulting and special project assignments and for staffing new and expanded programs and agencies. Such a roster, according to the chairman, would make possible the creation of a government-wide executive career ladder, and it would help keep the president informed about executive personnel resources for the executive branch. In terms of the interests of supergrade incumbents, the roster would offer them a means to make known voluntarily their experience, qualifications, and availability for other positions.

Unfortunately, once established, the roster included insufficient information on qualifications and provided no means for updating that information. Few of the government's career executives participated. In addition, acceptance by agency officials was uneven, and few utilized it. During the first three years of the roster's existence, only 29 federal agencies requested the commission's assistance in filling 134 supergrade positions.[20] The roster was "minimally utilized, poorly understood, and inadequate to meet the demands of an ever expanding supergrade system."[21]

However deficient the Executive Roster proved to be, the concept appeared sound, and it did serve to crystallize problems that required solution for a management system for executive personnel to become effective. Obviously, creation of such a system required much more research and planning. One conclusion appeared certain—in order to involve the agencies fully, legitimization by presidential and/or congressional action would be needed.

THE EXECUTIVE ASSIGNMENT SYSTEM

Momentum for the establishment of an effective system of executive personnel management accelerated during the first months of the administration of Democratic President Lyndon Johnson, who became president upon the assassination of John Kennedy in November 1963.

In an extraordinary all-day meeting of February 15, 1964, the chairman of the Civil Service Commission, John Macy, met with his top staff officers in a wide-ranging brain-storming discussion "to consider the issues involved in developing the highest possible quality of staff in the Upper Career Service." Perhaps the most important question posed by Macy was, Is the system bringing the best people to the top? The ensuing discussion implied that it was not, but the paucity of information made generalizations hazardous. One theme stood out. Agencies tended to promote from within to fill executive positions because they did not know of available outside talent. Hence there was little interagency mobility. What was needed was detailed information on all employees at the upper levels—in other words, "a meaningful inventory" of executive talent. Chairman Macy charged his staff with the development of a model system for jobs in grades GS-16–GS-18 which would include a plan for maintaining "100 percent statistical inventories" of the incumbents of those positions.[22]

Various studies were undertaken in the months following Macy's challenge to his staff. For example, proposals for "a new kind of appointment authority" for GS-16–GS-18 positions were put forward to establish a "competitive system flexible enough to meet the needs of policy-making officials for key assistants who will give them vigorous and imaginative support." One feature proposed that certain appointments could be made for up to three years—a proposal that was to emerge again in the next decade.[23]

Several means to implement a new executive appointment system were considered: by adoption of Civil Service Commission rules, by the president prescribing such regulations, or by executive order of the president. It is interesting to note that legislation by Congress was not even considered. Ultimately, the executive order method was selected and various drafts were framed by the commission's staff.

In August 1964 a draft proposal for an executive order to establish an Executive Assignment System was circulated among commission officers, which, among other features, projected establishment by the commission of an "Executive Placement Service to assist agencies in locating candidates for executive assignments from within the service." Shades of the British generalist tradition and the Second Hoover Commission's proposal for a Senior Civil Service were implicit in a section entitled "Mobility": "The Commission shall take steps to facilitate and encourage the movement of well-qualified employees into Executive Assignments from one assignment to another as may best suit the needs and convenience of the Government."[24]

Although more than two years were to pass before such an executive order would be forthcoming, commission staff already were considering how such a system would be implemented. The heart of the system, according to one appraisal, would be the Career Executive Roster, a current, comprehensive list of all persons in the federal service qualified for a career executive assignment. Information provided would have to be up to date, useful, accurate, and quickly retrievable. It would be necessary to have an arrangement "something like . . . an IBM card or tape system providing basic information about each person for quick referral to agencies and preliminary searches."[25]

While the Civil Service Commission was busy crystallizing its proposal, the prominent Committee for Economic Development, composed of two hundred business and academic leaders, recommended that all management responsibilities and functions concerning supergrade personnel be transferred from the commission to a new Office of Executive Personnel in the Executive Office of the President. Among its proposed functions were the preparation and maintenance of a complete inventory of each supergrade position and an inventory of prospective talent for these positions; and assistance to agency heads in their search for competent executives.[26] Although this reorganization proposal was not adopted, it did serve to focus attention on the fact that there was significant support from outside the government for a career executive system that would be more responsive to presidential and top political management, and for an effective system of executive assignment.

Clearly, the main business ahead now appeared to be to call for presidential action. This President Johnson promised in his State of the Union Address of January 14, 1966, when he said that he intended to "restructure our civil service in the top grades so that men and women can easily be assigned to jobs where they are most needed, and ability will be both required, as well as rewarded."[27]

On November 17, 1966, President Johnson fulfilled a major part of this pledge by issuing Executive Order 11315 creating the Executive Assignment System for GS-16–GS-18 positions and persons. Chairman Macy was convinced that the new system signaled "one of the most important advances in Federal management in recent years."[28] In signing the order, President Johnson stated that the new system would enlist the best available talent "to help achieve the goals of the Great Society."

> This new system will tell us whom we need and where they are. It will provide us with the flexibility to bring the right talent to the right job at the right time. Our Government will benefit from a more effective use of its top management. Our public servants will benefit from the increased opportunities for their career development and personal satisfaction. Our citizens will benefit from better administered programs which will provide full value for their tax dollar.[29]

The Executive Assignment System established by President Johnson was intended to: (1) provide for the establishment of cooperative planning efforts by the Civil Service Commission and the federal agencies whereby agency and government-wide personnel plans could be developed for staffing upper-level positions; (2) use an automated executive inventory to facilitate the identification of outstanding executive talent; (3) emphasize staffing procedures based on merit through a system of career executive assignments, but with sufficient flexibility to permit meeting emergency and short-term needs through limited executive assignments, and accommodating controversial, confidential, or political responsibilities through "non-career executive assignments"; (4) make known to agency heads the most capable executives from outside, as well as from inside, the federal service; and (5) foster "development of a Federal executive staff committed to the overall purposes of government rather than to a single agency or program."[30]

Disparities between law and practice, or between goals and performance, in public administration are inescapable; not all objectives of the Executive Assignment System were fully realized. Central to the whole system, nevertheless, was creation and use of the Executive Inventory, and it is with respect to the accomplishment of this objective that the Civil Service Commission registered perhaps its most outstanding success.

THE EXECUTIVE INVENTORY

On November 18, 1966, one day after the signing of Executive Order 11315 authorizing the Executive Assignment System, Chairman Macy announced the establishment of the Bureau of Executive Manpower in the Civil Service Commission to construct and administer the system. All aspects of executive personnel management were combined in the new bureau, including recruitment, selection, advancement, tenure, professional development, and utilization. Thus the bureau eliminated the fragmentation of responsibility which so plagued the commission's earlier attempts to establish an effective system of executive personnel management.

Critical to the Bureau of Executive Manpower's operation of the Executive Assignment System was the Executive Inventory. Whereas the Executive Assignment System referred to *positions*—about seven thousand positions by mid-1971 in grades GS-16–GS-18 in the executive branch of the federal government—the Executive Inventory referred to *people*—over thirty-five thousand federal executives by mid-1971 including those at grades GS-15–GS-18 and those serving at equivalent pay levels in pay systems other than the General Schedule.[31] The inventory was a prime source from which individuals could be selected to fill the positions in the system. It also provided the president and agency heads with a virtually complete computerized report on the top-level talent available to them, as contrasted with its incomplete and unautomated predecessor, the Executive Roster.

Each executive at GS-15–GS-18 and equivalents was required to complete a very detailed biographical questionnaire known as the Executive Inventory Record, which became each executive's personal statement.[32] Hence this information reflected each executive's own perception of his or her capabilities rather than as they might be interpreted by another person abstracting information from a personnel file. For example, besides making known factual data about their careers, executives gave narrative descriptions of their work experience reflecting their own perceptions of their background. This, perhaps, was the most important part of the record.

Assuming that an agency already had a vacant career position at the supergrade level, the position having been allocated from the government-wide quota by the Civil Service Commission or by special congressional authorization, then the first step in filling it was for that agency to identify and record the specific qualifications required for the particular job. The next phase was the search process—that is, use of the computer to perform the clerical function of screening the inventory files and printing out a preliminary list of persons who would meet both mandatory and desirable qualifications. This screening was purposely very broad so as not to exclude those who might reasonably meet the requirements.

Once the hiring agency eliminated from consideration those individuals in the computer printout who obviously were not among the better qualified, it would undertake a thorough evaluation of the remaining candidates. For this purpose, microfilm reproductions of the candidates' updated inventory records, including narrative material, would be made available by the Civil Service Commission, associates and superiors of the candidates might be consulted; and candidates would then be interviewed by the hiring agency.[33]

From November 17, 1967 (when the Executive Inventory became operational), to June 26, 1971 (the end of fiscal year 1971), the Civil Service Commission submitted a total of 1,318 lists comprising 7,542

63

names in response to executive searches. All but a few executive searches were conducted to help agencies fill supergrade positions. The inventory was used for other purposes as well, for example, to select members for special task forces, advisory groups, or committees, and to locate candidates for various short-term assignments.

If these statistics appear impressive, it should be understood that until March 1971 agencies were *required* to search the inventory to fill all supergrade positions despite the fact that they were not required to appoint candidates from lists referred to them by the commission. But the mandatory search requirements proved unsound, principally because in the frequent instances when an agency intended promoting from within rather than seeking candidates from outside, there was a tendency to regard the inventory search as more red tape. Indeed, only about 15 percent of all vacancies for supergrade positions were actually filled from the inventory.

This phenomenon, abetted by the predominance of organizational and occupational specializations (including occupational needs peculiar to certain agencies and expertise derived only from such agency service) and by the parochialism of professionalism, doubtlessly accounted for little interorganizational mobility among federal career executives. Commission inventory searches were often redundant or pro forma because agencies had already decided whom to appoint. Thus, the commission's executive director, Nicholas J. Oganovic, acknowledged:

> Despite the generally accepted program objectives, agencies have come to view a significant part of the search and referral process as red tape and often as a pro forma exercise. With increasing frequency, searches are started after the actual selection has been made. In some cases this is understandable—e.g., when an agency has a predominance of talent in a given occupational area and/or has a viable career development program for a given occupational area. In other cases, a lack of understanding or acceptance on the part of top agency managers causes the inventory search to be an after-the-fact operation.[34]

On March 5, 1971 the Civil Service Commission announced that no longer would an inventory search be mandatory for vacant career supergrade positions. Instead, each agency would be invited to nego-tiate an agreement with the commission to determine when a search might be waived. Thereafter, few such agency agreements were in fact negotiated with the commission, and the inventory search and referral process became—for all practical purposes—a matter of whether an agency wished to use it. Although the search and referral process did produce excellent candidates for many executive posi-tions, the effectiveness of the Executive Assignment System was eroded by the agencies' failure to utilize the Executive Inventory. Nevertheless, the inventory proved useful in other respects, princi-pally as a source of information. "We are able to supply information," asserted the executive director, "to the President, the Civil Service Commission, the Office of Management and Budget and Congress effectively and efficiently."[35] Most important, perhaps, was that the inventory made possible significant research and analyses of top ca-reer positions and executives in the federal government.

STUDIES BASED ON THE INVENTORY

By mid-1969 the Executive Inventory included information concern-ing approximately twenty-eight thousand individuals serving in grades GS-15–GS-18 and equivalent levels. Of these, one-fourth or roughly seven thousand were in the supergrades of GS-16–GS-18 and equivalents. For the first time, the Bureau of Executive Man-power was afforded the unprecedented opportunity to research this unique impressive data bank—a historically unparalleled system for making information readily available.

Warner, Van Riper, Martin, and Collins—in their outstanding collaborative 1963 study of federal executives—had stressed environ-mental factors such as father's education and occupation, parents' lin-eage, and marriage.[36] Interesting though such a sociological approach may be, this kind of information was unavailable in the Executive Inventory. It did, however, offer contemporary information more rel-evant to the study of careers of currently employed federal executives.

Besides current information concerning executives' last fifteen years of work experience, the inventory provided information relating to their education, preferences with respect to referral for assignment, professional activities, honors, and special qualifications; and certain additional data useful for statistical analyses of career patterns of federal executives as a group.

Beginning with publication of a brochure in November 1969 on characteristics of federal executives,[37] over a dozen analyses based on the inventory were in various stages of completion by mid-1971. Most were undertaken by staff of the Bureau of Executive Manpower, but others were undertaken by independent academicians retained as summer faculty of the commission to whom the bureau provided access to the inventory. Although few inventory studies were published, they were fully utilized as staff papers by the commission in its continuing efforts to improve personnel management of federal executives.

Characteristics of Federal Executives

The bureau's 1969 study of characteristics of the 28,000 federal executives (GS-15–GS-18 and equivalents), for whom adequate data were then available, found 81 percent were accounted for by the fourteen largest agencies (Veterans Affairs; National Aeronautics and Space Administration; Defense; Army; Navy; Air Force; Health, Education and Welfare; Treasury; Commerce; Agriculture; Transportation; Interior; Atomic Energy Commission; and Justice). Two-thirds had more than 20 years of service, and 54 percent were aged 55 or older. Only 21 percent listed themselves in the general occupation of administration, the remainder being distributed as follows: engineering 18 percent; medicine 14 percent; physical science 10 percent; law 7 percent; social science 6 percent; financial management 5 percent; business and industry 3 percent; biological science 3 percent; and the remaining 10 percent dispersed among other occupations. About 85 percent had at least one college degree and over 50 percent held a master's degree or higher.

The same study revealed that 42 percent had full federal careers, having entered below GS-9 and never having left; 22 percent entered at a senior level and never left; 20 percent entered at midcareer (GS 9-12) and never left; and the remaining 16 percent were in-and-outers (moved from federal employment and returned one or more times). Fifty-three percent worked in only one federal agency, and about 78 percent of those in supergrade positions were working in their present agency—cabinet department or independent agency—at the time they were first appointed to a supergrade position (and 80 percent of these were in the same bureau—the first organizational unit below the agency level—in the supergrade position to which they were first appointed). The median age at the time of the first supergrade appointment in the executive's agency was found to be 46.[38]

Although not all statistics in this initial inventory study differentiated the seven thousand supergrades from the approximately twenty-one thousand GS-15s and equivalents, for whom adequate data also were available, it is possible to sketch a rough likeness of a typical supergrade executive of 1969. The typical federal executive was likely to have been a specialist rather than a generalist; had at least a master's degree; had entered a federal bureau in a large agency below GS-9 and never moved from that bureau—even to another bureau in the same agency; had more than 20 years of federal service in that bureau; was aged 46 at the time of supergrade appointment; and was 55 or older at the time of the 1969 study. Results of this initial study were suggestive of subsequent analyses of the Executive Inventory by the Bureau of Executive Manpower.

Supergrade Scientists

In December 1970 a draft of a bureau study was completed of supergrade scientists, consisting of supergrades in these self-coded occupational categories: physical, biological, and medical sciences; mathematics; and engineering. Of 6,560 supergrades studied, 2,853 or 44 percent were scientists. This study conclusively dispelled any notion that many so-called executives were not truly managers of people, programs, and resources but were individual workers who either managed small teams or were "bench scientists." Only 12 percent of all supergrades, and only 11 percent of all supergrade scientists, were found to be self-designated individual workers.

In other respects, the self-coded scientists essentially shared the characteristics found in the initial study. The average supergrade scientist was a career executive performing managerial functions, had served in the federal government for 16 or more years, was aged 45–50, and was still working in the same bureau in which he or she was appointed to a supergrade position.[39]

Noncareer Executives

Prior to establishment of the Executive Assignment System, supergrade positions were commonly known as career and, for lack of better nomenclature, political—the latter term in reference to Schedule C appointments for persons serving in policy-determining or confidential capacities to political appointees or other key officials. In discussions within the Civil Service Commission, the term *political* caused concern. "It smacked more of partisan politics than of controversial policy aspects of a program." Accordingly, "the Commission eventually adopted the suggestion that Schedule C positions be referred to as 'non-career' rather than 'political.' This nomenclature provided a clear, meaningful distinction between Schedule C positions and others which did confer status while avoiding the unfortunate connotations of the adjective 'political.' "[40] The term *noncareer* then comprised positions in Schedule C as well as Schedules A and B (for which examinations were not practical). Schedule C supergrade positions were converted in 1967 to "noncareer executive assignments" and were broadened to include also supergrade positions in which the executive was deeply involved in so-called advocacy of administration programs and support of their controversial aspects. Although this change greatly increased the potential number of noncareer executive positions, a 1971 study of the inventory by the Bureau of Executive Manpower, found that career positions nevertheless represented 76 percent of the total supergrade positions. Moreover, this study found little difference between career and noncareer executives in terms of what they actually did on the job. Their inventory records revealed that most career as well as noncareer executives saw themselves as performing the executive functions primarily of managers or supervisors.[41] Hugh Heclo commented on the distinction between career and noncareer supergrades:

Hence for almost 7,000 people near the top of the government, the formal demarcation between bureaucrat and political appointee is far from obvious. Depending on who is doing the counting, noncareer "political" positions can be taken to mean only NEAs [noncareer executive assignments] or all positions exempt from the competitive career service. Thus anything from 9 percent to 25 percent of the executive supergrade positions can be considered as political appointments. That experienced government leaders disagree so widely on the actual proportions is itself indicative of the murky boundaries between political appointees and civil servants. Whatever the intricacies of body counts in the personnel system, the major point is that somewhere in this smudgy zone between top presidential appointees and the several thousand officials below them, the vital interface of political administration occurs, for better or worse in terms of government performance.[42]

Change of Administration

Not only was there little difference between career and noncareer supergrades in what they actually did as executives, but, contrary to widespread belief, most noncareer executives also stayed in federal service during or after a change of administrations. This surprising finding of one study of the inventory by the Bureau of Executive Manpower had significance for planning and development of executive personnel management.

The transition between Democrat President Johnson's and Republican President Nixon's administrations was the first for which adequate data had ever been available for the study of changes in employment status of federal executives—thanks to the Executive Inventory. Despite the change of *party* administrations, the bureau's study found that 37 percent of the incumbents of noncareer executive positions at the close of the Johnson administration were still in the same positions at the end of the first year of the Nixon administration. Furthermore, an additional 16.5 percent of the Johnson noncareer executives were still in the federal service in different positions at the end of the first year of the Nixon administration. Hence 53.5 percent of the Johnson administration's noncareer supergrade executives were still in the federal service at the end of the first year of the Nixon administration.

Even more striking, perhaps, was the finding that more than half of the Nixon group of noncareer executives and more than three-fourths of the Johnson group had completed ten or more years of federal service.[43]

Rate of Advancement

Still another study of the inventory sought to determine criteria of "success" in reaching GS-15 by a factor analysis of intercorrelations of the criterion of age at which an individual reached GS-15 with 39 other inventory variables. This mid-1971 study, however, found that the criterion of age, by itself, was not a controlling variable. Rather, the strongest factor derived was clearly what might be termed a generation factor—namely, that the age at reaching GS-15 was dependent on the generation in which the individual entered the federal service. Of those who entered before the Great Depression, 85 percent were found to have been aged 54 or older at the time of their GS-15 appointments, and none was younger than 50. The average age at appointment to GS-15 progressively decreased with each succeeding generation. For example, of those at GS-15 who entered federal service within the fifteen years preceding this study, only 14 percent were found to have been aged 54 or older at the time of their GS-15 appointment, and fully 45 percent were below age 42. Although this study analyzed the inventory in terms of reaching GS-15 rather than GS-16 or above, its conclusion could be equally descriptive of advancement to supergrade status.

> It seems evident that for both scientists and the nonscientists in grades GS-15 and above, the road to a senior grade is traveled fastest by playing according to the Government and agency rules, not the rules of a profession. The scientist who moves upward fastest is the one who came into the Government at a low level with poorer education than average (for his field), who has stayed with the Government, who has not been active in professional societies, who has not been productive professionally, and who has been recognized by his agency as contributing to agency goals. Much the same picture is presented for the upwardly mobile nonscientists.[44]

Interagency Mobility

Another inventory study worthy of mention concerned interagency mobility among federal executives. It was found that over 50 percent of all supergrades and equivalents (noncareer as well as career) and nearly 67 percent of the GS-15s had spent their entire federal career in a single agency, whereas only 12 percent of supergrades and 9 percent of GS-15s were "generalists" in that they held significant positions in three or more agencies.[45]

CONCLUSION

Facing a Congress controlled by opposition Democrats, President Eisenhower sought to salvage an emasculated semblance of the Second Hoover Commission's proposed Senior Executive Service by resort to executive orders creating a Career Executive Program outside the Civil Service Commission. Congressional hostility abruptly ended this endeavor, and the complicated and fragmented executive personnel system persisted.

Dwight Eisenhower's Democratic successors fared no better, and they too circumvented Congress in their attempts to rationalize executive personnel management. Unlike President Eisenhower, however, both Presidents Kennedy and Johnson relied on the Civil Service Commission to develop a new system.

First, the well-intentioned Executive Roster was attempted by the Kennedy administration primarily for filling supergrade positions. However, the roster was widely ignored and little used, and this system faltered. Next was the more ambitious computerized Executive Assignment System of the Johnson administration, but its mandatory search-and-referral Executive Inventory process degenerated into a pro forma exercise in red tape for many agencies. Accordingly, the inventory process became voluntary and failed to achieve the purpose for which it was intended.

The inventory, nevertheless, provided for the first time a rich resource for studies of federal executives. From various studies based on it, a composite portrait of federal executives began to emerge. In general, federal supergrade executives were immobile, highly educated specialists nearing retirement who had spent their entire careers in the federal government. Most entered the government at an early age and a low grade and worked in their specialties through the years in the same bureau, where they finally achieved executive status. This portrait began to be fragmented into significant differences when a generation factor was employed—that is, when executives were grouped according to time frames within which they first entered federal service. Nevertheless, though most in supergrades viewed themselves occupationally as scientists or other professional specialists rather than as administrators, there was little difference in what they actually did—all but a small minority performed the executive functions primarily of managers or supervisors. And this was true for noncareer as well as career executives. Though the former by definition had uncertain tenure in the government, most survived even a change of party administrations and had accumulated ten or more years of federal service.

Thus the inventory generated unprecedented statistical information and new knowledge and insights about federal executives. Armed with these studies, the Nixon administration was poised to frame its own proposal for a personnel management system for the federal executive and was even emboldened to resort to the legislative process for its establishment, as had been recommended by the Second Hoover Commission in 1955.

CHAPTER V

Nixon's Proposal for a Federal Executive Service

The Civil Service Commission (CSC) was an ambiguous entity from its inception, and it became more so after World War II, oscillating between more and less proximity to the president and White House and between its roles of policing and advising on personnel management. The commission's close access to two Democrat presidents, Kennedy and Johnson, through John W. Macy, its chairman and presidential advisor on personnel, ended with the presidential inauguration of Republican Richard Nixon in January 1969.[1]

The commission's intimate working relationship with the White House evoked distrust in Nixon's top staff. Accordingly, the Office of Management and Budget (formerly the Bureau of the Budget), established in mid-1970, added a new Division of Executive Development and Labor Relations charged with "advising the President on the development of new programs to recruit, train, motivate, and deploy and evaluate men and women who make up the top ranks of the civil service, in the broadest sense of that term."[2] Thus the Bureau of Executive Manpower began sharing its mission of developing a top-level executive personnel system with the new division of the Office of Management and Budget.

THE SUPERGRADE PUZZLE

After two years of operation, the Executive Assignment System had registered a number of successes. It had demonstrated to agencies its ability to refer highly qualified candidates on a continuing basis. The number of appointments across agency lines had increased. Agency heads and program managers had become actively involved. Some rationality in executive personnel planning had been introduced. And finally, the inventory had proven a rich resource for significant research of executive personnel and positions.

The Executive Assignment System, however, had to operate within a bewildering array of authorizations for supergrade positions and equivalents, concerning which the CSC's responsibilities were uneven and diverse. Over the years since World War II, a heterogeneous and fragmented complex of authorizations had been enacted by Congress governing the upper-level positions in the executive branch. Whatever semblance of a system existed was the product of valiant efforts of the CSC—through its Executive Assignment System—to institutionalize administratively some features of the Second Hoover Commission's proposal for a Senior Civil Service. But the CSC had been fighting a losing battle. Executive personnel management had to operate within a maze of statutory rigidities and flexibilities which created artificial, inhibiting, and illogical distinctions among various categories of upper-level positions.

Federal executive personnel management appeared more ascriptively than rationally determined. Categories of positions were differentiated by such factors as agencies, salary systems, types of programs, occupations, and professions. There were distinctions labeled career, noncareer, quota, nonquota, GS-16, -17, and -18, special agency authorizations, competitive, excepted, Schedule A, Schedule B, career executive assignments, Public Law types, and executive levels I–V, to mention only some of the categories. A despairing tone is implicit in this description by the CSC:

> There are numerical supergrade position quotas given to the Commission for classification action and allocation to various agencies; there are other positions granted directly to agencies but with classification action required by the Commission; there are positions for which no numerical limitations have been imposed, whereas almost the same types of positions in other agencies or pay systems are limited by specific numbers authorized by Congress; in some agencies positions must have the compensation and qualifications approved by the Civil Service Commission, whereas in others exactly the same types of positions are left for final determination by the agency head.[3]

The CSC defined federal executives as those in positions compensated at the salary range for GS-16–GS-18 or equivalents ($28,129–$36,000 in 1971). In March 1971 there were 10,431 federal executive positions of all types, of which 5,793 were in the General Schedule; 1,238 were Public Law (including former PL-313-type) positions; and 3,400 were positions of other federal personnel systems. The CSC had some responsibilities for most, but not all, GS and PL positions.

A total review of these top federal positions was long overdue. There was serious question whether the classification system should be applicable to executive positions. Not only did the career public services of many other countries, as we noted in chapter 1, have separate systems for executive personnel, but private industry in the United States also typically applied very different personnel practices to senior management. In 1963 the state of California had launched a separate career executive system that, by 1971, was healthy and appeared to be maturing into a viable and effective system.[4]

While the Executive Assignment System had brought about improvements in the staffing of federal supergrade positions, the problem of providing adequate numbers of these positions remained, particularly in light of the pressure for more supergrade positions at the outset of the Nixon administration. The government-wide quota of supergrade positions for the CSC to allocate to the various agencies appeared grievously insufficient. Accordingly, the commission intermittently appeared before the House Subcommittee on Manpower and Civil Service to request expansions of its supergrade pool. On one such occasion in March 1972, Subcommittee Chairman David Henderson expressed alarm about the "end runs" that were continuing to be made by various agencies to other congressional committees for spot authorizations of supergrade positions:

> At the present time, there are seven bills pending in the Congress which, if enacted into law, would create at least 90 additional supergrade positions.
>
> I cannot overemphasize the alarm that members of this subcommittee are experiencing over the number of bills—many of them administrative proposals—that are reaching the House floor with

provisions that violate the statutory standards and controls relating to Federal employment.

The Civil Service Commission, which is supposed to be the executive agency responsible for the overall administration of the Government's personnel system, seemingly has lost all control over top-level positions in the Federal Government. Instead, it appears that the Office of Management and Budget now is calling the shots in this area.

I deplore this situation and I, along with other members of this committee, do not intend to sit back and watch the Office of Management and Budget run roughshod over the standards and controls governing the employment and compensation of Federal employees.[5]

Beginning in 1949 with authorization of 400 positions in the government-wide quota, Congress had authorized additions of: 150 in 1954; 650 in 1955; 26 in 1956; 287 in 1958; 954 in 1961; 411 in 1962; 177 in 1966; 150 in 1969; and 7 in 1970. Only once—in 1959—had Congress reduced the government-wide quota, by 478. By mid-1970 the quota totaled 2,734 positions at GS-16–GS-18. Together with other authorizations, the total number of supergrade and PL-313-type positions was 7,020. Table 2 shows their distribution from 1947 to 1976 by year and by authority.

Table 2 shows that from 1954 to 1970, the total number of supergrades and equivalents had increased more than tenfold, or over 1,000 percent. During the same period the total number of federal civilian employees had increased only 27 percent.[6]

Congress had stipulated that, of the aggregate number of positions in the government-wide quota, no more than 12 percent could be allocated at GS-18 and no more than 25 percent at GS-17.[7] In 1963 a new nonquota category of supergrades was established by Congress which exempted from the government-wide quota professional positions in the physical or natural sciences and medicine, or engineering positions with the primary functions of research and development. This meant that an unlimited number of such positions could possibly be placed in GS-16–GS-18, so long as their duties and responsibilities were determined by the CSC to warrant the grade. In practice, the Bureau of Executive Manpower interpreted this authority broadly

TABLE 2. INCREASE IN SUPERGRADE POSITIONS, 1947–1976

YEAR	GOV'T-WIDE QUOTA	NON-QUOTA	SPECIAL AUTHORITY	PL-313-TYPE	TOTAL
1947				45	45
1948				50	50
1949	400			60	460
1950	400			90	490
1951	400		11	90	501
1952	400		19	90	509
1953	400		19	90	509
1954	550		19	90	659
1955	1,200		59	120	1,379
1956	1,226		65	220	1,511
1957	1,226		65	220	1,511
1958	1,513		174	737	2,424
1959	1,035		547	935	2,517
1960	1,035		547	1,030	2,612
1961	1,989		617	1,293	3,899
1962	2,400		633	1,301	4,334
1963	2,400	195	633	1,301	4,529
1964	2,400	1,014	882	1,301	5,597
1965	2,400	1,206	884	1,301	5,791
1966	2,577	1,420	977	1,334	6,308
1967	2,577	1,626	977	1,334	6,514
1968	2,577	1,776	981	1,334	6,668
1969	2,727	1,892	1,053	1,244	6,916
1970	2,734	1,953	1,095	1,238	7,020
1971	2,754	1,966	1,132	1,238	7,090
1972	2,754	1,806	1,221	1,238	7,019
1973	2,754	1,832	1,232	1,238	7,056
1974	2,754	1,855	1,442	1,238	7,289
1975	2,754	1,726	1,442	1,238	7,160
1976	2,754	1,704	1,492	1,238	7,192

Source: U.S. Bureau of Executive Personnel, Civil Service Commission, *Executive Personnel in the Federal Service* (Washington, D.C.: Government Printing Office, November 1977), 2.

and even approved, on occasion, such nonquota supergrade positions for psychologists, anthropologists, and economists. Insofar as agencies had successfully obtained nonquota supergrade positions, this development helped relieve some pressure on the commission's government-wide quota.

Nevertheless, the CSC continued to have the almost impossible task of providing an absolute minimum number of supergrade positions from its fixed government-wide quota to agencies responsible for implementing new high-priority programs. How did the commission meet this responsibility? Whence did it acquire the Solomon-like wisdom to allocate these positions among the competing agencies? There was probably no rational answer to this question. Some understanding of the process, however, may be gained by witnessing the commission's response to the late-1969 action of Congress (approved January 2, 1970) authorizing the CSC to establish 150 additional supergrade positions in the government-wide quota,[8] after many requests by the commission over several years.

On January 7, 1970, at the completion of the Nixon administration's first year, CSC Chairman Robert E. Hampton notified the heads of executive departments and agencies of the 150 supergrade positions that Congress had added because of new programs and responsibilities. He cautioned that even these positions "would not permit us to eliminate the inequities that exist or meet the needs that might arise in less critical programs." And he established the following guidelines for allocating the positions:

> Only programs of high Administration and Congressional importance will be considered.

> Allocations will be based on the total needs of an agency; that is, new programs will not get new positions unless existing authorized positions are optimally used.

> In those agencies with current accent on decentralization, we will look closely at what is being done to relocate current positions from headquarters to regions rather than solely requesting new positions for regional activities without decreasing the numbers in headquarters.

> We will need to keep a small reservoir of spaces to authorize key positions in future critical programs.[9]

In response to the chairman's memorandum, an assistant secretary of one executive department requested eight positions, based "strictly on priority programs," a request he labeled "modest, prudent." He wrote Hampton that these were positions the department needed immediately. In a revealing manner, he stated: "We are postponing requests for other very important positions only because we have found other, temporary means to get around the quota space problem." Among the eight requested positions, the first priority was a GS-18 position for executive assistant to the secretary the urgent need for which—again candidly stated—resulted from political pressures or, as he put it, "stems directly from congressional and presidential pressures."

Each agency, in requesting supergrade positions from the quota, attempted to impress on the CSC the great importance of its programs to the president and Congress. It was incumbent on the commission to be responsive to presidential and congressional leadership while, at the same time, maintaining the standards of fitness and merit for which it was responsible. The commission, and especially the Bureau of Executive Manpower, had to operate adroitly in a political milieu in administering its government-wide quota of supergrade positions. There were simply never enough positions in the quota to meet the program needs of the federal government. It became essential for the commission, therefore, to try to make the most efficient use of each quota space provided by law. In times of great demand for such spaces, the commission had taken steps to recapture vacant spaces. Accordingly, the commission ruled in 1970 that it would "automatically cancel any quota supergrade position which has been vacant for 180 days or more," so that such position might be relocated where most needed.[10]

THE COMMISSION'S STUDY

Soon after he entered the White House, President Richard Nixon requested the CSC to undertake a thorough and systematic analysis of the government's executive personnel management programs and to make recommendations for essential reforms. The bulk of the analysis was conducted by the Bureau of Executive Manpower and identified a now familiar litany of problems: (1) both career and noncareer executives must cope with a variety of *constraints* on their decisions to organize programs and on hiring, assigning, and removing their key career and noncareer subordinates; (2) executive personnel *planning* was grossly inadequate; (3) the bureaucracy lacked *responsiveness* to new political and program direction; (4) agency heads must confront a great variety of *pressures* concerning whom they chose for executive positions; (5) there was no assurance that the *best available executive talent* was being identified, developed, and utilized; and (6) there was inadequate centralized *leadership and responsibility* for management of executive resources.[11]

Unnecessary Constraints

Concerning unneeded contraints on executive decisions, the CSC cited the existence of over a dozen personnel programs governing executives, several of which inhibited many agency heads who had to deal with a variety of laws, regulations, pay systems, and career rights. These restrictions produced friction among different programs, difficulties in assigning people into and out of different programs, unnecessary administrative loads, and frustrations for executives who tried to understand and use these programs.

Each personnel program unnecessarily limited staffing options and program administration and led to: irrational distinctions among grade levels at GS-16, -17, and -18; overemphasis of prestige and status in determining grade levels; meaningless distinctions among positions designated career or noncareer; unwillingness of agency heads to fill important executive positions labeled as career with individuals whom they did not know well and whom they feared would become "locked in"; an appeals system for reduction-in-force actions unsuited to the executive work force; and inflexible authorizations for paying executives that led to inequities in particular situations within an agency or across agency lines. Agency heads, moreover, were severely limited in the number of executives they could appoint because of the various quotas. Because of these ceilings, neither the CSC nor the agencies could assign executive resources on a timely and rational basis in response to changing program needs.

Lack of Planning

In reference to the problem of planning, the commission flatly stated that there was "almost a complete lack of planning to identify and meet future executive manpower needs and to explore and develop sources of supply" With only a few exceptions, agencies were simply not forecasting executive needs to replace current executives or to meet changing program demands. The commission cited these examples: agencies had only general ideas of the number and kinds of executives to be replaced over the next five years; sources of supply to meet executive needs had not been identified (typically, legislation was proposed and approved for new programs without analysis of sources of required management talent); and program planning did not include executive personnel planning.

Unresponsiveness

The issue of responsiveness, according to the commission, was "how to insure that the bureaucracy reflects public policy expressed through the political process." Friction between career and political executives frequently accompanied changes in administration or administrators. Confronted by complex and constraining personnel programs, the new agency head found it difficult to depend on career subordinates to respond to political and program changes, particularly if the agency head perceived them to be locked in, and the head could not reassign them or appoint new subordinates through the establishment of new positions. Frequently restricted by incumbencies, the agency head's confidence became undermined, especially where career employees had been placed in political jobs, and, conversely, political ones in career posts. Accordingly, the commission complained, current personnel systems did not adequately recognize the value of providing to agency heads a reasonable number of "their own men" to serve as advocates. "This is not necessarily a partisan issue, but it is essential to building a unified and harmonious management team."

Pressures

In discussing the great variety of pressures on agency heads in selecting executives, the commission acknowledged the increasing impact on executive personnel management of greater professionalization of top management. Professionals in and out of government formed alliances to maintain professional credentials in agency staffs and to influence the direction and size of programs. Other staffing pressures came from such sources as interest groups for their advocates, partisan sources to reward party faithful, and Congress and constituent representation. The agency head needed some way to accommodate to these pressures.[12]

Needed Executive Talent

Demand for high-quality leadership with adequate managerial skills exceeded the supply, the commission suggested, thus frustrating the career growth of executives and hence the achievement of important program objectives. Clearly identified career fields, career goals, promotion ladders, or career development programs were simply not available in most agencies, where executive development had yet to become institutionalized or made an integral part of the total management process.

Lack of an Integrated System

Finally, the commission lamented the lack of any government-wide system of leadership and responsibility for management of executive resources. Even the president found it difficult to hold his appointees accountable for executive personnel management. Much more attention was devoted to financial resources than to personnel resources. No single agency—not even the CSC—had overall responsibility for executive personnel management, a situation that prevented the president from receiving periodic reports on the stewardship of executive resources or systematic reports for essential improvements. What was needed, the commission concluded, was a system to ensure effective, integrated, and coordinated management of executive resources *across* agency lines.

Having thus analyzed the six major problems, the commission's study restated the overall goal of federal executive personnel management: "to provide the right number of executives with the right skills and attitudes, in the right places, at the right time, motivated to perform in the most effective way." Within this broad goal, the commission redefined objectives of an effective executive personnel program:

Require that top agency executives carry out their responsibility for executive manpower management and assist them in doing so.

Insure that executives who have responsibility for government programs have commensurate authority over their executive resources in proper balance with the needs of the government as a whole and the long-run needs for a career work force.

Provide the quantity and quality of talent required by: forecasting needs; recruiting and developing potential talent at all levels; maintaining a pool of talent; and keeping it motivated.

Insure that the executives in the federal government are responsive to public policy as enunciated by the president and the Congress and responsive to the top political management of the government at all times.

Provide individual executives with opportunities to achieve their full potential for contributing to the nation's progress and for personal growth, recognition, and work satisfaction.

Assure that high-quality employees at entry level and at the mid-management level perceive that they can rise to the top and get important and influential jobs with reasonable security.

Provide a central source to review, analyze, and make recommendations on all aspects of executive personnel management, including a means for the president to hold agency heads accountable for the management of their executive manpower resources.[13]

PRESIDENT NIXON'S PROPOSAL FOR A FEDERAL EXECUTIVE SERVICE

All recommendations of the CSC were incorporated into President Nixon's proposal to Congress for establishment of the Federal Executive Service (FES).

The FES would include, with certain exceptions, the approximately 7,000 civilian executives then currently in grades GS-16–GS-18 and their equivalents. To correct the existing fragmentation of appointing authorities and personnel systems, FES coverage would be broad and based on levels of duties and salaries instead of job classifications.[14]

It followed, then, that centralized classification of positions by the CSC would be eliminated for authorizing executive resources, establishing qualifications and pay grades for individuals, and controlling assignments. Hence, prestige as a member of the FES would be substituted for grade as a status factor. Instead of centralized position classification, agencies would apply a position management approach, annually reviewing their executive manpower needs and requesting a specific number of executives for the ensuing fiscal year. The CSC, in its turn, in collaboration with the Office of Management and Budget, would review requests from agencies and forecast and authorize the number of executives for each agency on the basis of such factors as: current levels of program, budget, and executive staffing; anticipated program and budget requests; pending legislation; and the level of work to be done. The CSC would report the authorizations annually to Congress and they would become effective ninety days thereafter.

Appointments to the FES would be either career or noncareer. Noncareer appointments would be for executives whose employment would likely be of a temporary nature, such as executives whose relationships to agency heads would require an interdependence based on program philosophy, political agreement, or personal confidence; those who worked on relatively short-term projects; and those whose employment would be more oriented toward their professions or occupations. Though the proposal did not state how such relative professional orientation would be measured, it did identify this last group as "highly mobile people" who moved freely in and out of private employment, universities, private practice, and government in pursuit of their specialized interests, commonly known in government parlance as in-and-outers.[15] Noncareer officials would be appointed and removed at the pleasure of the agency head. All other members of the FES would be career merit appointments, which would require review and approval by especially established "qualification boards."

Actual positions and assignments, however, as distinguished from appointments, would not be designated as career or noncareer. Instead, each agency would be authorized a career/noncareer ratio by the CSC, in collaboration with the Office of Management and Budget, on the basis of its individual requirements. The aggregate government-wide number of noncareer executives would be limited to 25 percent of the total FES.[16] Annual authorized agency ratios would become effective ninety days after the CSC's annual report to Congress.

Within an overall government-wide salary range authorized for the FES by the CSC—approximately that encompassed by current GS-16–GS-18 positions—agency heads would have the authority to fix and adjust salaries of career and noncareer executive appointees. They would be able to increase, but not reduce, these salaries so long as the average salaries were within the authorized range and did not exceed the executive average set by the commission. Moreover, executives would automatically receive comparability pay increases and other benefits when they were authorized for other federal employees. These features, then, presumably would help the government to remain more competitive in attracting and keeping executive talent.

As has already been indicated, career and noncareer executives would be sharply distinguished in appointment and retention, but their actual assignments would not be designated career or noncareer. Since the FES would not provide for a government-wide system of position classification, heads of agencies would be able to reassign both career and noncareer executives, interchangeably, to any duties anywhere (organizationally or geographically) properly within the scope of the FES. It was reasoned that inhibitions to mobility would thus be reduced. Seymour Berlin, director of the Bureau of Executive Manpower explained:

> It has long been apparent that the present rigid distinction between "career" and "noncareer" positions does not reflect reality. In fact, executive positions in the Government lie along a continuum in respect to policy involvement, with only a comparative handful at either extreme which can be readily classified into these two categories. Furthermore, the tendency has been to categorize positions

of the highest responsibility as noncareer. This has resulted in a limitation of opportunity for those in the career service, since a career executive who elects to move into one of these top positions forfeits the career rights he has built up over the years. Under the FES, he may accept any assignment without such jeopardy.[17]

Although agency heads would continue to select their career executives, their initial appointments in the FES would require prior approval by the qualification boards that would be established by the CSC, the highly qualified membership of which would be appointed from within and outside the federal service. Not only would this requirement presumably encourage heads to select the individual best qualified, but it would also afford them a means to resist unreasonable pressure from interest groups on the subject of staffing.

Perhaps the most important and controversial feature of the proposed FES was the provision that employment of career executives would be governed by "employment agreements" for an initial, but renewable, period of three years. Under this agreement, the executive at any time could transfer to another agency, resign, or retire if eligible, but the agency could not remove the executive except for cause, disability, or refusal to accept a reassignment. Moreover, the executive would be specifically exempted from reduction-in-force procedures.

Once a career executive had completed the three-year period, the employing agency could: (1) offer a three-year renewal agreement; (2) offer a continuing GS-15 position in the competitive service; or (3) require the executive to retire if he or she had thirty years of federal service. Should the executive decline a renewal agreement, he or she would either be offered a continuing GS-15 appointment or be retired. Should a renewal agreement not be offered and should the executive decline the offer of a GS-15 appointment, he or she could receive, if otherwise eligible, severance pay or a discontinued service annuity. Were the executive to decline both renewal agreement and a GS-15 post, he or she would be entitled to neither severance pay nor a discontinued service annuity. Noncareer executives, on the other hand, would not receive employment agreements but would serve instead at the pleasure of the agency head. Obviously anticipating criticism of this unique feature, Seymour Berlin commented, "Far from creating an untouchable elite corps, the FES proposal recognizes that the country's needs demand that the executive group be composed only of individuals *currently* making an exceptional contribution, and that persons serving in career executive positions are periodically reviewed for retention in the group."[18]

Should an executive be transferred to another agency during a three-year agreement period, the agreement with the new agency would expire at the end of the existing one, with the usual three-year renewal options thereafter. This provision allegedly would facilitate organizational mobility, but meanwhile it would assure that executives would not move to avoid having their continuing service reviewed. Meanwhile, organizational mobility would continue to be encouraged through the existing executive inventory and by the increased variety of assignments for which an FES executive would be peculiarly qualified and available, thus "broadening his experience and preventing the excessive specialization that today stands in the way of mobility."[19]

CONGRESSIONAL REACTIONS

On February 2, 1971, President Nixon's message to the Democrat-controlled Congress urged "prompt and favorable consideration of this landmark legislation." Recalling his 1971 State of the Union Address, in which he proposed to Congress a sweeping reorganization of the executive branch, the president linked the need for this "best of structures" to the need for the "best people," and he added: "We need both dedication and high performance from our Federal executives. Mere competence is not enough. Mere continuity is self-defeating. We must create an environment in the Government service in which excellence and ingenuity can flourish—and in which these qualities are both encouraged and rewarded."[20] Hailing the proposal as "a milestone in the eighty-eight-year evolution of the merit system," CSC Chairman Hampton hoped "that Congress will enact the proposal substantially as submitted to Congress, for we are confident that it will help to make the merit system more responsive to modern needs."[21]

On May 10, 1971, a two-hour hearing was held on the FES bill by the Senate Committee on Post Office and Civil Service. Hampton was the only witness. After covering much of the substance of the commission's study, he identified three problem areas that the FES was designed to address. The most evident was the lack of a personnel system for government executives. "What we have is a hodgepodge of authorities and pay systems, all under different ground rules, with no one agency accountable for the effectiveness of executive manpower management." Also, agency managers lack the authority to manage their executive resources. And finally, an executive might remain an executive as long as he or she wished even after ceasing to make a high-level contribution. "We have the means of dealing with outright incompetence," Chairman Hampton declared, "but mediocrity remains a problem." And he added that a single weak executive, "on the weakest link principle," could jeopardize an entire program.[22]

Much of the Senate hearing consisted of discussion of salary ranges for federal executives and their lack of comparability with the compensation of executives outside government.[23] The hearing was "mild in tone," according to a Washington columnist, Mike Causey, committee members giving Hampton "an easy time."[24]

In the following month, however, the chairman of the Senate committee, Democrat Senator Gail McGee, wrote to Hampton about "a number of misgivings" expressed by his committee members, including the following features: the FES "philosophy," the mobility issue, nonquota positions, fall-back to GS-15, political implications, the career/noncareer ratio, the impact on the career service, and retirement.[25] Hampton quickly responded in detail, addressing each of the committee's concerns.[26]

Over a year passed between the hearing and the Senate committee's report recommending passage of the FES bill with its amendments. Among the amendments proposed by the committee were the following: (1) The committee rejected the part of the bill providing exceptions from the FES and proposed instead that the president determine exceptions after recommendation by the CSC. (2) The committee also rejected the bill's provision for a three-year contract as too "revolutionary." (3) The committee rejected the requirement that the commission collaborate with the Office of Management and Budget, as diffusing the commission's responsibility. (4) Instead of the agency having complete latitude to determine the pay of an FES executive (between GS-16 and Level V), the committee proposed that the agency choose from among eleven specified pay rates covering the same range. (5) And, finally, instead of the head of an agency having exclusive authority to determine the qualifications of noncareer employees without any restraints on which positions should be noncareer, the committee proposed requiring the CSC to approve the qualifications of individuals prior to noncareer appointments.[27]

Meanwhile, on April 18, 21, and 25, 1972, the delayed House hearings on the FES were much more extensive and contentious than the Senate hearing. Hampton again appeared and covered much the same ground, but twelve other witnesses also appeared, including administration spokespersons favoring the bill and officials of government employee unions opposing it. Opponents criticized the three-year renewable contract and the projected career/noncareer mix (75 percent/25 percent) as politicizing the FES. Elmer B. Staats, comptroller general of the United States, stated the General Accounting Office criticism that the provision for a three-year renewable contract would create "a needless disincentive, and might invite abuses," and would "tend to diminish rather than enhance the Government's attractiveness as an employer."[28] According to Causey, criticism by the General Accounting Office was a critical blow and its advice to Congress would "gut" the bill.[29]

OTHER REACTIONS

Government critics of the FES gained a prominent ally from outside the government—George A. Graham, executive director of the prestigous National Academy of Public Administration. In a pungent article in the *Public Administration Review*, Graham charged the CSC with attempting to escape "political pressures" by the FES provision to vest the function of qualifying "men" for positions in "department boards."

> How many of the 75 percent reserved-area positions will be filled by men who have never worked a day for Uncle Sam before? When

their numbers are totaled (particularly after a new administration) how many of the FES jobs will be left in the reserved area for the qualified men who have demonstrated their worth by the best of all tests—working for the government? . . . Who is responsible for the relocation of career men who are not reappointed to an FES position? Is anyone? Yes, of course, the displaced person has a hunting license to find a job back in grade 15 somewhere—but where? . . . Can anyone doubt that the mortality rate will be terrific? Claiming that most career executives would wind up at the bottom of FES, Graham predicted that FES would "truncate" the entire Federal career service. In short, FES is "full of holes."[30]

But the "fatal flaw," according to Graham, was the three-year renewable agreement. Inaction—not action—would get rid of the career executive, Graham claimed. For one who achieved GS-15 ranking rapidly and was offered an FES appointment in his or her early 40s, the offer made it probable that he or she would be "eased out of the government when he is at his peak." Whatever it may be called, "this is not a career." Instead, the three-year agreement scheme was "disastrously dysfunctional" and "a camouflaged way of cutting out accumulated dead wood." It will result, however, in "a cutting of live roots." A "less disastrous way" would be to "wipe the slate clean" of tenure provisions, with all FES executives serving at the pleasure of department heads, who would have "free discretion" to remove them. The "quality control function" of approving career appointments to the 75 percent reserved area should be vested in an independent government-wide "Citizen Board" of twelve to fifteen eminent citizens from outside the government, and the provision for three-year contracts should be stricken.[31]

In a rebuttal article in the same issue, Roger W. Jones, a consultant with the Office of Management and Budget, could not accept Graham's "negative prejudgment." The flexibility of agency heads to establish a "more effective mix" of career and noncareer executives, together with annual review by the CSC and the Office of Management and Budget, would be "more constructive" than current maneuvering on Schedule C appointments, which resembled the children's game of "Pin the Tail on the Donkey" or "Pin the Trunk on the Elephant." Quality control for entrance into FES career ranks would be vested in qualification boards as agents of the CSC—not in departmental boards as Graham feared.[32]

The three-year renewable agreement, wrote Jones, would be "rational, and as fair as any selection-out system can be," and "far better than no tenure, which Mr. Graham seems to favor," which would permit "arbitrary and capricious removal." Furthermore, Graham's suggestion that each holder of a three-year contract would ultimately disappear into limbo so long as a timid agency head did nothing was a "patently farfetched assumption" that would not be permitted to become a general rule or an option of any agency head. Finally, "the entire concept of the Federal Executive Service gives greatly needed and long overdue leverage for manpower planning, accompanied by better incentives for useful mobility than now exist."[33]

CONCLUSION

The Senate never acted on the FES bill, and after the hearing in the House of Representatives, the bill was never reported from the House Subcommittee. Inaction by both houses, therefore, killed the proposal. Still, top officials of the CSC and the White House sought to salvage it by planning to introduce a modified version in a nonelection year after the 1972 presidential and congressional elections, which they hoped would reelect Republican President Richard Nixon and shift control of the Congress from Democrats to Republicans. In his column of May 17, 1972, Causey conjectured: "If Mr. Nixon wins again, the present CSC team is . . . likely to reintroduce the idea of contracts for top career officials. They think it would have a better chance in 1973 with a president in his last term recommending it as a genuine civil service reform, and better able to blunt criticism that it was a set-up to clean out well-entrenched Democrats."[34] Although Richard Nixon did win reelection in November 1972, a favorable political climate for a revised FES (even one stripped of the three-year contract provision) was never to materialize during the Nixon era, and the CSC put the proposal quietly on the shelf.[35]

Nixon's FES initiative had simply become overwhelmed and obscured by other developments in a larger political landscape. These developments included: Nixon's effort to politicize the higher civil service and the suspicions and mistrust thereby aroused; his effort to establish "the imperial presidency"; other abuses of executive authority; and the resurgence of congressional oversight.

President Nixon reputedly was resolved to purge the higher civil service of Democrat civil servants and replace them with Republicans. "Distrust of the bureaucracy was a recurring theme in almost all of Nixon's public statements," and a major objective of his strategy was "to contain and neutralize the bureaucracy."[36] This was hardly a posture designed to evoke support for the Nixon-sponsored FES package.

CHAPTER VI

The Making of the Senior Executive Service

The abuses of executive authority associated with the Nixon presidency tolled the death knell of the Federal Executive Service. In the maelstrom of Vietnam, Watergate, impoundments, and coups sponsored by the Central Intelligence Agency, Congress was not about to provide the president with more authority over the bureaucracy. Indeed, the entire tide of legislative resurgence in the early 1970s—embodied in the War Powers Act, the Congressional Budget Reform and Impoundment Control Act, invigorated congressional oversight of intelligence activities, and so forth— pointed in the opposite direction and seemed to doom any structural reforms that could be construed as augmenting the power of the executive branch.

Paradoxically, it was exactly this political turmoil that created a climate hospitable to a new round of reform. Reinforced by a series of scandals in Congress, the perfidies of Watergate soon broadened in the public mind to encompass the whole "mess in Washington." Politics itself, not the political balance between the two ends of Pennsylvania Avenue, became identified as the problem. The way was then clear for Jimmy Carter, a self-described outsider untainted by experience in the federal government, to reframe the debate. What the irrationalities of politicians had torn asunder, the cool logic of a businessman, armed with reorganization plans and zero-based budgets, would put right.

Central to Carter's campaign for the presidency in 1976 was an attack on what he called the "horrible bureaucratic mess" in Washington.[1] The federal bureaucracy, Carter charged, is "wasteful" and "disorganized."

There is a pervasive tendency in government toward unrestrained growth in salaries, number of personnel and expenditure of funds. This growth often bears little relationship to the actual need for government services. . . . The first piece of legislation I will send to Congress will initiate a complete overhaul of our federal bureaucracy and budgeting systems. The second part, as a follow-up to the first, would initiate the reorganization of our federal bureaucratic structure. . . . The greatest need facing the United States today is for a well-managed structure of government—one that is simple, efficient and economical.[2]

THE FEDERAL PERSONNEL MANAGEMENT PROJECT

After his election, Carter moved quickly to redeem these campaign promises by asking his transition planner (and soon to be the executive associate director of the Office of Management and Budget) Harrison Wellford, to coordinate a study of the organization and operation of the federal bureaucracy. Reporting in April 1977, Wellford's team described a federal executive establishment that was bloated, redundant, and inefficient.

In an effort to address some of these problems, President Carter established in May 1977 the Federal Personnel Management Project under the joint leadership of the Civil Service Commission and the Office of Management and Budget. With the then chairman of the CSC, Alan Campbell, as its chairman and Wayne Granquist, associate director of the Office of Management and Budget, as its vice chairman, the project was charged specifically with the responsibility of undertaking a "full-scale review of federal personnel management laws, principles, policies, processes, and organization."[3]

Overseen by its executive director, Dwight Ink, the day-to-day work of the Federal Personnel Management Project was undertaken by nine subject matter task forces led by distinguished federal officials, private sector executives, and academic experts and staffed by more than one hundred federal employees. As table 3 indicates, these task forces—covering the whole gamut of civil service issues, from equal employment opportunity to labor-management relations— were to identify problems and develop detailed options for reform. Task Force #2, headed by Sally Greenberg, a senior official at the

TABLE 3. TASK FORCES OF THE FEDERAL PERSONNEL
MANAGEMENT PROJECT

TASK FORCE	CHAIR
1. Composition and Dynamics of the Federal Work Force	Joseph T. Davis, IRS
2. Executive Service	Sally Greenberg, CSC
3. The Staffing Process	Charles E. Weithoner, FAA
4. Equal Employment Opportunity and Affirmative Action	Harriet Jenkins, NASA
5. Job Evaluation, Pay, and Benefit Systems	William D. Conley, Honeywell, Inc.
6. Labor-Management Relations	Chester A. Newland, University of Southern California
7. Development of Employees, Supervisors, Managers, and Executives	James W. Brogan, CSC
8. Roles, Functions, and Organizations for Personnel Management	Walter G. Held, Brookings Institution
9. Federal, State, and Local Interaction in Personnel Management	Joseph R. Coupal, Jr., House of Representatives Staff

Source: James McGrath, "Federal Civil Service Reform: The Federal Personnel Management Project and Proposed Changes in the Federal Civil Service System," Library of Congress, March 30, 1978.

Civil Service Commission, was devoted exclusively to the problems of the higher civil service.[4]

In addition to the nine subject-specific task forces, the Federal Personnel Management Project included a "Working Group" co-chaired by Jule Sugarman of the Civil Service Commission and Howard Messner of the Office of Management and Budget and composed of the assistant secretaries of administration of all departments and major agencies. The group was to act, in effect, as a steering committee for the project. To circumvent what had been one of the chief obstacles to earlier reform efforts—opposition from federal agencies—it was agreed that nothing was to be proposed which did not have the full support of this committee.[5] Table 4 provides a complete list of the members of the working group.

The task forces worked through the summer and early fall of 1977.

Table 4. Working Group of the Federal Personnel
Management Project

Cochairmen

Messner, Howard M.	Office of Management and Budget
Sugarman, Jule M.	Civil Service Commission

Members

Allnut, Robert F.	Energy Research and Development Administration
Beckham Jr., William J.	Treasury Department
Burkhardt, Francis	Labor Department
Conway, James R. V.	Postal Service
Cooke, David O.	Defense Department
Drayton, William	Environmental Protection Agency
Gabusi, John	Community Services Administration
Kallaur, Walter V.	General Services Administration
King, J. Fred	Agriculture Department
Kline, Ray	National Aeronautics and Space Administration
Laise, Carol	State Department
Medina, William	Housing and Urban Development Department
Mendelsohn, Robert	Interior Department
McFee, Thomas	Health, Education, and Welfare Department
Porter, Elsa A.	Commerce Department
Rooney, Kevin D.	Justice Department
Scott Jr., Edward W.	Transportation Department
Taylor, Eldon D.	National Science Foundation
Vaughn, Robert D.	Veterans Administration

By October of that year they had issued a total of seven "option papers," the results of which were vetted by the Working Group and distilled into a set of more than one hundred specific reform proposals in the final staff report of the Federal Personnel Management Project, completed in December 1977. The first volume of the report, containing the recommendations themselves, was released to the public in January 1978, with volumes 2 and 3, which presented the option papers and other supplements, following in February.

THE EXECUTIVE SERVICE TASK FORCE AND ITS RECOMMENDATIONS

The option paper dealing with problems of the higher civil service, nearly sixty pages in length, including several detailed appendixes, was completed first, at the end of July 1977. Its major finding was the now familiar refrain that the extant system of executive personnel management failed "to foster efficient, effective and equitable administration of Government programs." Eleven (also familiar) problems were identified as especially critical:

1. Neither the Congress nor the president has effective control over the total numbers in the executive cadre.

2. The numbers of executives authorized have little relationship to current needs, and the system cannot adapt rapidly to program changes.

3. The multiplicity of hiring authorities with different requirements and provisions results in individuals with substantially similar responsibilities being employed and compensated under very different standards. It is susceptible to manipulation and fosters the use of questionable, albeit legal, maneuvers.

4. Individuals with little or no adequate managerial expertise can be placed in positions responsible for managing billion-dollar federal programs and for supervising thousands of employees.

5. Career employees have little opportunity to undertake positions of the highest responsibility without relinquishing their career tenure.

6. Whenever there is a change in political leadership, there is a period in many agencies during which the work of the government is done at a minimum maintenance level. New initiatives are rare and even ongoing programs operate in low gear.

7. There are critically important executive positions classified as career positions which new administrations would like to fill with executives of their own choosing, but reassignment of incumbents is very difficult to make, principally because of the existing protection of rank and inflexibilities of the system.

8. It is commonly observed by both career and noncareer ex-

97

ecutives that some career managers are functioning less than optimally, in some instances because they are in positions that make greater demands on them than they are capable of meeting, in other cases because they have no incentive to do their best. It is difficult to remove such managers.

9. Compensation of executives has been a serious problem in recent years, with most senior executives frozen in pay for long periods while their subordinates' pay, compensation for comparable positions in the private sector, and the cost of living have all risen dramatically.

10. The present process for establishing and filling an executive position is time-consuming and inefficient.

11. Minorities and women have been virtually excluded from top management ranks.[6]

Revisions of the existing system of executive personnel management would not, in the view of Task Force #2, suffice to remedy these problems. Instead, the task force proposed an entirely new "Executive Service" that would "seek a balance between giving agency heads flexibility in the use of executive resources and ensuring meaningful career protection to employees."[7] The Executive Service would include all managerial positions in the supergrades (GS-16–GS-18) and in Executive Levels IV and V across all agencies and personnel systems in the federal government—including the CIA, FBI, Tennessee Valley Authority, and the Foreign Service—with provision for presidential exceptions.[8] The service would encompass both career and noncareer appointees, although it would be divided into a Career Managerial Service and a Noncareer Managerial Service. No more than 15 percent of the overall Executive Service would consist of noncareer members. Certain positions covered by the service, particularly those involving audit and inspection, contracts and grants, investigations and security, and so forth, would be designated "career reserved"; that is, they could be filled only by a member of the Career Managerial Service (or by a "limited term" appointee).[9] Remaining positions (an anticipated 50–70 percent of the total) would be designated as general, to be filled by officials from either career or noncareer ranks.

Members of the Career Managerial Service would attain tenure in the Executive Service—though never in a specific position—after serving a one-year probationary period. A tenured member of the service removed from a position for cause or poor performance would be guaranteed either another assignment in the Executive Service (in the same agency or a different one) or reassignment to another service at a pay level no lower than 85 percent of his or her current Executive Service salary; he or she would also be allowed to retire, if eligible.[10] No involuntary reassignment or transfer of a member of the Career Managerial Service could take place within 120 days of the appointment of a noncareer employee who was closest to (and above) him or her in the supervisory chain; similarly, no performance ratings would be made within six months of a change in administration.

A rank-in-person classification system would prevail in the Executive Service, with three compensation levels, designated A, B, and C. To guard against uncontrolled grade escalation, the task force recommended limiting the A level to 8 percent of the service and the B level to 37 percent, with C members constituting the remaining 55 percent. Longevity increases would be prohibited. Pay would instead be pegged solely to individual and organizational performance, which would be evaluated annually by panels in each agency. Top performers could expect to receive bonuses of up to 20 percent of base pay. Additional benefits and incentives—recruitment bonuses, deferred compensation, annual leave carry-overs, expense accounts, and so forth—would be made available to increase the attractiveness of the service so as to enhance recruitment and retention. To maintain the overall level of excellence, participation in executive development programs would be mandatory for both career entry and continuation.

These features of the Executive Service, Task Force #2 maintained, would speak directly to the eleven critical problems identified above. The president and Congress would have more effective control over total staffing levels in the executive cadre. Executive personnel could be flexibly deployed when and where needed. The number and complexity of hiring authorities would be drastically reduced. Demonstrated managerial ability would be necessary before an individual could be placed in an important administrative post. Career public executives would be able to accept top policy-making positions without relinquishing their career status. Policy continuity would be provided during periods of political transition, while at the same time a new administration would eventually be able to assemble a philosophically compatible staff.

Agency heads, moreover, would have considerable latitude to shift personnel. Regular performance reviews, coupled with performance-based pay and selections-out, would improve the overall calibre of the executive cadre. Incentive pay and deferred compensation plans would loosen some of the constraints on executive salary levels and would narrow, though not close, the gap between public and private sector executive pay. Personnel authority would be considerably decentralized, and bottlenecks in filling positions would be reduced. And an emphasis on systematic executive development would open new career opportunities for women and minorities.

In designing this system, the task force considered two alternative higher civil service models, which emerged in part from their consultation with more than four hundred groups "representing a broad spectrum of interests," and from their meetings with approximately two hundred senior executives. The first alternative was basically a private industry model, in which top management has "a free hand to assign, pay and remove executives." The second was basically a European-style civil service model, characterized by a permanent cadre of professional managers, with service tenure, rank-in-person, and a highly structured, closed-career-ladder system. The task force's summary assessment of these systems and its consequent strategy are revealing in light of later developments:

> The study group considered both of these philosophies carefully and devised two systems reflecting these views. In neither case were we satisfied that the system dealt adequately with the full range of problems associated with executive personnel. We, therefore, attempted to construct a system which incorporated some of the best features of the other two systems. It is this system that we have recommended.[11]

The final staff report of the Federal Personnel Management Project cast Task Force #2's proposals into fourteen discrete recommendations (as set forth in table 5) with annotations as to the method of implementation—legislative action, executive order, and so on—which would be required. Combining these recommendations with proposals from the other task forces, the project formally transmitted this report to the White House in December 1977.

The Carter administration accepted these recommendations without substantive revision, a fact that reinforced the beliefs of some critics that the entire process of the Federal Personnel Management Project's hearings and option papers had been something of a charade, that the recommendations that the chairman of the Civil Service Commission, Alan Campbell, had elicited from the policy machine in December were exactly the recommendations he had put into the machine the preceding spring.[12] A more charitable (and accurate) interpretation is that careful attention to the politics of reform from the earliest days of the Federal Personnel Management Project—widespread consultation with leading members of Congress, key interest groups, and a broad cross-section of agency officials—meant that the administration received a set of proposals that virtually everyone, or at least everyone who seemingly mattered politically, could live with. This is to say that there was no replay here of the Eisenhower-era Senior Civil Service reform initiative, where critics were not confronted until it was too late.

THE SENIOR EXECUTIVE SERVICE IN CONGRESS

Following a nationally televised speech on March 1, 1978, in which he outlined the major provisions of his proposals, on March 2, President Carter sent his message on civil service reform to Congress. On March 3, 1978, legislation entitled the Civil Service Reform Act of 1978 was introduced in both the House of Representatives (H.R. 11280) and the Senate (S. 2640) with bipartisan sponsorship.[13] For the reasons noted above, most provisions of the proposed Civil Service Reform Act—particularly title IV, which dealt with senior executives—simply mirrored Federal Personnel Management Project's recommendations. With respect to title IV, the only change of conse-

TABLE 5. RECOMMENDATIONS OF THE FEDERAL PERSONNEL MANAGEMENT PROJECT

1. Create a wholly new personnel management structure for selecting, developing, and managing top level Federal executives.

2. Bring all executive branch systems and agencies into the Executive Service, but provide for Presidential exceptions.

3. Include in the new Executive Service all managerial positions at the present GS-16, -17, and -18 supergrade levels and in Executive Levels V and IV.

4. Set total executive strength Government-wide and for each agency, using a zero-base determination of need, subject to Congressional review.

5. Delegate authority to agency heads to determine whether an individual meets the specific qualification requirements for a particular Executive Service position (as opposed to managerial qualifications, in general).

6. Identify positions which should be administered on a strictly non-partisan basis and those concerned exclusively with managing on-going programs without major policy formulation. Reserve those positions solely for career employees. Permit all remaining positions to be filled by career or noncareer managers, at the discretion of the agency head. To prevent an increasing politicization of the remaining positions, set a statutory ceiling limiting the total proportion of noncareer managers in the workforce to current levels.

7. Shift from the current rank-in-position to a rank-in-person personnel system. Develop appropriate limitations to prevent members of the Executive Service from all rising to the upper end of the pay scale.

8. Eliminate protection against reduction in rank and other aspects of veterans' preference within the Executive Service.

9. Establish a system of accountability for organizational performance, linked with both compensation and tenure of executives.

10. Protect career executives against capricious, improperly motivated, or illegal discriminatory actions. Except for misconduct, prohibit a newly appointed noncareer executive from moving subordinate career executives out of their positions until at least 120 days after the noncareer executive is appointed.

11. Eliminate longevity pay increases for executives. Substitute one-time incentive payments based on excellence of performance and not subject to pay ceilings.

12. Require systematic executive development with full attention to the necessity for bringing women, minorities and other excluded groups into the managerial mainstream.

13. Require individuals to demonstrate managerial capability before entering the Executive Service.

14. Give present incumbents of positions incorporated into the Executive Service the option of being "grandfathered" into the Service or of remaining in their present positions, retaining all the rights, compensation, and benefits to which they are presently entitled.

Source: U.S. Personnel Management Project, *Final Staff Report*, vol. 1, sec. 8, "Establishing an Executive Service" (Washington, D.C.: Civil Service Commission, July 1977–February 1978), 186–200, recommendations 78–91.

quence was in the name, from the project's Executive Service to Senior Executive Service (SES).

Given the resistance earlier reform initiatives had met, the response—or nonresponse— of Congress to the proposed SES was extraordinary. It slipped through Congress wholly unscathed, with all of its major provisions intact. In thirteen days of hearings before the House Committee on Post Office and Civil Service and twelve days of hearings before the Senate Committee on Government Affairs, attention was focused primarily on other elements of the president's civil service package—veteran's preference, merit pay, labor rights, affirmative action, dismissal procedures, and so forth.[14] For supporters of the SES, the only real cause for concern came when the House Committee on Post Office and Civil Service approved an amendment—ultimately defeated in conference—introduced by Representative Gladys Spellman (D-Maryland) that sought to limit the system to a two-year experiment in three agencies.

This is not to say that legislators—in asking questions of administration officials or representatives of various interest groups offering testimony—ignored the SES. Concerns about title IV, particularly about potential politicization of the upper reaches of the career bureaucracy, were clearly voiced.[15] The point, however, is that sailing for the SES in Congress was exceptionally smooth, far smoother than anyone familiar with the legislative history of earlier reform initiatives would have expected.

Final congressional approval of the Civil Service Reform Act provided a fitting coda to the administration's orchestration of the legislation: the Senate accepted the conference report on October 4, 1978, by voice vote; the House passed it by a vote of 365 to 8 on October 6. One week later, on October 13, President Carter signed the bill into law. As provided by the statute, the SES was inaugurated nine months later, on July 13, 1979.

PROVISIONS OF THE SENIOR EXECUTIVE SERVICE: AN ANALYTICAL SUMMARY

Exactly what did the Congress authorize in title IV of the Civil Service Reform Act of 1978? Many features of Nixon's ill-fated Federal

Executive Service were incorporated. As we have noted, moreover, most features of the SES as set forth in the act are identical to those proposed by the Federal Personnel Management Project, which have already been described in some detail. It is appropriate to review the key provisions of the legislation here, however, both to underscore the continuity of the proposals and to provide a firm point of departure for the analysis of the SES undertaken in the next chapter. These provisions were:

Uniform Executive Personnel System

All GS-16, -17 and -18 positions falling under the General Schedule in all federal agencies (with certain specified exceptions, such as intelligence agencies, the FBI and government corporations) plus positions in levels IV and V of the Executive Schedule were collapsed into the SES. Most of the more than sixty separate appointing authorities were eliminated.

Rank-in-Person, Not in Position

The use of position classification for senior executive jobs was abolished. Unlike employees within the standard GS system, members of the SES carry their rank (in effect, their status and pay grade) wherever they go, just as in the military. Thus rank in the SES inheres in the person, not in the particular job being done.

Redesignation of Executive Positions

Distinctions between political and nonpolitical jobs were relaxed. Managerial positions are no longer as rigidly classified as career or noncareer (or political). Although some positions remain "career reserved," most have been designated general, which means that they may be filled by either careerists or noncareerists. The main intent of this provision was to provide opportunities for careerists to assume positions of greater responsibility and authority without sacrificing their career civil service status. To prevent the SES from becoming dominated by political appointees, the Civil Service Reform Act placed a statutory limit of 10 percent on the number of noncareerists in the service (and 25 percent in any one agency).

104

Flexibility in Assignments

To encourage broader experience and perspective among senior officials and to accommodate the changing needs of agencies, the CSRA allowed agency managers to shift SES members from position to position as deemed necessary.

Performance Appraisal

Each member of the SES would be subject to annual performance evaluations that take into consideration both individual and organizational performance. Consistently unsatisfactory performance would result in removal from the service and reversion to a GS-15 position, or, where feasible, and desirable, optional retirement.

Performance Awards

Up to 50 percent of career SES members in each agency were to be eligible to receive annual cash performance bonuses. These bonuses, which might not exceed 20 percent of an employee's base pay, would be linked to the annual performance reviews.[16]

Special Ranks

Each year, the president could, upon recommendation of the Office of Personnel Management and the agencies, confer the rank of meritorious executive or distinguished executive on career appointees; no more than 5 percent of the SES could receive the former rank in any given year; and no more than 1 percent could receive the latter. Recipients of the meritorious executive rank were to receive one-time, lump-sum bonuses of $10,000; recipients of the distinguished executive rank were to receive $20,000.[17]

Executive Development

Under the general supervision of the Office of Personnel Management, agencies were to establish programs to recruit and develop candidates for senior executive positions and to provide development opportunities, including sabbaticals, for continuing members of the SES.

WHY WAS THE PROPOSAL FOR THE SENIOR EXECUTIVE SERVICE ADOPTED?

Although the SES is distinctive in certain respects, the similarities between it and earlier reform initiatives are striking. Rank in person, consolidated appointment authority, and executive mobility, as well as stress on enhanced compensation, were at the heart of the Senior Civil Service and Federal Executive Service proposals as well. This raises an interesting and important question: Why did the SES proposal succeed—legislatively, at least—where its predecessors had failed?

At least five factors were critical to the early success of the SES. Although these have been alluded to above, it is worth restating them here. First, far more than Dwight Eisenhower and even more than Richard Nixon, Jimmy Carter made civil service reform a presidential priority. It was the centerpiece of his plan to reorganize the federal government, and he devoted much of his time and energy to seeing it implemented. Although earlier presidents had interests in civil service reform, Carter's zeal and personal commitment were unusual. He talked about the need for reform in cabinet meetings and persuaded his top officials, including the secretaries of state and defense, to adopt the issue as their own and to use their influence in Congress to promote it. Earlier rounds of reform, the Federal Executive Service partially excepted, were clearly initiatives by civil service professionals (in the broad sense) who managed to obtain a formal stamp of presidential approval. The Civil Service Reform Act, in general, and the SES in particular, were widely perceived as something squarely on President Carter's agenda. This made them more difficult to resist.

Second, and even more important, was the politically astute manner in which the reform was moved forward. Opposition was anticipated and, wherever possible, co-opted. The Federal Personnel Management Project's strategy of broad participation, manifest both in the hearings and in the use of the Working Group, was extremely effective. The administration also made a concerted effort to breathe life into what is ordinarily seen as a lifeless issue. The chairman of the Civil Service Commission, Alan Campbell, for instance, met with the editorial boards of dozens of major U.S. newspapers. Whenever the reform bill seemed about to become bogged down in Congress, a new flurry of editorials would appear in support of it. And, by bundling the SES together with other, more politically attractive reforms, such as merit pay and changes in federal labor relations practices, a broader coalition could be constructed.

Third, Congress and the country had changed. The first stirrings of the tax revolt were under way, deficits were rising, and bureaucrats were even less popular than usual. Proponents of reform played on these themes, carefully packaging the Civil Service Reform Act to fit the antigovernment tenor of the times. Congressional defenders of public employees had an especially difficult time opposing a bill that would ostensibly make government more efficient, accountable, and well managed. And, not incidentally, we now had a Democratic president, early in his second year in office, addressing Democratic majorities in both the House and the Senate.

Fourth, the SES was not the Senior Civil Service. Although similar in many respects, the SES clearly embodied different values. Responsiveness, not neutral competence, was its hallmark. This was a key difference, for unlike the intangible and somewhat distant benefits of earlier initiatives, the allures of the SES (and other features of the Civil Service Reform Act) for the president and his top advisers were real and immediate. The new leverage over the bureaucracy that it conferred made the SES worth the expenditure of political capital; although the Federal Executive Service may have been worth such expenditure, too, by the time it reached Congress, President Nixon had precious little political capital left.

Fifth, and perhaps most important, the SES was perceived as the proverbial elephant in the midst of the proverbial blind men. Members of Congress, representatives of interest groups, administration officials, and senior executives themselves saw in the SES—in part, because of astute political management, *were encouraged to see* in the SES—what they wanted to see. Did the SES represent a reinforcement of traditional civil service values of nonpartisanship and neutral competence or an opportunity for greater managerial control and responsiveness to policy? Would the SES look like an elite European administrative cadre, the roster of junior vice presidents in Fortune 500 corporations, or an assemblage of trusted lieutenants in a political machine? In effect, the answer to all these questions was Yes. So disparate were the images of the SES in 1977–1978 that one could construe the proposed service as virtually anything one wished. Whether they were themselves unclear as to the real purposes of the SES or whether they simply found the confusion politically advantageous, administration officials did little to bring conceptual order to the issue.[18] The long-term consequences of this strategy—or oversight—is the subject of chapter 7.

CHAPTER VII

Reform in Action:
The Senior Executive Service, 1979–1994

The creation of the Senior Executive Service (SES) in 1978 was an achievement of historic proportions. What a generation of reformers had tried and failed to accomplish in a myriad of vehicles, from the Senior Civil Service to the Federal Executive Service, had seemingly finally come to pass. By the time the SES went officially into effect on July 13, 1979, more than 98.5 percent of eligible senior managers in nearly 70 federal agencies had chosen to convert from grades GS-16 and above to SES status, creating a corps nearly 7,000 members strong. By 1994 the SES covered 8,200 top civilian executives in over 70 federal agencies (see table 6).[1]

Yet while the SES has survived, it has not thrived. The weakness in its pulse may be felt particularly from levels of turnover that consistently approached 10 percent a year through the 1980s; from survey data that show depressingly low morale; and from recurrent attempts to alter the structure of the system. In 1988, for instance, a General Accounting Office study found that only 12.6 percent of SESers would recommend public sector employment to someone just beginning a career.[2] Another GAO analysis indicated rather ominously that many of these senior executives might be taking their own advice: of all SES members who separated from the service in 1985, more than 25 percent were less than 50 years of age; over 42 percent were less than 55; and over 75 percent were less than 60. When the full effects of the federal government's new retirement system—which removed the "golden handcuffs" from employees through pension portability—are felt, the attrition rates may become even greater.[3] If, as it is reasonable to assume, SESers represent much of the institutional

Table 6. Agencies with More Than 75 SES Members, 1994

AGENCY	NUMBER OF SES MEMBERS	% OF SES TOTAL
Defense Department	1,488	18
Department of Health and Human Services	653	8
Treasury Department	601	7
NASA	577	7
Energy Department	513	6
Commerce Department	449	5
Transportation Department	417	5
Agriculture Department	381	5
Department of Veterans Affairs	330	4
Justice Department	316	4
Environmental Protection Agency	288	4
Interior Department	286	3
National Regulatory Commission	214	3
Labor Department	171	2
State Department	140	2
General Services Administration	121	1
Department of Housing and Urban Development	113	1
National Science Foundation	107	1
Education Department	91	1
Office of Management and Budget	78	1
Total of 20 Agencies	7,334	89
Other Agencies	866	11
Total government-wide	8,200	100

Source: Internal unpublished statistical summaries in the Office of Executive and Management Policy of the Office of Personnel Management (February 1994).

memory of the federal government, as well as the deepest repository of managerial skill and substantive expertise, such low levels of morale and high levels of turnover are worrisome, to say the least.

Underlying these symptoms are many of the same seemingly intractable problems that have dogged the senior federal executive personnel system for years—compensation, career/noncareer relations, and executive development and mobility. This chapter explores how the SES has addressed these problems over the past fifteen years and discusses four sets of proposals—made by the Volcker Commission, the Twentieth Century Fund and other groups—to alter further the structure of the senior executive personnel system.

To provide a proper context for understanding these problems and proposals, however, we begin with a brief discussion of the political environment of the higher federal service during the 1980s. This was a critical period, for within months of its inception, the SES was confronted with the 1980 election of Ronald Reagan, the most avowedly antigovernment president in generations. Not only would the fledgling SES have to weather the turmoil of a change of party control of the executive and Senate, but its career executives would also become the new administration's "obvious and immediate target."[4]

THE SENIOR EXECUTIVE SERVICE UNDER THE REAGAN ADMINISTRATION

The new Office of Personnel Management had barely begun to function when its first director, Alan Campbell, left the government in December 1980, thus increasing OPM's uncertainty amid the presidential transition to Republican Ronald Reagan. Campbell's replacement was Donald Devine, who sought to reverse the direction of civil service reform by replacing the management orientation of career executives with their "unswerving emphasis on responsiveness . . . to political direction."[5] Describing Devine as "a favorite of the far right," Brownstein and Easton elaborated: "Only in a government at war with its own employees, where political appointees view themselves as the French at Dien Bien Phu, could a man like Devine be appointed to run the OPM. . . . Devine has surrounded himself with political appointees . . . and has virtually ignored career personnel, resulting in often poorly informed decisions and plummeting morale at OPM."[6] During Devine's four-year term at the helm of the Office of Personnel Management, the number of its career professionals fell 18 percent, while the number of its political appointees increased 169 percent.[7] Bernard Rosen, a former executive director of the Civil Service Commission, observed that many of Devine's political appointees had little or no relevant experience for their positions at the Office of Personnel Management.[8]

The Reagan administration undertook several measures to guarantee that career civil servants became responsive to executive "political" direction. First, the number of noncareer SES appointees was increased and for the first time accounted for over 10 percent of the executive population by September 1983.[9] Second, the number of "limited term" executive appointments (also exempt from career controls) and Schedule C political appointments to lower-level positions was substantially increased. Finally, the number of forced reassignments of career executives within the SES, including geographic reassignments, was greatly increased, jumping to 1,226 in 1982 followed by another 1,100 in 1983. More than 40 percent of the career executives who had converted to the SES in July 1979 had left government service by the end of March 1983.[10]

To acquire better understanding of what was behind these statistics, we turn now to a more detailed look at three major problems: compensation, career/noncareer relations, and executive development and mobility.

Compensation

As we have seen, every major study of the civil service for the last forty years has warned that noncompetitive low salaries of senior executives threaten to undermine the federal government's ability to attract and retain competent managers. Salaries have been so eroded by inflation and years of neglect that public service may be priced out of the reach of the middle class. Indeed, one study group, after reviewing the compensation picture for all top federal officials, grimly predicted that we were "drifting toward a government led by the wealthy and by those with no current family obligations."[11]

Recognition of this problem provided a major rationale for the establishment of the SES. Promises of significantly increased compensation were dangled in front of senior executives. Although the risks of enlisting in the SES would be real (one could be fired or transferred without appeal and would in any event be held closely accountable for one's own performance and that of one's organization), the rewards nevertheless would be commensurate. Fifty percent of the service would be eligible for annual performance bonuses of up to 20 percent of base pay. Meritorious executives (a presidential rank limited to 5 percent of the service per year) would be given one-time cash payments of $10,000; distinguished executives (a rank limited to 1 percent of the service) would be granted $20,000. In theory a high-flying, top-performing SESer earning $47,500 in base pay in 1979 could take home $77,000, not an insignificant amount of money by any standards at that time.

In the end the facts did not bear out the theory, at least not for many years. Almost immediately Congress clapped lids on the bonus provisions, first limiting eligibility to 25 percent, then to 20 percent of the service. Although these restrictions were later eased, considerable damage to morale had already been done. A survey of SES members conducted by the General Accounting Office in 1987 revealed that 61 percent of executives were either "dissatisfied" or "very dissatisfied" with their current salary levels.[12] As one SESer put it, "The SES [was] given a bad check. We signed a contract and the other side violated it."[13]

While it is true that many people grumble about pay, and while it is also true that it may be hard to muster sympathy for a group of people whose base salary in 1989 averaged nearly $75,000, it is important to maintain perspective. To begin with, there had been a steady decline in SES salaries, measured in constant dollars, over the first ten years of the service's existence. For example, a member who received a salary of $47,500 in 1979 (the rate for an ES-4, the level at which approximately 50 percent of SES members are pegged) earned $47,447 in 1987 inflation-adjusted dollars.[14] Although other wage earners had similarly seen small paper increases in salaries undercut by inflation over the same period, salary levels for federal executives were exceptionally low (relatively speaking) to start with. From 1969 to 1979, for instance—a period when corporate executives saw a 60 percent *increase* in real purchasing power—federal executives experienced a 31 percent decline in their purchasing power.[15]

Indeed, given the turnover rates of the 1980s, it was the ever growing gap in pay between the public and private sectors which was particularly troubling. While SES pay was declining in real terms from 1979 to 1987, compensation for executives in comparable positions in the private sector increased over the same period by nearly $2,000 in inflation-adjusted dollars. And because the SES started from a position of deficit (the gap between the two groups in 1979 was $14,315 or 30.3 percent) the gap grew proportionally larger. In 1987 the difference was $25,392 in nominal dollars or $16,414 in constant dollars (34.8 percent). The higher one rose in the SES, moreover, the more aggravated became the problem. At the top of the SES pay scale, the gap between SESers and their private sector counterparts in average cash compensation reached 58 percent by the end of the 1980s, a number that was reduced only slightly when total compensation packages (including retirement benefits) were taken into consideration.[16]

Pay *compression* was a related problem. Because Congress could not muster the political will to raise legislative salaries, which in turn served as an effective ceiling on administrative pay, throughout the late 1970s and early 1980s everyone in the SES—and many employees in GS grades below the SES—earned exactly the same salary. Even as the ceilings were raised in the mid-1980s, compression remained a problem. Within the SES itself, the nominal pay differential from ES-1 to ES-6 in 1988 was approximately 17 percent, although because few SESers were actually classed in the lower (ES-1 and ES-2) pay grades, the effective differential was 8 percent. And it was still the case that a mid-to-high-grade GS-15 earned more in base salary than a low-grade SESer (in 1988, for instance, a GS-15, step 8, received $67,717, a step 9, $69,547, and a step 10, $71,377 in base pay; an SES ES-1 earned only $65,994).[17]

The Career/Noncareer Nexus

Although salary has been a serious problem for the SES, it has not, interestingly, been the *most* serious one, at least from the perspective of its members. In fact, when the General Accounting Office surveyed those who left the SES in 1985, salary did not even make the list of the top ten reasons cited for leaving. What did fill the list were grievances about politicization, meddling by top management, and restrictions on professional autonomy.[18] Critics complained that increased politicization was accompanied by a significant reduction in the policy roles of the top levels of the career civil service.[19] Patricia Wilson's research of the reasons senior executives leave the federal government confirms that SES members are most motivated by public policy interest—their dominant motivating need is to influence public policy.[20]

All these complaints seem to reflect the fact that the top of the U.S. bureaucracy is an unsettled and uneasy melange of career executives and political (noncareer) appointees. In 1991 there were in the U.S. government some 508 agency heads and other political appointees arrayed just below the president. The SES contained another 722 noncareer appointees. Political appointments to the executive branch made under Schedule C authority—some of which are to policy/managerial jobs, most of which are not—added another 1,832.[21] Taken together, this total of 3,062 is an extraordinarily large number of noncareer officials, far exceeding in proportion anything found in other industrial democracies. The reasons for and merits of this mix have been much discussed and need not be dissected here in any detail.[22] Suffice it to say that it is problematic for the SES, in part because of the inevitable friction that follows the day-to-day collision of partisan and professional judgment. It is problematic also because every top job filled by a political appointee is one job fewer open to a career official.[23]

As with compensation, the SES was supposed to have solved, or at least mitigated, these problems. Presumably, it was to have been a large and fairly harmonious service, with no distinctions between career and noncareer members—other than that certain jobs requiring exceptional "impartiality," designated "career reserved," were to be off limits to noncareer officials. Undue politicization of the senior management ranks would also be prevented by limiting the number of noncareer SES officials to 10 percent of the total service (and to 25 percent of any one agency). And by moving to a rank-in-person system and erasing the distinction between political and nonpolitical jobs, in theory the SES permitted a career member to take any position—even one requiring a presidential appointment and senatorial confirmation—without giving up career status. By law, the worst that can happen to SESers who take sensitive, "political" assignments and then find themselves out of a job following a change in administration (or any other happenstance), is a reversion to a GS-15. Indeed, the expectation was that normally the displaced SES official would simply be shifted to another SES assignment. The system was designed to open a whole new world of professional opportunities for career officials.

But as with compensation, the reality has been different. From 1979 through 1991, for example, only 116 career SES members were appointed by the president to policy-sensitive positions requiring Senate confirmation (PAS positions). This number actually overstates the case for upward mobility, as 35 of these appointments were to inspector general posts, which, while of undoubted importance, are not generally considered policy-making in character. Overall numbers of political appointees (PAS, noncareer SES, and Schedule C) increased from 2,481 in 1979 to 3,062 in 1991. Only two of 508 PAS appointments in 1991 were filled by career SES members.[24] Clearly career SESers have not overrun the battlements of senior policy positions.

It is somewhat less clear how effective the SES has been in mitigating day-to-day friction between career and noncareer appointees. Although most studies have failed to find evidence of wholesale politicization, evidence has not been adduced that relations among officials have improved since the advent of SES.[25] The weight of anecdotes describing favoritism, political retribution, unfair decisions about bonuses and other political shenanigans, whatever their worth, suggests that tensions between career and noncareer officials have remained troublesome.[26]

Executive Development and Mobility

If the first truth about U.S. bureaucracy is that it has an exceptionally large number of political appointees, the second is that it is highly fragmented. To talk of *the* federal bureaucracy is, for most purposes, illusory. Our administrative state is best seen as a congeries of nearly independent fiefdoms, each with its own territory and culture, each managing its own programs with blithe disregard for any other, occasional border skirmishes notwithstanding.

One of the purposes of the SES—and of its aborted predecessors—was to bring a measure of coherence to this fragmentation. Although few expected or wanted absolute uniformity to be imposed on the agencies, it was intended that the SES would serve as the basis for a genuinely government-wide senior personnel system.

In his testimony on the Civil Service Reform Act before the House Committee on Post Office and Civil Service, the then chairman of the Civil Service Commission, Alan Campbell (who would later become the first Director of the Office of Personnel Management) noted that the traditional fragmented approach to career building, in which an administrator spends his or her entire life within one agency, "deprives both the government and the employee of the rich benefits in competence and understanding which accrue from experience gained in a variety of agencies and programs." The SES, he maintained, would place a "strong emphasis" on executive mobility and development, with the Office of Personnel Management having a "positive duty to encourage and assist career employees in moving among agencies."[27]

In effect, SESers would be a corps of executive smoke jumpers, ready to drop in and quell administrative brushfires wherever they might break out. To help them develop the managerial skills they would need to do this, the Civil Service Reform Act directed the Office of Personnel Management to "establish programs for the systematic development of candidates for the Senior Executive Service and for the continuing development of senior executives."[28] The legislation also provided for a system of sabbaticals—up to eleven months long—whereby career executives would be encouraged to take study leaves and hone skills that they could bring back to their work in the federal government.

Once again, expectations have not been met. By the end of 1986, only four federal agencies—the Defense Contract Audit Agency, the Environmental Protection Agency, the Department of the Interior, and the Department of the Navy—were operating rotation programs, under which a total of 86 career SESers received new assignments. And these, it should be stressed, represented only *intraagency* rotations. No formal mechanism is in place to encourage or facilitate interagency mobility, except for a list of SES vacancies published by the Office of Personnel Management. Only 54 SES members (or 0.7 percent) were transferred between agencies in 1991.[29] By the same token, executive training and development programs for SES officials have been meager, at best. In 1988, the Office of Personnel Management initiated an SES fellows program, through which "SES members have the opportunity to design an individually tailored developmental experience"—but for which only six fellows were selected.[30] By the middle of 1991, moreover, only 32 sabbaticals had been granted since the inception of the SES.[31]

Most worrisome, perhaps, has been the inattention by agencies and the Office of Personnel Management to the beginning of the SES pipeline—to those career civil servants in GS-13–GS-15 ranks who are presumably the SESers of tomorrow. Despite the requirement in the Civil Service Reform Act that the Office of Personnel Management establish (or cause agencies to establish) "Candidate Development Programs" (CDPs) for the SES, little progress has been made in this area. The General Accounting Office reported in 1986 that while fifty agencies had in fact established such programs, few actually used them. Eighty-seven percent of initial career SES appointments in the years 1982–1984 went to people who had not gone through one. Fewer than half of those who did participate received an SES appointment (in 1990, the Office of Personnel Management identified 166 graduates of development programs who had not been selected for SES positions). And about half of those who failed to receive an SES appointment after finishing a program wound up being assigned to a job that was *less* responsible than that which they had left.[32]

At least some of the responsibility for this continued fragmentation must be borne by the Office of Personnel Management. A major management review of the central personnel agency sent to Congress in 1989 by the General Accounting Office concluded that "during the last 10 years, OPM has not provided the leadership necessary to sustain attention to identifying and resolving critical human resource problems affecting federal operations and preparing for the future."[33] At least since 1981, the Office of Personnel Management has construed its role very narrowly, farming out to agencies virtually all responsibility for recruitment, hiring, training, and work force planning. Although considerable personnel deregulation and decentralization was clearly intended by the Civil Service Reform Act, abdication of responsibility by the Office of Personnel Management, particularly with respect to the SES, was not.

PROPOSALS FOR FURTHER REFORM

One clear indication of the extent to which the SES has failed to meet the initial expectations of reformers is the number of proposals that have surfaced to refashion the system. Conceptual dissensus, moreover, is reflected by the unusual variety of such proposals.

Proposal #1: Jettison the Nonexecutives

One of the earliest and most radical proposals for change came from the President's Private Sector Survey on Cost Control, more familiarly known as the Grace Commission, after its chairman, Peter Grace. Established by President Reagan in 1982, the Grace Commission was charged with identifying waste and inefficiencies in the federal government and with making recommendations for change. Among its 47 reports containing nearly 2,500 suggestions on over 750 issues were a series of recommendations, from the commission's task force on personnel, aimed at the SES.[34]

In brief, the task force argued that the SES was too large and included too many people who were not "true executives." The SES's overinclusiveness was said to be a problem chiefly because it limited the potential effectiveness of the performance bonus system: too few dollars had to be used to reward too many senior officials. The Office of Personnel Management, the task force concluded, should take a hard look at SES membership, eliminating positions that did not involve substantial managerial responsibilities. An exercise of this sort would lead to an SES cut from its then current level of nearly 7,000 members to somewhere in the neighborhood of 1,000–3,500 executives. To help recruit and retain executives for this streamlined SES, the Grace Commission also recommended an immediate 20 percent increase in pay.

The Grace proposal spoke to some genuine concerns, pay problems not least among them, and in limited ways made some sense. It is true that many members of the SES are not executives in the private sector's use of the term. Some do serve primarily in a technical or professional capacity, as high-level attorneys, engineers, or bench scientists. And a case can be made, as is discussed below, that it may be more appropriate to develop separate personnel systems or separate personnel tracks for nonmanagerial specialists.

Yet the narrowness of the definition on which the commission seemed to insist was misplaced in the context of the federal government. Although they may not be the mirror images of division vice presidents in large corporations—the apparent analogue of the commission—many SESers who would be cut out of the service by this proposal do play significant management roles.

The government of the United States is not—and should not be construed as—USA, Inc. The lines of authority in a set of agencies necessarily entangled in the web of democracy cannot be made as neat and tidy as those to be found in IBM or AT&T. Anyone who believes that the president sits at the apex of "his" bureaucracy, issuing unchallengeable commands to "his" administrative agencies, should check with Congress and the courts. Moreover, sharp distinctions between executive and nonexecutive jobs are difficult to discover in a system that primarily makes policy rather than breakfast cereal or automobiles.

The Grace Commission also ignored the fact that Congress deliberately cast a wide net in defining *executive* in the 1978 legislation. The SES was to be not just a scheme for paying a few people more money but a system for nurturing managerial talent through executive development programs. The exclusivity embraced by the Grace Commission would have undercut this goal. It would also have meant, as Edie Goldenberg pointed out, a return to the old rank-in-job system for most senior executives, thereby reducing flexibility in reassignment, another important aim of the Civil Service Reform Act.[35]

Perhaps the most troubling aspect of the commission's proposal, though, was its largely unarticulated assumption that career administrators cannot be trusted to be responsible. Elevating accountability to the president to the position of first principle, the commission envisaged a pared-down SES that would be comprised, as a General

Accounting Office report concluded, "mostly of political appointees"—well-paid political appointees at that.[36]

Proposal #2: Jettison Political Appointees

A second major set of proposals aimed at fixing perceived problems with the SES was issued in early 1984 by the Senior Executives Association, which is the major professional association of SES members.[37] Some of the association's proposals, which were timed to coincide with Congress's statutorily mandated five-year review of the SES, were, from the perspective of an outsider, relatively technical in nature, having to do with relocation allowances, retirement benefits, reassignments, reduction-in-force provisions, and so forth. Many others, not surprisingly, had to do with the inadequacy of SES pay and complaints about limitations of the bonus system.

The Senior Executives Association's most controversial recommendations, like those of the Grace Commission, were aimed at the basic structure of the SES. Unlike the Grace Commission, however, the association located the system's chief structural flaw not in its purported excess of nonexecutives but instead in the "mistake" of trying to include both career and noncareer officials in the same system. The SES, in the SEA's view, should be a career-only system. Political appointees ought to be restricted to the Executive Schedule. Trying to force both groups to live together within the same system "has had little positive value, and . . . has added unnecessary irritants to an already stressful relationship between career and non-career appointees."[38]

The Senior Executives Association found little support for this position outside its own ranks, however. As the General Accounting Office pointed out in summarizing reaction to the proposal, "convincing arguments have not been made that combining career and noncareer employees in SES has increased tension, or that separation would reduce tension."[39]

Although the association is undoubtedly correct in pointing to serious conflicts between career and noncareer officials, its solution misses the point: it is the heavy reliance on political appointees in the

U.S. government in general, not the personnel system into which they are folded, that is the source of the tension.

Proposal #3: Separate the "Specialists"

A third set of proposals sought to strip the SES of yet a different cohort.[40] Aimed at addressing what are seen as the unique problems of scientists, engineers, and other technical specialists in the SES, these proposals actually fall into one of two categories, which we can label *separate service* and *separate track* plans. Both are based on the assumption that technical specialists have needs that are distinct from and sometimes at odds with general managers.

As the name suggests, proposals for a *separate service* aimed to break scientists and engineers completely away from the SES and create a separate, technically oriented, senior personnel service (or services). These proposals had their roots in studies conducted by the National Institutes of Health (the Chen Committee) and the Federal Laboratory Review Panel (the Packard Panel), both of which focused on the interrelated problems of pay, recruitment, and performance appraisal for scientists.[41] The National Institutes of Health proposal called for senior technical personnel within its compass to be taken out of the SES and organized into a scientific faculty, modeled on the personnel systems of universities.[42] The Packard Panel also recommended the establishment of a new scientific/technical personnel system, called the Senior Scientific and Technical Personnel Service, which would parallel the SES.

Unlike the proposals for a separate service, which clearly would require action by Congress to alter the structure of the SES and other affected personnel systems, the proposals for a *separate track* would retain the general legal structure of the SES while instituting distinct career ladders or tracks within the service for technical personnel. One such proposal, developed by the Naval Material Command, suggested reorganizing the SES into three separate tracks: technical specialist–expert, functional manager, and executive manager. Technical specialists–experts would be defined as scientists, economists, lawyers, engineers, and other specialists who did not have any managerial duties. Functional managers were defined as those who, while acting as managers, would hold jobs that required a high degree of technical competence. And executive managers were defined as non-technical generalists. As with all such systems, each track would have attached to it separate systems for recruitment, performance appraisal, and career development.[43]

A similar proposal, developed by the Naval Research Laboratory, envisaged a distinction between SES general managers (SES GM) and SES technical managers (SES TM). An SES GM position would require general managerial ability but no specific scientific or technical expertise. An SES TM position, on the other hand, assumed advanced training and expert knowledge in the natural sciences or engineering, as well as managerial competence. SES TMs, unlike SES GMs, would be automatically exempt from the navy's mandatory five-year rotation requirement for SES members.[44]

One tracking system that has actually been installed and used with some success is the Senior Scientific Service operated by the Department of Health and Human Services. The service, which encompasses approximately 23 percent of the department's SES positions, entails (1) a separate performance management system, which gives greater weight to scientific excellence than managerial achievement; (2) a proportionate set-aside of the SES bonus pool for members of the Senior Scientific Service, who compete only against one another for this additional compensation; and (3) the use of distinguished members of the outside scientific community on qualifications review boards in recognition of the greater weight given scientific competence in judging the credentials of candidates.[45]

Although these proposals for separating specialists and generalists have considerable surface appeal, some important issues remain to be resolved. First, what are the relative merits of a separate service as opposed to a separate track? One disadvantage of the former is that it may prove to be just the beginning of the emasculation or disembowelling of the SES, a prospect not to be dismissed lightly given the various constituencies that have expressed an interest in slicing away one part of the service or another. Furthermore, the establishment of a wholly separate service would raise the fear, warranted or not, in the minds of scientists that they would be relegated to a second-class senior personnel system, one that would not be looked to readily as a recruiting ground for top managerial jobs; certainly the British experience suggests caution on this point. Although a tracking system would raise similar questions, as long as the structural integrity of the overall system remained intact, the potential for trouble would be muted.

Second, how many tracks would need to be created? Even if the problem of nonscientific specialists is set aside, it is not clear, as the Naval Material Command proposal reminds us, that two tracks would be sufficient. Once other nongeneralists—lawyers, economists, and so forth—are taken into account, the number of potential tracks increases apace. While in some sense it may suffice simply to identify a single nonmanagerial track that would encompass all specialist groups, the usefulness of this strategy would hinge on the purposes to which the tracking scheme is turned. If tracks are looked to as loci for organizing career development and mobility plans—and a strong case can be made that they should be—then a track that is defined essentially as a residual category (i.e., nongeneralist managers) will not be effective.

Third, at what level of government would the tracking take place? Would the SES as a whole have two (or more) tracks, as defined and supervised by the Office of Personnel Management? Or would agencies be permitted to develop and operate their own tracking plans? Too decentralized a system would once again clearly redefine the SES as nothing more than an employment vehicle.

Fourth is a related issue that concerns the mechanism by which executives are recruited to or selected for a particular track. Although some degree of self-selection will presumably pertain, what kind of central review will be needed? At what point in an executive's career will tracking begin?

Finally, there remains the issue of the relationship among tracks. If the experience of the Foreign Service with its four "cones"— political, economic, consular, and administrative—is any guide, we can anticipate that a tracked SES would tend to become a hierarchically stratified SES. Some SES members might come to be seen as more equal than others, depending on which track they had followed

Would certain top jobs, for better or worse, become the exclusive preserve of members of one track or another? How easy would it be for an executive whose interests have changed to move from out of one track and into another?

Proposal #4: Don't Jettison Anyone,
but Upgrade Status and Pay

In 1986 the Twentieth Century Fund, a private, nonprofit research foundation based in New York, organized a task force devoted entirely to the problems of the SES. Chaired by former Virginia Governor (later Senator) Charles Robb and comprised of sixteen prominent public officials, executives from the private sector, and academics, this group embraced the basic objectives of the Civil Service Reform Act and argued that "since its inception, the SES has demonstrated that it can be a building block for the kind of elite system of senior executives that this nation needs." Rejecting the fundamental structural changes urged by the Grace Commission, the Senior Executives Association, and the various bodies calling for the excision of scientists and other technical personnel, the task force found the current blend of career and noncareer officials in the SES "about right" and recommended that the SES "maintain its current mix of generalists and specialists."[46]

The real problems with the SES, argued the Twentieth Century Fund task force, stem from status, not structure. We as a nation needed to change our attitudes toward public service and cease the "bureaucrat bashing" that reached a crescendo during the 1980s. Senior executives must be able "to advance into high positions" and be recognized for their contributions. Our "political leaders must . . . reawaken the sense of pride in government that can alone tap the latent patriotism and enthusiasm of the young." More "ceremonial benefits" and greater recognition of excellence should be accorded SESers by both the White House and the private sector. A change in name—to the U.S. Executive Service—should be considered "to add some fresh luster to [the SES's] image." More substantively, the task force also urged increased pay and a "more assertive" Office of Personnel Management.[47]

Similar proposals were issued in 1989 by the National Commission on the Public Service, a prestigious nongovernmental group led by Paul Volcker, the former chairman of the board of governors of the Federal Reserve System. Fundamental to the message of the Volcker Commission was a "call for a renewed sense of commitment by all Americans to the highest traditions of the public service." To accomplish this aim, "bureaucrat bashing" must stop: "Presidents, their chief lieutenants and Congress must articulate early and often the necessary and honorable role that public servants play in the democratic process."[48]

Like the Twentieth Century Fund, the Volcker Commission also called for giving career appointees more responsibility, more training, and more money. It also recommended upgrading the role of the Office of Personnel Management, especially in the areas of executive recruitment and development. The commission went farther in several areas, though, urging a significant reduction (from 3,000 to 2,000) in the total number of political appointees in the federal government and a lower cap on the number within any one agency, a restoration of purchasing power for senior executives to 1969 levels, and, if necessary, a severing of the link between congressional and executive pay.[49]

Eschewing quick structural fixes for the problems of the SES, both the Twentieth Century Fund task force and the Volcker Commission properly focused attention on the deepest and most enduring sources of strain in the federal executive establishment, which they understood to be the historical lack of political consensus in the United States about the role of senior administrative officials in the federal government. Both the fund and commission knew that any meaningful and lasting administrative reform in this area would require such a consensus. To that end they have written what amount to treatises in applied political thought, laying the theoretical groundwork for our collective acceptance of a strong and spirited corps of senior executives in the U.S. government. Whether their calls will be heard is a question to which we now turn.

THE PROSPECTS FOR CHANGE

A remarkable amount of attention has been focused on the SES in the past decade. Scarcely a year has gone by without some major study of the system issuing forth from a congressional committee, the General Accounting Office, or one nongovernmental body or another. Friends of the higher civil service may well take heart from this attention and find in it causes to believe that the nation's decades-long search for a higher civil service may be, if not at an end, at least making some progress. After all, if getting an issue on the public agenda is the first step in shaping a change in policy, and if widespread discussion is any sign of an issue being on the public agenda, then there can be little doubt that some sort of change is in the wind.

We may also take heart from the shift in political winds that began in the 1988 election. The inauguration of George Bush as president in January 1989 produced a new director of the Office of Personnel Management, Constance Newman, and a new attitude toward the SES. For his first address outside the White House, a week after his inauguration, President Bush spoke at a meeting of some three thousand federal career executives. He spoke of his respect and appreciation for public service as "a noble calling and a public trust" and called for "a spirit of teamwork between political and career officials." The career executives gave him a two-minute standing ovation.[50]

Clearly, a new spirit of optimism among SESers began to emerge. It was during the tenure of President Bush that they finally received a substantial pay increase. Congressional pay reform in 1990 solved, at least temporarily, many of their pay problems. In January 1991, SES pay rates increased 18–25 percent. Moreover, the lowest level of SES pay (ES-1) had to equal at least 120 percent of the GS-15, step 1 pay. Almost half of SES members in 1991 were paid at the ES-4 level. After the pay raise, annual retirements in the SES dropped from about 8 percent to 2 percent. SES pay was still not competitive with the private sector, but 1993–1994 rates, displayed in table 7, were not insubstantial.[51]

Although the Clinton administration, by the end of its first year, had not offered any particular support for the SES, neither had it signaled a return to the bureaucrat bashing of the 1980s.[52]

Table 7. SES Pay Rates, 1993–1994

ES-1	$ 92,900
ES-2	97,400
ES-3	101,800
ES-4	107,300
ES-5	111,800
ES-6	115,700

Source: U.S. Code, Title V, Sec. 5332, Schedule 4, Executive Order No. 12826, December 30, 1992.

Yet our optimism needs to be tempered. The only feature of our fifteen-year-long conversation about the SES more striking than its volume is its discord. While almost everyone seems to agree that something needs to be done about the SES, there the agreement stops. What for the Grace Commission is a system insufficiently accountable to political leaders is to the Senior Executives Association a system overly politicized. What the Twentieth Century Fund sees as an appropriate balance between generalists and specialists is a hopeless mishmash of incompatible occupations to the Office of Scientific and Technology Policy and others. The Volcker Commission's diagnosis of a government overrun by too many political appointees runs afoul of the perspectives of the Grace Commission and the Twentieth Century Fund—not to mention the appointees and their appointers— while receiving only partial spiritual support from the Senior Executives Association.

Only on the issue of pay—particularly the need to raise it—has there been anything approaching general agreement. But even here we have to be careful. Arguments remain sharp about how to raise pay—across the board, by performance bonuses, by locality adjustments, and so forth—and how much to raise it.[53] So, if "Fix the SES!" is a banner under which everyone can march, many such banners will have to be painted because the parade is bound to be striding off in more than a few directions simultaneously.

None of this should be too surprising. The lack of consensus about what is wrong with the SES today is a direct reflection of the lack of consensus about what it was supposed to be in the first place, a point developed in detail in chapter 8.

CHAPTER VIII

Images of the U.S. Higher Civil Service

Institutions of government, like any institutions of human devising, are in a sense basically abstractions.[1] Although Congress, for instance, may be identified with the elegantly arranged marble that rises to a dome on one end of Pennsylvania Avenue or with the 535 particular men and women who are sent to Washington by U.S. voters, these physical manifestations of the institution do not begin to capture what we mean when we say things like "Congress is overstaffed" or "Congress has too little influence in foreign affairs." In the sense of these two statements, Congress is not palpable. It is, rather, an image, a set of ideas—about the Constitution, law, politics—which people carry around in their heads.

While some of the ideas we have about institutions of government are rooted squarely in fact and thus widely shared (e.g., "Members of Congress are elected"), many of our ideas, especially those that seem actually to animate our behavior, are slippery amalgams of facts, prejudices, values, and beliefs that resist empirical validation and often vary from one person to another (i.e., "Yes, members of Congress are elected. But given the power of special interests, elections are meaningless"). Thus the image of Congress that P. J. O'Rourke carries around in his head is likely rather different from the one that resides in the head of Senator Robert Byrd of West Virginia.[2]

Conflicts among images, while occasionally troublesome, generally do little more than enliven democratic debate when institutions are old and established. When institutions are in their infancy, however, such conflicts can be fatal. "Habits of the heart," to use Tocqueville's phrase, take time to develop. Institutions require a certain degree of conceptual consensus simply to survive, much less to thrive. Had the anti-Federalists been slightly more persuasive in 1787, for example, it is unlikely that Robert Byrd would today have a Senate to champion.

Such was the unrecognized dilemma of the men and women who created the Senior Executive Service (SES). Like the designers of Congress two centuries ago, the framers of the SES brought to the table fundamentally conflicting ideas about what an American institution—in their case, a higher civil service—ought to look like, ideas that had, at turns, shaped a series of unsuccessful reform efforts over the preceding thirty years.

For some the SES was to be the reincarnation of the aborted Senior Civil Service, an elite, European-style corps of generalist civilian executives. For others, it was a second chance at a Federal Executive Service, a system that would help elected officials and their appointees get a firmer political grip on the vast federal bureaucracy. Still others saw the SES primarily as a vehicle for bringing the supposed rigor of private sector management techniques to the federal government or as a backdoor way to increase the pay and perquisites of civil servants.

But rather than try to meet these contradictions head on, as the founders had done in the Constitutional Convention and its aftermath, the creators of the SES chose to overlook them and to give the SES such a nebulous definition that everyone could believe whatever he or she liked about it. The result: support as shallow as it was broad, useful in the near term to pass a law, but useless in the long run to build an institution.

We discuss in this chapter four contending images of the U.S. higher civil service, which we have distilled from our earlier analyses of the long history of attempts to reform the civil service in the United States. We consider these images as ideal-types, as purely analytical constructs that have no one-to-one correspondence with any one reform proposal or any one group's view. Nevertheless, because they embody the jumbled set of archetypes or Platonic forms of upper administration on which the framers of the SES were able to draw, an understanding of these images and their assumptions and implications goes a long way toward explaining how the SES was born, why it never matured, and what now needs to be done.

IMAGE #1: THE HIGHER CIVIL SERVICE AS AGENCY SPECIALISTS

The first, and ultimately the most potent, image was what we shall term the *traditional agency perspective*. This view assumes that the higher civil service is and ought to be simply the name we give to those people who happen to occupy the top jobs in various federal agencies. They have nothing in common other than a pay grade. These upper-level employees are assumed to be professionals and specialists—engineers, scientists, lawyers, physicians, economists, and the like—who may (or may not) exercise general managerial authority. Beyond one's profession, one's primary loyalty is to one's bureau or agency. In theory, careers unfold within bureaus or agencies, although in some cases lateral movement within the profession—between the agency and a university, research institute, or industry—is considered appropriate. Interdepartmental mobility is not viewed as desirable, for specialized skills are not readily transferable among agencies.

Management, according to this view, is considered both an undefinable, unteachable art and a necessary evil. Good managers—a term to be used advisedly—are always competent specialists first, steeped in the traditions and rituals of the agency/profession. Managers seek to retain their identity as professionals and are among the harshest critics of "bureaucracy," "paper pushing," and "red tape." If one has the misfortune to be considered good at management, sooner or later one will be forced away from the laboratory bench or equivalent specialist venue and dragooned into a position of supervisory responsibility.

The more decentralized the personnel system, the better, according to the traditional agency perspective. First the Civil Service Commission and later the Office of Personnel Management have been "bottlenecks." Far from performing any useful services for agencies, these central staff agencies have simply made it more difficult to do the real work of government, especially by making it difficult, through onerous procedures, to recruit candidates for top jobs—candidates best known and judged by people already in the agency.

The chief problem with the U.S. higher civil service, aside from interference from the commission and its successor, is pay. Pay levels are too low to attract and retain the best people. Reform proposals from this perspective, then, are centered on making salary and benefits more competitive with those available to comparable professionals outside the federal government.

IMAGE #2: THE HIGHER CIVIL SERVICE AS EUROPEAN-STYLE ELITE CORPS

The second image of the U.S. higher civil service that emerged during this period was sharply at odds with the first. It was what we may call the *elite corps perspective*. According to this view, the federal government is more than a collection of disparate agencies performing discrete, technical, caretaking services for the public. Instead, there is an appreciation of government as a whole and a concomitant understanding that government exists, or ought to exist, to play an active, positive role in society.

This fundamental assumption leads in turn to the belief that administrators, especially higher administrators, need first and foremost to view themselves as guardians of the broad public interest. They need to identify not with the narrow perspectives of an agency or profession but with the central idea of public service. To that end, they need to be set apart from the rest of the civil service and put into a distinctive, government-wide, corps that can provide the necessary socialization and career development.

Administrative generalists, not technical specialists, are the mainstay of the higher civil service. This is necessary because only generalists are likely to have both the catholic perspectives and broad skills necessary to translate elusive public purposes into government action. Experts, the aphorism has it, should be on tap, not on top.

This is not to say that the higher civil service is conterminous with some generic idea of "management." The perspective that views the higher civil service as an elite corps decisively rejects the notion that the private sector is home to some magic managerial potions that can be transferred wholesale to the arena of government, either in the persons of managers from the private sector or through the importation of techniques themselves. Indeed, the core assumption of this perspective is, as Paul Appleby put it, that "government is different." Government management requires far more political acumen, bargaining ability, and sensitivity to diverse constituencies than private management. Most important, it requires a particular commitment to public service and an attitude that one's work is more than meeting some objectified goal or milestone.

The only way these managerial skills can be instilled is through the development of a from-the-bottom-up career system. Great attention needs to be paid to recruitment, training, and career development. Likely candidates for high administrative office need to be identified very early on, preferably at the time they enter the system as college graduates or holders of newly minted graduate degrees. Much on the model of the military or foreign service, heavy investments in training, both in house and university based, need to be made throughout the career cycle. And, on the same model, regular rotation from agency to agency, and from field to headquarters, should be the norm. Systematic performance reviews by senior career administrators should be used both to reinforce proper public service values and to guide career development and pare down cohorts, so that there is ultimately a proper match between the number of higher administrators and the number of available positions.

Given the extraordinary fragmentation of the U.S. government, considerable centralization in the personnel system is required to perform these functions. Only a government-wide staff agency can nurture a government-wide perspective in senior civil servants. The real problem with the Civil Service Commission, now the Office of Personnel Management, has been not that these offices have retained central authority; rather, it is that they have exercised it poorly, squandering their efforts on developing and overseeing an antiquated system of position classification. A strong and activist bureau of executive personnel needs to be responsible for recruiting, selecting, training, placing, and appraising higher administrators.

Finally, this image anticipates a major reduction in the number of political appointees in executive positions. The increased use of political appointees in subcabinet-level jobs has been problematic for two reasons. First, it has diminished the effectiveness of government by turning over ever greater administrative authority to men and women with little experience in public service—and, worse, little commitment to public service. Second, by effectively denying career executives access to some of the most interesting and challenging jobs in government, it has made it more difficult to recruit and retain the most talented public servants. This image rejects simple distinctions drawn between politics and administration and recognizes the extent to which top bureaucrats are inevitably involved in shaping as well as executing public policy. It assumes, however, that central to the definition of the role of career executives is a belief that, within the law, any elected administration should be served loyally and responsibly.

IMAGE #3: THE HIGHER CIVIL SERVICE AS POLITICAL MACHINE

The third image of the U.S. higher civil service that evolved during the post–World War II period shares with the second the idea that the traditional civil service has deteriorated into a congeries of narrow, calcified, and unintegrated agency fiefdoms. Consequently, it shares, too, the assumption that greater breadth of perspective, flexibility, and coherence should be brought to the system. Where this image parts company is in its insistence that *political responsiveness* ought to be the primary aim of any reform.

Central to this perspective is the belief that bureaucracy is naturally resistant to the authority of elected political leaders. Career executives identify with the programs for which they are responsible. They measure success by their ability to protect and expand their administrative domains, and they develop close strategic alliances with interest groups and members of Congress who have similar programmatic interests. Consequently, presidents who desire change are frequently stymied. Much of the impetus for the steady increases in the size of presidential staff in the past fifty years can be attributed to efforts to circumvent the career bureaucracy, as can the tendency to fill greater numbers of jobs within line agencies with short-term political appointees.

The model higher civil service from this perspective is one that would reduce the need for these palliatives. Senior career administrators should be highly responsive to the government of the day and in effect should be direct appendages of the president in the agencies. This view is grounded in one powerful (if unsophisticated) strand of democratic theory: in a democracy, free elections are the only legitimate vehicle for the articulation of the public interest. Career administrators have no right independently to make judgments about policy. Because it is impossible rigidly to separate political and administrative roles, it is essential that bureaucrats derive their values from elected officials. It is essential, that is to say, that they be absolutely responsive.

How can such responsiveness be ensured? First and foremost, administrators must be made accountable for their performance. The grip of tenure must be relaxed so that political leaders have the ability to remove at will unresponsive or poorly performing executives from office, though not necessarily from the civil service. Second, upper administration should be permeable. While the preponderance of top officials will likely always be drawn from the career ranks because of the need for technical expertise, presidents should have wide discretion to make political appointments to "administrative" offices. Closing the higher civil service to outsiders or reserving key positions for career executives only exacerbates the problem of accountability.

IMAGE #4: THE HIGHER CIVIL SERVICE AS CORPORATE MANAGERS

The final image of the higher civil service that emerged during this period bears the stamp of the private sector. According to this *corporate perspective*, the U.S. government ought to emulate U.S. business in its managerial practices. Although government is not a money-making activity, like business it is primarily about accomplishing goals. The president of the United States is equivalent to the chief executive officer of a large conglomerate, members of his cabinet akin to the heads of major operating divisions.

Like any top executives, the president and his appointees cannot be expected to accomplish their goals without full control over the necessary resources, one of the most important of which is personnel. The civil service system bequeathed by the Pendleton Act has been far too insulated and buffered to be an effective management tool. No one would expect the president of IBM or General Motors to try to run the company with employees who answer only to an independent commission (and then only minimally), so why should we expect the president of the United States to do so? Personnel administration needs to be recognized as a central management function in the public sector, just as it is in the private sector. The central personnel agency should be headed by a single person directly responsible to the president, not to an independent commission.

A related and even more troublesome problem is that employees have no real incentives to perform at high levels of productivity, since they know that their pay and promotion chances have little to do with their output. Although this is a problem throughout the system, it is especially vexing at the highest levels, where leadership and initiative are critical. "Pay-for-performance" should be the guiding principle of the higher civil service, performance being measured with reference to clearly articulated, established goals. To provide even greater incentives, cash bonuses should be available for executives whose performance is clearly exemplary.

Reflecting changes in the experience of the private sector, this perspective has shifted positions over the years on the generalist/specialist question, although the current mainstream view generally de-emphasizes the idea of a manager for all seasons. At the same time, unlike image #1, image #4 includes a strong belief in the value of management and the relevance of the techniques generated by various theories of management. Hence this view encourages exchanges, if not permanent lateral movements, by executives between public and private sectors and so shows a major disagreement with the closed-career perspective of image #2.

Political questions that are central to images #2 and #3 are given scant attention by image #4. What is important is whether an executive is getting the job done, not whether he or she is political or career by background. Because of its emphasis on managerial flexibility, however, this perspective leads by default to a higher civil service that is structurally similar to that proposed by image #3, the political responsiveness model; that is, tenure is relaxed and at-will employment the rule. The chief difference is that there is an implicit distaste for "politics" in the corporate model—politics generally being perceived as an extraneous, efficiency-impeding element in management. Thus, image #4 places greater stress on presumably unbiased, analytically detached measures of job performance, applied to political appointees as well as career executives, which may come indirectly to limit at least certain kinds of responsiveness.

As we noted at the beginning of this chapter, these four images have been presented as ideal-types. Although strong traces of the images can be found in the pre-SES proposals for reform, we have deliberately not linked them, so as to avoid any suggestion of a one-to-one correspondence. The post–World War II period did not serve up, seriatim, convenient little reform packages just waiting to be analyzed. The Senior Civil Service embodied a considerable chunk of image #2, to be sure; but image #2 is also reflected in other proposals, just as the Senior Civil Service incorporated other images.

The advantage of using ideal-types is that they exhibit strong coherence, at least if constructed properly. One knows that if one accepts a particular set of assumptions, then others naturally follow. For example, the assumptions of image #2 about closed careers compel further assumptions about centralized personnel management, mobility, generalists, and so forth—and vice versa. There is, in other words, a "strain to consistency." One can thus predict that assumptions drawn from two or more different images will, in general, create conflict and instability.[3]

SHAPING THE SENIOR EXECUTIVE SERVICE: A KALEIDOSCOPE OF IMAGES

Which of these images underlies the SES? The answer is, All of them. More than any other attempt at reform of the higher civil service since World War II, the SES rests on a kaleidoscope of images, a veritable mulligan stew of ideas: a little pay-for-performance here, a little political responsiveness there, with a splash of opportunity for career executives and a dollop of decentralization.

Although it is impossible to reconstruct precisely the collective assumptions and perceptions of the framers of the SES, the documentary record from this period—the Federal Personnel Management Project issue papers and recommendations, congressional hearings, the SES provisions (title #4) of the Civil Service Reform Act itself—is quite complete and affords considerable insight into the sorts of image that guided their work. And it is clear that, at the very beginning of the discussions about the SES, a deliberate decision was made to trade intellectual coherence for intellectual balance. Consider, for instance, the following passage from the final report of the Federal Personnel Management Project's task force on the SES:

> The study group gave serious consideration to three complete system designs, each of which has a different focus and each of which received some support among the many groups and individuals with whom we consulted:
>
>   1. A system designed to maximize the agency head's autonomy in managing his executive resources—similar to systems prevailing in some large *private sector organizations.*
>   2. A system establishing *a cadre of professional career managers* along the lines of an officer corps.
>   3. A system which *balances* the need of agency heads for flexibility in the use of executive resources and the need of employees for career opportunities and protection, with special attention to the rights of the public for effective, efficient and impartial administration of Federal programs.[4]

Although the task force found "some evident advantages" in the first two systems, they decided that the balance of system three, which they labeled "the Executive Service," was of paramount importance. Indeed, members of the task force complained that, in discussing various options with over four hundred different groups and two hundred current executives:

> a very common difficulty was the fact that most respondents were unacquainted with the totality of the executive personnel management picture and, consequently, did not recognize the existence of

the full range of problems the study group was trying to address. The result in many instances was that such respondents would advance fragmentary systems which would solve the particular problems of which they were aware but would leave others unaddressed or even aggravated. *The study group thus found it impossible to adopt in its totality any of the systems suggested to us. We were, however, able to appropriate many innovative features from the many helpful comments that were received.*[5]

So it was that the panel recommended a system that seemingly had something for everyone, rhetorically and substantively.

Image #1 (*traditional agency perspective*) was tapped by removing certain noxious central controls over agency autonomy exercised by the Civil Service Commission—such as classification of executive positions, approval of the qualifications of an agency's nominees in cases of movement within the system, case-by-case authorization of spaces, and so on—and by drawing the boundaries of the service broadly enough to include virtually all functional specialties.[6]

Image #2 (*elite corps perspective*) received its due in passages extolling the virtues of "a highly professional cadre of career managers" and in recommendations for a rank-in-person system, opportunities for career executives to take noncareer jobs without jeopardizing their career status, the establishment of career-reserved positions, and various protections against political abuses of merit principles.[7]

Although the post-Watergate climate of 1977 discouraged some of the more direct and strident rhetorical flourishes of image #3 (*political responsiveness perspective*), the goals of greater political responsiveness did not go unrepresented in the Federal Personnel Management Project's proposals. Agency managers were given greater flexibility to fill positions with noncareer appointees and to reassign executives when, in the agency manager's judgment, such actions became necessary to ensure responsiveness and "to relieve the frustration that the political leadership often feels when confronted with the bureaucracy."[8]

Finally, the project's papers are filled with image #4 (*corporate perspective*) allusions: words such as *efficiency, effectiveness, accountability,* and *performance* frame almost every sentence. Moveover, replacing "longevity pay," which is a "practice that runs counter to that of the private sector," with pay for performance "will make it possible both to reward the outstanding performer and to motivate the marginal and mediocre employee."[9]

As one would expect, congressional testimony about the SES was less consistently inconsistent, at least when taken in discrete chunks. Scores of individuals and groups drew on these images in supporting the proposal (and rarely in opposing it) in ways that revealed wholly different understandings of what the SES was to be about. In fact, if one did not know better and failed to see the same three letters— *SES*—used by all who commented, one would come away from reading the more than three thousand pages of hearings and supporting documents with the idea that these people must have been talking about different reform initiatives.[10]

The remarks, for example, of Roy Ash and William Eberle, representing the Committee for Economic Development, were virtually a pure projection of image #4, with their constant references to private sector practices and consistent emphasis on "managerial authority," performance appraisals, and financial incentives. Similar comments were forthcoming from representatives of the American Society for Personnel Administration.[11] For these people, and many others, the SES was appealing because it would allow, in their view, the federal government to function more like a large private corporation.

On the other hand, a statement prepared by the National Treasury Employees Union, used the logic of image #1 to *oppose* most features of the SES, which they deemed highly vulnerable to political abuse. "Though the opportunity existed to return a great deal of personnel authority to individual agencies, where it rightfully belongs, the President has chosen instead to concentrate all power over this 'elite corps' in his own political appointees." Almost identical comments were made by representatives of the National Federation of Professional Organizations, who described the proposed SES as "a blatant political patronage grab . . . just as odious as the 1972 [Federal Executive Service] proposal"; and by spokesmen for the National Association of Supervisors, who viewed the SES as simply adding "8,000 more political jobs." At the same time, image #1 values were occasionally invoked to *support* (with some reservations) the idea of the

SES. Albert Grant of the American Society of Civil Engineers endorsed the system, asking only that the importance of "engineering, scientific and technical expertise" be recognized, as did George Auman of the Federal Professional Association, who urged that "specialists . . . be afforded the same opportunities for rewards and varying assignments as those in the Senior Executive Service."[12]

A few others drew on image #1 to praise the financial inducements in the SES or to note the loosened controls over the autonomy of agencies. In general, it is fair to say that the greatest skepticism voiced about the SES came from those who held image #1 views of the U.S. higher civil service. In one sense, this is not surprising, for image #1 represented the traditional way of doing things whereas the SES, whatever else it was, was something new and thus potentially threatening to the status quo. The irony, of course, is that it is this image of the higher civil service that the SES has come most closely to approximate.

One of the strongest image #3 conceptions of the SES expressed during the hearings, paradoxically enough, came from a member of Congress, Leo Ryan (D-California). In a remarkable extended exchange, worth quoting at length, with James Peirce, president of the National Federation of Federal Employees, and with Nathan Wolkomir, former president of that organization, Ryan insisted on the paramount importance of responsiveness on the part of career executives to political appointees and elected officials.

> *Mr. Ryan.* Isn't the career employee required to take orders from a person who has been appointed by the President?
>
> *Mr. Peirce.* Very definitely, but the thing that we pointed out here is that with the approach that is revealed in this SES system, we would most surely have employees . . . afraid to give an opinion based on their expertise and background.
>
> *Mr. Ryan.* Especially if they disagreed with the person who appointed them, and put them in there to carry out the policies of the President; right?
>
> *Mr. Peirce.* I think that's true. I think also it restricts—
>
> *Mr. Ryan.* Is that wrong?

Mr. Peirce. The initiative and initiation on their part to bring forth ideas. And this would tend to kill those ideas coming to the surface.

Mr. Ryan. I can think of a particular regional director of a particular Federal agency in San Francisco right now who is diametrically opposed to what the President wants, and so far, he has gotten away with it.

Is he right?

Mr. Peirce. He could be.

Mr. Ryan. What is right? What the people want as expressed through their elected officials, or the career employee who doesn't necessarily feel compelled to respond to the sense of the people?

Mr. Wolkomir. You are saying because the President is elected, he is infallible.

Mr. Ryan. You are saying, if I understand you, you are saying the career employees should be protected by the politician when he says—

Mr. Wolkomir. We are saying he should have the right for redress. Under the proposal, he has none, and a man in a democracy has got a right to say what he thinks.

He has got a right to come to you, hasn't he? Are you saying because he is a Federal employee he should keep quiet and just follow orders, because the President was elected?

Mr. Ryan. He must follow orders of the President and his surrogates in the various departments at the top; you are darn right.[13]

Ralph Nader expressed similar, if more tempered, thoughts about the need for political responsiveness. "Obviously, any form of SES will result in a certain amount of politicization of high level career officials, but we do not believe that all politicization is necessarily bad. When a majority of those citizens who rejected Gerald Ford and elected Jimmy Carter, they announced in a gross fashion that they did not endorse the way the Republicans were running the government."[14] As was the case with SES supporters who came at the system using other images, Nader expressed reservations, calling for better protection for whistle-blowers in particular. But the point is that he, and several others, supported the SES because he believed that it embodied a particular image of a higher civil service of which he approved—an image that was strikingly different from those seen by other SES advocates.

Less conspicuous during the hearings were well-articulated analyses of the SES along the lines of image #2. Although scores of witnesses expressed concerns about undue politicization of the civil service under the provisions of title 4 almost without exception they did so in a manner that emphasized their commitment to a traditional image #1 vision of top executives. The reason for this near lacuna, we suspect, is that language embracing the values of a European-style cadre of elite administrators has little political appeal in general in the United States, and it certainly had little appeal in the antigovernment atmosphere of the late 1970s. Even those who apparently saw the SES in terms of image #2—especially those academics who supported what the Federal Personnel Management Project outlined as a "system two" approach to building a higher civil service (see above)—chose to couch their support mainly in other terms.[15]

Again, what is remarkable about this collected testimony is not that different people had different reasons for supporting the SES; it is hardly unusual for a piece of legislation to tap multiple motives in various constituencies. What is peculiar is the extent to which the reasons were fundamentally at odds or incompatible with one another, drawn as they were from contradictory understandings of what a higher civil service should look like.

Table 8 summarizes this paradox by listing the major features of the SES, indicating the image(s) from which each is drawn and the image(s) that each contradicts.

Table 8 looks too much like a Chinese menu to resist the hackneyed parallel: it appears as if the SES's designers and supporters had sat around a table in 1977 and 1978 and, in an effort to satisfy every-

Table 8. Key SES Features and Images of the
Higher Civil Service

SES FEATURE	SUPPORTING IMAGE(S)	CONTRADICTORY IMAGE(S)
Government-wide personnel system	2 & 3	1
Rank-in-person	2	1
Decentralization of recruitment and training	1 & 4	2
Relaxed tenure, managerial flexibility	3 & 4	1 & 2
Responsiveness through political appointments to career jobs	3	1, 2 & 4
Careerist opportunities through career appointments to political jobs	2	3
Pay-for-performance	3 & 4	2
Emphasis on general management	2	1
Mobility	2	1
Accountability through measurable performance goals and appraisals	3 & 4	2

Key:
   Image #1 Traditional agency perspective
   Image #2 Elite corps perspective
   Image #3 Political responsiveness perspective
   Image #4 Corporate perspective
Note: Not all images are located on each dimension because, at least as we interpret them, certain dimensions are either irrelevant or not logically required for certain images. For instance, Image #3 does not really address the issue of rank-in-person versus rank-in-position, just as Image #1 is agnostic on the type of pay schemes.

one's appetite, picked a few dishes, cafeteria-style, from column A, a few from column B, and so on.

CONCLUSION

What are the implications of this analysis for the SES? Again, we would not argue that, had SES been more conceptually coherent, it would necessarily have been more successful. Most of the evidence, in fact, including the cases reviewed in this book, points in the opposite direction. Coherence is probably a necessary condition of success, but it is certainly not sufficient.

Nor would we argue that parts of the SES at least would have been markedly more successful, even given the basic design, if certain things had just broken in the right way. For instance, one popular explanation for the SES's problems hinges on Congress's failure to fund the bonus provisions fully and the consequent souring of senior executives toward the whole idea. Another has it that if President Carter had won re-election in 1980 and kept Alan Campbell and company on at the Office of Personnel Management things would have worked out. Although the SES may have been better off had both scenarios happened, we doubt that either was critical.

The confusion over the SES ultimately echoes deeper confusion in the American political tradition. The SES will not prosper— indeed no real higher civil service for the United States can be created—until American political theory finds a place for higher administration. It is to this and related questions that we turn in our concluding chapter.

Conclusion:
Whither the Senior Executive Service?

The foregoing chapters chronicle the frustrated efforts of two generations of administrative reformers to create a higher civil service in the United States. We now turn to two questions that arise naturally from this history: Why has reform proved so elusive? And what, if anything, can be done?

WHY HAS THE UNITED STATES FAILED TO DEVELOP A HIGHER CIVIL SERVICE?

Some might object that even to pose this first question is to assume a fact not in evidence. The Senior Executive Service (SES) may not be perfect, it may be argued, but certainly it *is* a higher civil service. We believe, however, that such an argument is true only in terms of the narrowest of definitions. The SES is a *higher* civil service only in contrast to the *lower* civil service, a distinction of dubious utility. Most of the structures that political scientists and other close observers refer to as higher civil services in the rest of the world have in common a set of characteristics that the SES almost wholly lacks: prestige, esprit de corps, closed career paths, domination of top managerial positions, and so forth. Indeed, we define a higher civil service, as we noted at the beginning of this book, as *an elite corps of career public officials who fill key positions in governmental administration.* By this definition, which we believe captures general usage quite well, the SES is simply not a higher civil service.[1]

The real U.S. counterparts of the mandarins of Britain, France, Germany, and Japan are political appointees, not civil servants. Nor are Britain, France, Germany, and Japan the only countries that provide such contrast with the United States. As was discussed in chapter 1, virtually every other nation in the world—certainly every other nation in the developed world—has created a higher civil service. It is the striking singularity of the American experience that makes this question—Why not the United States?—so compelling.

This is not to say, by the way, that these higher civil services are somehow better across the board than what the United States has produced. Indeed, Milton Esman believes "the growing complexity of government favors the U.S. pattern," which encourages the movement of program specialists into senior civil service posts.[2] Moreover, the United States may well tap men and women to manage its public institutions who are brighter, more competent, more ethical, more representative, and more responsible and accountable than those who occupy similar positions in some other countries. Furthermore, as we noted in chapter 2, all top public managers, whether nominally civil servants or political appointees, are by the nature of their work political actors. Indeed, it is undoubtedly true that top civil servants in some nations exhibit less neutral competence and more bald partisanship than many political appointees in the United States. These caveats notwithstanding, the fact remains that the United States has walked a markedly different administrative path from the rest of the world. Why?

The answer reflects both history and ideas, or—better—the interplay between history and ideas. Unlike those in European states, the U.S. bureaucracy was not wrought from long-standing legacies. To begin with, public administration in America started with a fairly clean slate, or at least as clean a slate as any nation is ever likely to find. As European states began in the late eighteenth and early nineteenth centuries, and Japan in the late nineteenth century, to construct what we now know as their higher civil services, they were mindful of existing structures and often built on top of them, propelled as they were by conflicts, forces, and ideas centuries in the making. It is not coincidental that Japan's elite bureaucrats are deemed latter-day samurai or that members of France's *grand corps* trace their lineage past Napoleon to Colbert. Americans, on the other hand, had no state-building Frederick the Great or Louis the XIV in their past, no Colbertian minions of kings to build an apparatus of control, no established church to provide a template for hierarchy and centralized administrative management.[3]

Moreover, notwithstanding some exogenous influences, the United States became a nation (and began building its administrative structures) at a time when the model that Americans might logically have used—Great Britain, the former colonial power—was scarcely in a position to teach sound administrative lessons to anyone else. British institutions of public administration were rightly regarded, at home and abroad, as corrupt and inefficient. Indeed, Britons were made to wait nearly three-quarters of a century after the American Revolution before they saw the stirrings of administrative reform.[4] Though latent ill-feeling toward the former colonial master may also have played a part in rejecting the generalist/elite British model, the record of other new nations suggests otherwise. The experiences of former British, French, and even Portuguese dependencies in the past thirty years, and of Latin American states beginning in the early nineteenth century, demostrate—as our discussion in chapter 1 attests— that colonial administrative forms have great staying power.[5]

If Americans had anything at all written on their otherwise blank administrative page, it was ringing "self-evident truths" from the Declaration of Independence about equality, rights, and consent of the governed and a litany of abuses committed by King George III. Our oft noted distrust of executive authority and disdain for officialdom were not simply present at our creation; they were *reasons* for our creation. Alexis de Tocqueville, that peripatetic and perspicacious Frenchman, observed that Americans' natural inclination is to diffuse and decentralize power: an administrative function concentrated in one powerful official in France, he noted, is spread over nineteen minor—and publicly accountable—magistrates in America.[6] There seemed little basis for a higher civil service in a system that generally deconcentrates power and distributes most governmental functions over a multiplicity of states and localities.

Founding ideals aside, perhaps the most crucial historical factor that explains the failure of the United States to develop a higher civil service is the timing of the emergence of widespread political participation relative to the development of strong state institutions. Simply put, in Europe and Japan administration preceded participation. In the United States participation preceded administration. In those different sequences lay tremendous variation in administrative development.

The administrative structures of the old world evolved over centuries in service to various princely sovereign authorities, sacral and secular. Not until they were wholly woven into the fabric of their respective political cultures—not until they became institutionalized, to use Samuel Huntington's term—were they made subject to the demands of the people at large.[7] By this time, the old-world institutions were strong, their traditions deep. Like mighty oaks, they could withstand the buffets of the populist gale. But they did so not by standing rigid in the wind but by bending when necessary. As participation grew, administration adapted. Though they remained steadfastly elitist in structure and in most cases even continued to recruit almost exclusively from upper social and economic strata,[8] the old bureaucracies proved extraordinarily capable of serving democratic purposes.[9]

In the United States participation was widespread from the outset, at least relatively speaking. The winds blew strong before the seeds could even take root. America's administrative structures—and administrative outcomes—were thus bent to popular participation to an extent unparalleled in Europe or anywhere else in the world. Not only could virtually all white males vote but, as Tocqueville pointed out, virtually all were, in a sense, administrators.

> In America the power that conducts the administration is far less regular, less enlightened, and less skillful, but a hundredfold greater than in Europe. In no country in the world do the citizens make such exertions for the common weal. I know of no people who have established schools so numerous and efficacious, places of public worship better suited to the wants of the inhabitants, or roads kept in better repair.[10]

One practical effect of this early and widespread participation was to create a self-perpetuating civic assumption: government, at all levels and in all its institutional manifestations, can and should be in the hands of those who are governed. Why suffer the ministrations of separate and self-inflated elites? Government is not complicated. It does nothing beyond the reach and ken of the common man. Or to use Andrew Jackson's more eloquent words, "The duties of all public officers are, or at least admit of being made, so plain and simple that men of intelligence may readily qualify themselves for their performance; and I can not but believe that more is lost by the long continuance of men in office than is generally to be gained by their experience."[11] Indeed, throughout the early years of the Republic, the duties of administrators *were* plain and simple. Leonard White's portrait of early-nineteenth-century officials in the United States is instructive.

> Most civil servants were engaged in finance, record keeping, and the ordinary type of clerical operations, chiefly plain copying. The professional side of the service was modest indeed, comprising the judges, the district attorneys and an occasional legal counsel elsewhere, and a small number of physicians and surgeons in the army, navy, and marine hospitals. Add a few surveyors in the western wilderness, a few engineers in the army and a naval constructor, and the roll of professionally trained officials is complete. Science— other than the professions—was absent. Statisticians were unknown and professional economists could not be found on the North American continent, much less in the departments of State. It was not an age of experts.[12]

This civic assumption maintains, furthermore, that those public officials whom American democracy simply cannot do without— elected or otherwise—need constant reminding that they are no higher and no better than anyone else. Americans maintain this system, Tocqueville averred, by refusing to elevate officials over the citizenry. Public officials here are accessible, "uniformly simple in manner," without airs or robes of office. They are also attentive, obliging, and open. And by offering only "drudgery and subsistence . . . to those entrusted with . . . administration," Americans have, in Jefferson's words, taken "a wise and necessary precaution against the degeneracy of the public servants."[13]

Self-interest bolstered this ethic, of course. Throughout the nineteenth century, public contracts and public jobs were viewed as a sort of booty to be claimed by privateers who, with each election, swept in on the not particularly fat but nonetheless undefended ship of state. Patronage was the order of the day, with rotation its great principle and corruption its great result. But who was there to resist? The permanent government was small, the hungry ranks of the parties, especially after 1828, swelling. Britain had its corruption, too, of course, but because it was less democratic, it was easier to tame. In the United States, seemingly everyone was either part of the game or hoped after the next election to get to play. "So the gas lights don't work because the contractor down the street did a lousy job for too much money. . . . Why change the system? Next year, *I* could be that contractor."

And whatever selfishness failed to stimulate, partisanship provided. President John Adams arguably set the cycle in motion with a series of "midnight appointments" shortly before leaving office in 1801. As the first non-Federalist to take office, Thomas Jefferson, Adams's successor, felt bound to undo these and to appoint loyal Republicans as further vacancies arose.[14] Although the threat from Federalists faded through the terms of Presidents Madison and Monroe, the practice of appointing loyalists became accepted. With the election of Jackson and the simultaneous reflowering of a serious partisan opposition in the Whigs the practice became a principle.[15]

Deterioration of urban life in the late nineteenth century, moral revulsion toward corruption, and fear of the rising power of immigrant-based political machines touched off a wave of administrative and political reform. Primaries, short ballots, city managers, executive budgets, and civil service merit systems are all legacies of this period.[16] But while possibly salutary in other respects, none of these reforms addressed the needs of the higher reaches of the civil service. If anything, the rhetoric of this period exacerbated the problem. Civil service reform was sold as something without real political implications. Public administration was just business administration in another venue, according to Woodrow Wilson.[17]

The political ethos of the times ordained that civil servants—higher or otherwise—have no role in government except as executors of policy made by elected officials or their appointees. Why bother

building elaborate systems on the European model which would socialize elite administrators and inculcate appropriate republican values? We need only keep our bureaucrats on a short political leash and
subject them to close checks by legislators and elected executives.
And certainly we did not need to encourage the development of a
generalist class of higher administrators. The Pendleton Act ordained
that entrance tests be practical—better and safer for American democracy that we have only narrow specialists, men and women disin-
clined and ill equipped to look beyond their disciplines of engineering, medicine, or accounting.[18]

Thus, by the time the U.S. national government began in the late
nineteenth century to take on those functions that require a significant administrative infrastructure—economic and social regulation,
broad internal improvements, active foreign policy—U.S. "higher"
administration looked substantially different from that found anywhere else in the world. Riddled with politics, uninsulated from legislative interference, and viewed with little or no respect by the public,
the federal service was dominated—where there were careerists at
all—by specialists and was seemingly dedicated to the proposition
that anything smacking of an elite, including adequate pay, appropriate training, and a closed, bottom-up system of recruitment, would
contaminate democracy's blood. With all this as prolegomenon, it is
little wonder that the Senior Civil Service foundered, the Federal
Executive Service failed, and the Senior Executive Service fizzled.

WHERE DO WE GO FROM HERE?

An obvious conclusion to draw from the above analysis is that a genuine higher civil service is not in the American future. The burden of
U.S. history and the weight of U.S. culture are fundamentally at odds
with the notion of elite public administration. Even if some such system were to be foisted on the federal government, it would soon be
reshaped to conform to existing biases. The SES is a case in point.
And what is not possible is ultimately not desirable. The American
people are best served—according to these widely held, myth-
sustained values—by truly American institutions, institutions that reflect their own distinctive climate and temper.

This conclusion is obvious but, in our judgment, dubious. It suffers, to begin with, from a kind of simple-minded historicism. Although the past certainly conditions the public policy choices of the present and the future, it does not determine them. Nothing is already scripted. Political and administrative institutions are the product of collective human decisions made and remade constantly. We need to give habit and tradition their due in decision making but not to ignore the role of reason altogether. As we read the historical record, reason has been insinuating itself ever more insistently into the process over the past forty years. As anemic as the Senior Civil Service, Federal Executive Service, and SES were and are, their existence provides unmistakable markers of change.

And what does reason suggest? First and most important, reason suggests that no nation can prosper in the modern world without a neutrally competent higher civil service at the core of its government. The day of a public service filled with Cincinnatuses leaving for a turn plow and farm has passed. So, too, has the day of the canny partisan who changes overnight from speech writing or managing literature drops to managing major federal programs. Both images are romantic. Both resonate with basic chords of American democracy. But neither is realistic. Continuity, steadiness, experience, expertise: these are the values that higher administrators need especially to embody in an age of complexity—along with virtue and a sense of responsibility, which all public officials, elected or otherwise, ought to share.

To move us farther in this direction, we offer here four sets of specific proposals. Some of them are modest and may easily be accommodated within the structure of the SES. Others require more fundamental change.

Eliminate All Political Appointments Below That of Assistant Secretary

In 1991, as we noted in chapter 7, approximately 3,000 federal jobs encompassing everything from cabinet secretary to cook were subject to the vagaries of the political appointment process. Included were 508 positions that fell into the PAS category—presidential appointments subject to Senate confirmation; 722 were noncareer SES positions; another 1,832 fell under Schedule C and included primarily nonmanagerial jobs—chauffeurs, personal aides, and assistants.[19]

The need in a republic for certain of these jobs to be filled by political appointment is beyond serious dispute. Cabinet secretaries and their chief deputies need to have the absolute confidence of the president and to be prepared to advance the president's agenda with partisan enthusiasm. Somewhere around the level of assistant secretary, however, the balance of required skills shifts. More time is spent on the pith of day-to-day management, less on strategy, speechmaking, and consultation with partisan movers and shakers. Needed here are the talents of the experienced professional: rationality, substantive expertise, disinterested judgment.

No sharp line separates one sort of job from another. Officials below the level of assistant secretary, moreover, do behave "politically" and make decisions that have policy implications, as is emphasized in chapter 2. But most of what they do most of the time is *not* political in any meaningful sense of that term. And the fact that their decisions and actions may have policy implications is immaterial. No evidence exists to suggest that the overwhelming majority of career civil servants is anything other than loyal to the government of the day.

Bureaucratic sabotage, where it exists, is a function of program and turf, not of party. In any event, to expect some White House–vetted commissar to come in from the outside to kick the troops into line and to prevent administrative sabotage is fantasy. Organizations do not function that way in general,[20] nor do large public organizations behave that way in particular. They have sophisticated cultures and are enmeshed in intricate webs of relationships with other actors.[21] It takes time and experience to learn to lead them in new directions.

The ironic fact is that presidents would be better served if they did not put their "own people" in place. They, like the American people at large, benefit most when wise decisions are made and programs run smoothly.[22] Who, then, gains from the present system, and who would lose most through reform? Individual members of Congress, to begin with. Their ability to get themselves re-elected is a function of their ability to dispense favors and largesse, which in turn is a function, at least in part, of the wheels they can turn and buttons they can push in the bureaucracy. And administrative appointments are themselves favors, of course. It was Congress, after all, that created the spoils system, and it was Congress that had to be dragged kicking and screaming into making even minor modifications in it.[23] Lobbyists, think tank scribes and consultants, representatives of interest groups of various sorts—including those from self-described public interest groups[24]—and even some academics—often have a vested interest in the prevailing system as well and would stand to lose from reform. The revolving door pivots past their offices too. How else can the Sierra Club get its man in the Environmental Protection Agency or the coal industy its woman in Interior? How would the Heritage Foundation have done without the Reagan administration? The Kennedy School without Clinton?

Some may object that our proposal to eliminate most political appointees resurrects and leans on the timeworn dichotomy between politics and administration. Perhaps it does. But in response we would say two things. First, anyone who doesn't advocate turning all administrators into political appointees (or vice versa) leans on this dichotomy to some extent. The question for most people is not whether, but where, the line should be drawn. Second, we find some attacks on this distinction too epistemologically slippery by half. To observe correctly, for example, that high civil servants do make policy and then conclude that *therefore* there is no difference between policy and administration is to strip two perfectly good and useful words—*policy* and *administration*—of meaning and distinction. Such tortuous logic exemplifies much of the destructive nonsense known as postmodern analysis.[25]

Establish Clear Career Tracks for Senior Executives

Where are the dedicated and talented senior administrators of tomorrow going to come from? So far the federal government has assumed, like the baseball-loving farmer in *Field of Dreams*, "that if we need them, they will come." And so far that has worked fairly well. Sufficient numbers of qualified GS-14s and -15s have been interested in entering the senior ranks to satisfy demand. But as we observed in earlier chapters, levels of satisfaction with federal service have been declining. And alternatives for midcareer managers, especially given a new pension system, have been looking brighter. In any event, while this system often promotes excellent people, it does so ultimately as a result of serendipity. Why wait until individuals have reached the top rung of the General Schedule and are perhaps in their late forties or early fifties to begin considering and grooming them for senior positions? This system approaches what John Armstrong has labeled the "maximum deferred achievement" model of recruitment.[26] In effect, no decisions are made about who shall be chosen for top posts until the day it happens. For good reason, most successful businesses choose not to operate that way, nor for that matter do academic departments.

What is needed is a system that identifies potential senior executives early, preferably at the point of college graduation, and then move them along through progressively more responsible positions, providing further education and training at regular intervals. Ideally, this program of career development would involve considerable rotation of assignments, both within and outside the primary agency.[27] Indeed, a structured system of postings to nonfederal and even nongovernmental organizations has considerable merit, as the French have discovered. An expanded version of the Presidential Management Intern Program would be a good first step in this direction. Loosening the iron bands of rank-in-job classification in the middle levels of the civil service would be a good second step.

Another measure would be to follow the lead of the military services and create an academy for civilian officers, an idea that has surfaced occasionally over the years.[28] We believe this idea makes eminent good sense. At one level the military academies exist to provide training in certain technical skills that each service needs. Far more important, though, they *socialize* our future senior commanders. They use their uniquely intense and insulated atmospheres to inculcate a set of values—honor, commitment, responsibility—that the services themselves, and U.S. society as a whole, consider useful. By what logic do we assume that our civilian administrators are less important to the nation's future and can be left to their own devices or to those of the general culture to imbibe appropriate values?[29]

Put Specialists and Generalists in Separate Tracks

American bureaucracy has long been dominated by technical specialists, men and women who, first and foremost, are capable chemists, economists, virologists, accountants, and so forth. In this regard our public service is at the opposite end of the spectrum from the British, which, as we have seen, has traditionally prized the generalist. Long and ultimately fruitless debates have taken place as to which system is better.[30]

It is clear to us that the upper reaches of administration need specialists *and* generalists. It is equally clear, however, that a single personnel system cannot accommodate the needs of both groups. A system that rewards broad management skills tends to undervalue, and thus to discourage, good science. A system built wholly of technical experts is ineffective and undirected.

Although the SES tried, in effect, to meld the two by putting the same sorts of people (specialists) into a putatively more generalist-oriented, rank-in-person structure, it wound up with the worst of both worlds. Because the SES is the only route upward for talented people at top levels of the General Schedule, excellent bench scientists (and their equivalents in other disciplines) are forced to choose between promotion and better pay, on the one hand, and what they do best, on the other. By the same token, because the SES has done nothing to encourage the cultivation of generalist talents at the front end of the process (see the preceding section), the best that can be done is to take middle-aged men and women who are good specialists, give them a course or two at the Federal Executive Institute, and hope that they become good general managers in the SES. In operation this is not quite the so-called Peter Principle, but it is close.

We believe that it makes more sense to adopt a two-track system. Parallel to (and equal with, in terms of pay and status) a generalist-oriented SES, a senior specialist corps is needed, modeled perhaps on the Department of Health and Human Service's Senior Scientific Service.[31] This would keep experts on tap and at least next to the top.

157

It would meet the needs of specialists and the organizations they serve while allowing the SES or a similar system to develop its generalist potential more fully.

Treat Senior Administrators as Public Officials as Well as Public Servants

American administrators have never had a well-defined role in our system of governance. American political theory does not accommodate them. The Constitution neither anticipates nor mentions public administration, as many political science professors tell their students.

The logic that seems to be operating here is that because elections are the only way to confer legitimacy in a democratic system, appointed administrators cannot be given anything important to do, at least not without being watched closely and checked by legislators, elected executives, political appointees, and assorted others. It follows, then, that certainly such administrators cannot be allowed (again, in theory) broad discretionary power, or have the status of official conferred upon them. To do so would violate the precepts of popular sovereignty, and hence the essence of the Constitution. Or at least such is the argument.[32]

As Hugh Heclo has put it, we "have tried to dance around the problem," either by pretending "that career personnel have ... duties separate from policy or political roles" or by the "dangerous delusion" that personnel techniques borrowed from the private sector can substitute for serious thought about what a higher civil service ought to look like.[33]

Can the existence of an active higher civil service be reconciled with the Constitution? John Rohr, for one, seems to think so and has done some especially creative and useful analysis on this point. He begins by pointing out that while the Constitution omits mention of the word *administration* specifically, administration was nevertheless among the framers' foremost concerns, at least if *Publius* is any guide: "The word *administration* and its cognates appear 124 times through the *Federalist Papers;* more frequently than *Congress, President,* or *Supreme Court.*"[34] Rohr argues very persuasively that our administrative state *is* fundamentally compatible with the plan of the founders; that the higher civil service today fulfills executive functions originally intended for but relinquished by the Senate; and that public administration further "heals a defect" in our body politic by overcoming the inadequate representation in the House of Representatives.[35]

We agree with Rohr's analysis and would add that a strong case can be made that the founders envisaged an administrative system that looked far more like what we recommend here than that which exists. First, despite the example of the states, where many executive officers were popularly elected, the founders insisted on appointment to fill all subordinate executive positions. Second, Washington and Hamilton chose for senior administrative posts the best and brightest of their day, with little regard for party, and kept them in place; some key officials, in fact, lasted well into the post-Jeffersonian Republican administrations. Third, chief clerks, the top career administrators in the government of that time, were subordinate only to the secretary of their department and were in fact charged with running its affairs in the secretary's absence.[36] Fourth, and perhaps most important, the dictates of democracy, which seem to be the touchstone of defenders of the current system, held little interest for James Madison and his colleagues. Their concern was creating and preserving a *republic*.

To treat senior administrators as public *officials* as well as public *servants*, then, is to accept them as a legitimate part of government. It implies recognizing the constitutionality as well as the reasonableness of broad, though bounded, grants of administrative discretion. The three principal branches of the U.S. government—Congress, President, and Supreme Court—ought to return to their primary constitutional functions and leave administration to administrators. Congress needs to quit trying to micromanage federal programs; the president needs to forgo his army of political appointees; and the courts need to hew to the old principle that administrators are the best judges of matters in their own domain.

But what about administrative responsibility? How could a democracy regard bureaucrats with such equanimity? Who would make them accountable to the public interest?

Before we answer directly, consider the following parable. Two friends, John and Ed, purchased identical Labrador dogs. John took the trouble to train his dog, whereas Ed let his run as free as he wished. Both dogs could pick a duck out of a pond or plunge into a thicket and bring back a downed woodcock and in that sense would do what was wanted. It is just that John's trained dog would do it every time. Ed's dog might or might not, depending on how he felt, what else was available to do, what one bribed him with, or how high the setting was on his shock collar.

The point is that bureaucracy can be regulated with checks that are internal as well as controls that are external. Internal checks can be more effective and efficient. Careful training is always better than a stout leash. In the opening salvo of his famous exchange with Herman Finer, Carl Friedrich wrote:

> Responsible conduct of administrative functions is not so much enforced as it is elicited. . . . Even under the most tyrannical despot administrative officials will escape effective control. . . . The problem of how to bring about responsible conduct of the administrative staff of a large organization is, particularly in a democratic society, very largely a question of sound work rules and effective morale.[37]

In the final analysis the most compelling argument in favor of our vision of an American higher civil service is neither historical nor constitutional. It is an argument from necessity: In an increasingly complex, competitive, and interdependent world, the United States needs a government that is as sagacious, steady, and responsible as it can possibly get. We can no longer afford the costs attendant upon an apparatus that looks as though it were cooked up by Mr. Dooley in the smoke-filled back room of a nineteenth-century political club. Although the connection is seldom made, virtually every major government scandal and policy disaster of recent years can be traced to the system of political administration that suppresses the wisdom and values of career professionals and gives free rein to the lightly toasted ideas and short-term interests of political appointees. How many Watergates, Irangates, Challenger disasters, and Department of Housing and Urban Development scandals do we have to suffer before we recognize the ineptitude and corruption this system encourages? Not many, we hope.

Opposition to these proposals will come from many of the same quarters that opposed the spirit of the Senior Civil Service, the Federal Executive Service, and the SES; from congressional micro-managers, members and staff, who see electoral advantage in being able to influence appointment and direct the outcome of particular administrative cases, from denizens of the think tanks and Beltway bandits who furnish so many of the in-and-outers who prosper under the current arrangements; from interest groups and lobbyists fearful of losing access. Indeed, even to cite these sources of opposition is to remind ourselves that meaningful administrative reform, as always, requires broader political reform. Changes in campaign finance, the structure of congressional committees, and ethics legislation are crucial.

Do we as a people have the political will to make these changes? If will can spring from despair, perhaps so. But those who looked to the return of a Democrat in the White House in 1993 were to be disappointed. By the middle of 1993, Bill Clinton's first year as president, public disgust with governmental performance had reached historic proportions. Spending was seen as out of control, the deficit nearly beyond reckoning. Government was in gridlock, to use the popular phrase. Antigovernment gadfly Ross Perot, whom the *New Republic* labeled the "pox populi," was more popular than ever. President Clinton's standings in the polls were lower than had ever been recorded for a president at that point in his term. Congress seemed to be faring even worse: following check kiting, sexual harrassment, and post office money-laundering scandals, members of Congress had finally fallen behind used-car salesmen in public trust and esteem. To paraphrase columnist George Will, government was not just going through another of its bad patches. Rather, it had settled into a deep trough and lacked the strength to lift itself out.[38]

Although conditions improved by the end of Clinton's first year as president, with the economy recovering, gridlock seemingly broken, and Clinton's popularity rising, the SES continued to falter. On February 10, 1993, in the second month of his presidency, Clinton took executive action to "reduce the federal bureaucracy by at least 100,000 positions." Whereas each executive department and agency with over 100 employees was ordered to eliminate not less than 4 percent of its civilian positions over the next three years, Clinton stipulated that "at least 10 percent of the reductions shall come from the Senior Executive Service, GS-15 and GS-14 levels or equivalent."[39]

At the same time, President Clinton announced that there would be no pay increases for federal employees in 1994, and increases would be 1 percent less than current law for each of the three years after that. "It is time for government to demonstrate in the condition we're in," said Clinton, "that we can be as frugal as any household in America."[40] By freezing federal pay for his first two years at the level fixed by President Bush for 1993 and promising reduced increases thereafter, President Clinton effectively assured that the gap in pay between the SES and the private sector would widen still more.

Finally, neither Clinton's promise to "reinvent government" nor the resulting Gore Report included any proposal to improve the SES.[41] Indeed, by calling for a massive decrease in management positions, the Gore Report would accelerate the long-term trend toward a higher ratio of political appointees to career executives.[42]

In these grim circumstances we still find solace. Though we know with Aeschylus "how men in exile feed on dreams of hope,"[43] we prefer the optimism of Oliver Goldsmith:

> *Hope, like the gleaming taper's light,*
> *Adorns and cheers our way;*
> *And still, as darker grows the night,*
> *Emits a brighter ray.*[44]

Notes

Bibliography

Index

Notes

1. BUREAUCRATIC ELITES IN HISTORY

1. Dwight Waldo, *The Enterprise of Public Administration* (Novato, Calif.: Chandler & Sharp Publishers, 1980), 6–10.

2. Brian Chapman, *The Profession of Government: The Public Service in Europe* (London: Unwin University Books, 1959), 9.

3. Joseph LaPalombara, "Values and Ideologies in the Administrative Evolution of Western Constitutional Systems," in Ralph Braibanti, ed., *Political and Administrative Development* (Durham, N.C.: Duke University Press, 1969), 171.

4. Ferrel Heady, *Public Administration: A Comparative Perspective*, 4th ed. (New York: Marcel Dekker, 1991), 159, 163, 165.

5. Lawrence J. R. Herson, "China's Imperial Bureaucracy: Its Direction and Control," *Public Administration Review* 17 (Winter 1957): 44.

6. Mattei Dogan, "The Political Power of the Western Mandarins," in Mattei Dogan, ed., *The Mandarins of Western Europe: The Political Role of Top Civil Servants* (New York: John Wiley & Sons, 1975), 4. Similarly, Professor Liu has observed: "In spite of the basic divergence in cultural patterns and the vast differences in institutional settings between the Sung bureaucracy and contemporary Western society, general similarities and common problems do exist" (James T. C. Liu, "Eleventh-Century Chinese Bureaucrats: Some Historical Classifications and Behavioral Types," *Administrative Science Quarterly* 4, [September 1959]: 208).

7. John A. Armstrong, *The European Administrative Elite* (Princeton, N.J.: Princeton University Press, 1973).

8. Rupert Wilkinson, *Gentlemanly Power, British Leadership, and the Public School Tradition: A Comparative Study in the Making of Rulers* (London: Oxford University Press, 1964). It is curious, indeed, that Armstrong, *European Administrative Elite*, makes no mention in his 1973 book of Wil-

kinson's 1964 study, since both books emphasize the role of education in preparation and recruitment for the public service.

9. Dr. Sun Yat-sen was the first provisional president of the Republic of China. He delivered an address, from which this passage is quoted, on the origin and theory of the so-called Five-Power Constitution in July 1921 before a group of Kuomintang party members in Canton, China (*Sun Yat-sen: His Political and Social Ideals*, trans. Leonard S. Hsu [University Park, Los Angeles: University of Southern California Press, 1933], 112, emphasis added).

10. In his comprehensive history of public administration, E. N. Gladden acknowledges that the "steadying" influence of the Chinese bureaucracy was the main factor contributing to the "remarkable staying power" of Chinese civilization (Gladden, *A History of Public Administration* [London: Frank Cass & Co., 1972], 2: 227).

11. E. A. Kracke Jr., *Civil Service in Early Sung China* (Cambridge: Harvard University Press, 1953), vii, 1. For Weber's characteristics of modern bureaucracy, see *From Max Weber: Essays in Sociology*, trans. H. H. Gerth and C. Wright Mills (New York: Oxford University Press, 1946), 196, 207, 243. On the fact that these characteristics were fully developed in imperial China, see also H. G. Creel, "The Beginnings of Bureaucracy in China: The Origin of the *Hsien*," *Journal of Asian Studies* 23 (1964): 155–85, esp. 155–59. "The substitution of the *hsien*, as an administrative district governed by an official appointed by and responsible to the central government, for the fief governed by a feudal lord, represented the territorial aspect of the transition from feudalism to centralized bureaucratic government in ancient China. . . . It is an event of some importance in world history" (161). For comparison of the longevity of the Chinese and Roman empires, see John K. Fairbank, Edwin O. Reischauer, and Albert N. Craig, *East Asia: Tradition and Transformation* (Boston: Houghton Mifflin Co., 1973), 93, 150. "The long duration of the Chinese empire is . . . solely and altogether owing to the good government which consists in the advancement of men of talent and merit only" (Thomas Taylor Meadows, *Desultory Notes on the Government and People of China and on the Chinese Language* [London: William H. Allen and Co., 1847], 124).

12. James Legge, *The Chinese Classics: With a Translation, Critical and Exegetical Notes, Prolegomena, and Copious Indexes* (Hong Kong: Hong Kong University Press, 1960), vol. 3, *The Shoo King, or The Book of Historical Documents*, pt. 2, p. 50.

13. Harry Krantz, *The Participatory Bureaucracy: Women and Minorities*

in a More Representative Public Service (Lexington, Mass.: D.C. Heath & Co., 1976), 2. Cheng F. Zhang, describing Imperial China's mandarin system, states: "Thus, the basic belief was that it should be men with general knowledge and ability who provided the backbone for the administration of empire. . . . Therefore, even officials in charge of specialized departments were themselves generalists. . . . Under the system of competitive examination, recruitment examination questions always revolved around the Confucian classics . . . and assessed whether the modes of thinking of candidates were conducive to virtue" (Cheng F. Zhang, "Public Administration in China," in Miriam K. Mills and Stuart S. Nagel, eds., *Public Administration in China* [Westport, Conn.: Greenwood Press, 1993], 7).

14. See, e.g., Donald F. Lach, *Asia in the Making of Europe* (Chicago: University of Chicago Press, 1965), vol. 1, bk. 2, ch. 9, esp. pp. 804, 812. Presumably, the reason why Marco Polo had made no reference to China's examination system was its discontinuance for over six decades (1257–1315), a period dominated by the Mongols, during which Marco Polo was in China (1271–1295).

15. Ssu-yu Teng, "Chinese Influence on the Western Examination System," *Harvard Journal of Asiatic Studies* 7 (1943): 267–312.

16. Y. Z. Chang, "China and English Civil Service Reform," *American Historical Review* 42 (April 1942), 544.

17. Teng, "Chinese Influence," 295, quoting R. Ingles, "Manner in Which the Literary Examinations are Conducted," *Chinese Respository* 4 (July 1835), 127–28.

18. Philip Woodruff, *The Men Who Ruled India* (New York: Shocken Books, 1953), vol. 2, *The Guardians*. "District officers" were otherwise known as "deputy commissioners" and "collectors."

19. Armstrong, *European Administrative Elite*, 271–72.

20. Richard A. Chapman, *The Higher Civil Service in Britain* (London: Constable & Company, 1970), 8–9.

21. Meadows, as quoted by Teng, "Chinese Influence," 289. In 1856, Meadows advocated the admission to competition of "coloured natives" in the East India Company's examinations; Thomas Taylor Meadows, *The Chinese and Their Rebellions* (Stanford, Calif.: Academic Reprints, 1856), xxvii.

22. See the Macauley Report of November 1854, reprinted in the so-called Fulton Committee Report of 1968: Lord Fulton, Chairman, *The*

Civil Service, Report of the Committee, 1966–1968 (London: Her Majesty's Stationery Office, 1970), vol. 1, app. B, pp. 119, 120, 124–25; hereafter cited as the *Fulton Committee Report.* The Northcote-Trevelyan Report of November 1853 is also reprinted in app. B, pp. 108–18.

23. See, e.g.: Teng "Chinese Influence," 296–300. Fred Riggs has commented that the use of the term *mandarin,* meaning "a powerful generalist bureaucrat in an elite corps recruited an an early age by examination," is applicable to the highest officials in most parliamentary systems as well as to those in imperial China. In observing that the two systems are historically linked and virtually the same, Riggs has pointed out that this is especially true in Britain where the administrative class mirrored the colonial Indian civil service, which, in turn, was borrowed from imperial China's mandarin system. See Fred W. Riggs, "Why Has Bureaucracy Not Smothered Democracy in America," Occasional Paper series, Section on International and Comparative Administration, American Society of Public Administration, Prelminary Draft, October 12, 1992, n. 13, p. 14. See, also Fred Riggs, "Bureaucratic Links between Administration and Politics," in Ali Farazmand, ed., *Handbook of Comparative and Development Public Administration* (New York: Marcel Dekker, 1991), 488.

24. For discussion of the British civil service reform movement, see, e.g. Richard Chapman, *Higher Civil Service in Britain;* E. N. Gladden, *Civil Services of the United Kingdom, 1855–1970* (London: Frank Cass & Co., 1976); G. A. Campbell, *The Civil Services in Britain* (London: Whitefriars Press, 1955); R. G. S. Brown, *The Administrative Process in Britain* (London: Methuen & Co., 1971).

25. Heady, *Public Administration,* 226.

26. Brian Smith, "The United Kingdom," in Donald C. Rowat, ed., *Public Administration in Developed Democracies: A Comparative Study* (New York and Basel: Marcel Dekker, 1988), 73–74.

27. *Fulton Committee Report,* 1: 11.

28. Stanley Rothman, Howard Scarrow, and Martin Schain, *European Society and Politics* (St. Paul, Minn.: West Publishing Co. 1976), 331.

29. Macauley Report, in *Fulton Committee Report,* 1: 120.

30. V. Subramanian, "A Socio-Historical Overview," in Rowat, *Public Administration in Developed Democracies,* 91.

31. Patricia A. Maley, "Comparative Administrative Personnel Practices in Commonwealth Higher Civil Services: A Study of Systemic Emulation over Time," M.A. thesis, University of Delaware, 1981, 36.

32. Subramanian, "Socio-Historical Overview," 95–96.

33. See Wolfgang Franke, *The Reform and Abolition of the Traditional Chinese Examination System* (Cambridge: Harvard University Press, 1960).

34. See, e.g., A. Doak Barnett and Ezra Vogel, *Cadres, Bureaucracy, and Political Power in Communist China* (New York: Columbia University Press, 1967), 19.

35. Chung-kuang Chiang, "The Politics of Revolutionary Higher Education in the People's Republic of China with Emphasis on Beijing University," Ph.D. dissertation, University of Delaware, 1985, 130.

36. Quoted by Anne Friedman and Mary Chan Morgan, "Controlling Bureaucracy in Communist China (1949–1980)," in Krishna K. Tummala, ed., *Administrative Systems Abroad* (Lanham, Maryland: University Press of America, 1982), 248. Oliver Williams has observed: "Beginning in the mid-1950s, the party became an even greater force in the political process as a result of Mao's desire to place power in the hands of ideologically committed generalists instead of technically proficient specialists. . . . When Deng came to power, moderates championed a reduction in the party's exercise of control over administrative matters. . . . Party cadres, recruited for their 'redness' rather than expertise, lacked the skills to manage the details of administrative work" (Oliver Williams, "An Outsider's Perspective," in Mills and Nagel, eds., *Public Administration in China*, 147–48).

37. See Fairbank, Reischauer, and Craig, *East Asia*, 305.

38. "Most of the higher civil servants are brought into the bureaucracy through the expedient and relatively lenient channel of 'special appointment' ". (Suk-choon Cho, "The Bureaucracy," in Edward Reynolds Wright, ed., *Korean Politics in Transition* [Seattle: University of Washington Press, 1975], 78).

39. According to one Korean scholar, graduates of Seoul National University occupied 36.8 percent of South Korea's administrative posts during 1948–1967, and 42.9 percent in 1980. By contrast, 63.2 percent of top bureaucrats in the 20 departments of Japan's central government were Tokyo University graduates, whereas the largest number of high administrators in the United States produced by a single university comprised no more than 3.4 percent of the total (Wan Ki Paik, "The Formation of the Governing Elites in Korean Society," in Gerald E. Caiden and Bun Woong Kim, eds., *A Dragon's Progress: Development Administration in Korea* [West Hartford, Conn.: Kumarian Press, 1991], 51).

40. Hahn-Been Lee, *Korea: Time, Change, and Administration* (Honolulu: East-West Center Press, University of Hawaii, 1968), 5.

41. David I. Steinberg, *The Republic of Korea: Economic Transformation and Social Change* (Boulder, Colo.: Westview Press, 1989), 92.

42. Ku Tashiro, "Japan," in Rowat, *Public Administration in Developed Democracies*, 391. See also Akira Kubota, *Higher Civil Servants in Postwar Japan: Their Social Origins, Educational Backgrounds, and Career Patterns* (Princeton, N.J.: Princeton University Press, 1969).

43. Richard P. Suttmeier, "The *Gikan* Question in Japanese Government: Bureaucratic Curiosity or Institutional Failure," *Asian Survey* 18 (October 1978): 1048. For generalists' attitudes toward specialists in imperial China, see Joseph R. Levinson, *Confucian China and Its Modern Fate* (Berkeley, and Los Angeles: University of California Press, 1968). China finally abandoned its examination system in 1905, after the Russo-Japanese War of 1904–1905 and the growth of the revolutionary movement demonstrated that top generalist officials were inadequately trained "to deal with the new tasks" (Franke, *Chinese Examination System*, 69). See also Ichisada Miyazaki, *China's Examination Hell: The Civil Service Examinations of Imperial China* (New York: Weatherhill, 1976), 124–27.

44. Heady, *Public Administration*, ch. 5, esp. p. 192.

45. Teng, "Chinese Influence," 281, 283.

46. Ezra N. Suleiman, "From Right to Left: Bureaucracy and Politics in France," in Ezra N. Suleiman, ed., *Bureaucrats and Policy Making: A Comparative Overview* (New York: Holmes & Meier, 1984), 117.

47. See, e.g., Ezra N. Suleiman, *Politics, Power and Bureaucracy in France: The Administrative Elite* (Princeton, N.J.: Princeton University Press, 1974); *Fulton Committee Report*, app. C, esp. p. 133; Yves Meny, "France," in Rowat, *Public Administration in Developed Democracies*, 273–92.

48. James W. Fesler, "The Political Role of Field Administration," in Ferrel Heady and Sybil L. Stokes, eds., *Papers in Comparative Administration* (Ann Arbor: Institute of Public Administration, University of Michigan, 1962), 120, 121.

49. Heady, *Public Administration*, 209–10.

50. Paul P. Van Riper, *History of the United States Civil Service* (Evanston, Ill.: Row, Peterson and Co., 1958), 63.

51. U.S. Congress, House, Joint Select Committee on Retrenchment,

Report: Civil Service of the United States, 40th Congress, 2d Session, H Rep. 47, May 25, 1868 (Washington, D.C.: Government Printing Office, 1868), 110–202.

52. U.S. Congress, House, *Report of the Civil Service Commission to the President*, 43rd Congress, 1st Session, Exec. Doc. 221, April 15, 1874 (Washington, D.C.: Government Printing Office, 1874), 24.

53. Teng, "Chinese Influence," 306–08.

54. Quoted in Van Riper, *History of the U.S. Civil Service*, 100.

55. Frederick C. Mosher, *Democracy and the Public Service* (New York: Oxford University Press, 1968), 37–38.

56. F. F. Ridley, ed., *Specialists and Generalists* (New York: Barnes & Noble, 1968) treats the issue as it relates to the public services of Great Britain, Australia, France, West Germany, Sweden, and the United States. For a U.S. view of the issue in Great Britain, see Robert Presthus, "Decline of the Generalist Myth," *Public Administration Review* 26 (December 1964): 211–16. See also Robert T. Golembiewki, "Specialist or Generalist? Structure as a Crucial Factor," *Public Administration Review* 25 (June 1965): 135–41; Frederick T. Bent, "The Civil Servant: Gentleman or Professional?" *Public Administration Review* 31 (September–October 1971): 577–81.

57. See, e.g., Samuel Krislov, *Representative Bureaucracy* (Englewood Cliffs, N.J.: Prentice-Hall, 1974); Kenneth John Meier, "Representative Bureaucracy: An Empirical Analysis," *American Political Science Review* 69 (June 1975): 526–42; Joel D. Aberbach, Robert D. Putnam, and Bert A. Rockman, *Bureaucrats and Politicians in Western Democracies* (Cambridge: Harvard University Press, 1981).

2. BACKGROUND TO THE SUPERGRADES

1. Arthur W. Macmahon and John D. Millet's study, *Federal Administrators: A Biographical Approach to the Problem of Departmental Management* (New York: Columbia University Press, 1939) was concerned with those "individuals who hold positions in the national departments between the Secretary and the operating divisions in the bureaus" (vii). Accordingly, this study was limited to assistant secretaries, under secretaries, and bureau heads. No questionnaires were employed; the methodology was impressionistic and historical, with some use of interviews. Aggregate data sources were not included. Likewise, John J. Corson, *Executives for the Federal Service: A Program for Action in Time of Crisis* (New York: Columbia University Press, 1952), lacked empirical underpinning and consisted

mainly of an argument for procurement of "top-level" executives rather than being a study of incumbent federal executives. Paul T. David and Ross Pollock, *Executives for Government: Central Issues of Federal Personnel Administration* (Washington, D.C.: Brookings Institution, 1957), similarly consisted of a proposal rather than an empirical analysis, in this instance a study of issues of, and alternatives for, establishment of a career executive program. Marver H. Bernstein limited his study to political executives, namely those appointees outside the civil service who have "policy-making duties," in his *The Job of the Federal Executive* (Washington, D.C.: Brookings Institution, 1958), and this is true even to a greater degree of the following: Dean E. Mann, *The Assistant Secretaries: Problems and Processes of Appointment* (Washington, D.C.: Brookings Institution, 1965); David T. Stanley, Dean E. Mann, and James W. Doig, *Men Who Govern: A Biographical Profile of Federal Political Executives* (Washington, D.C.: Brookings Institution, 1967); John W. Macy, Bruce Adams, and J. Jackson Walter, *America's Unelected Government: Appointing the President's Team* (Cambridge, Mass.: Ballinger Publishing Co., 1983); G. Calvin Mackenzie, ed., *The In-and-Outers: Presidential Appointees and Transient Government in Washington* (Baltimore: Johns Hopkins University Press, 1987).

2. See, e.g., Richard Bendix, *Higher Civil Servants in American Society: A Study of the Social Origins, the Careers, and the Power-Position of Higher Federal Administrations* (Boulder: University of Colorado Press, 1949), reprinted by Westport, Conn.: Greenwood Press, 1974; W. Lloyd Warner, Paul P. Van Riper, Norman H. Martin, and Orvis F. Collins, *The American Federal Executive: A Study of the Social and Personal Characteristics of the Civilian and Military Leaders of the United States Federal Government* (New Haven: Yale University Press, 1963), which reported on 12,929 civilian and military executives from cabinet level to GS-14 or equivalent, only 7,640 of whom, however, were in the civil service. See also David T. Stanley, *The Higher Civil Service: An Evaluation of Federal Personnel Practices* (Washington, D.C.: Brookings Institution, 1964), a brief study of some 16,000 executives and professionals in grades GS-15–GS-18; Franklin F. Kilpatrick, Milton C. Cummings Jr., and M. Kent Jennings, *The Image of the Federal Service* (Washington, D.C.: Brookings Institution, 1964); John J. Corson and R. Shale Paul, *Men Near the Top: Filling Key Posts in the Federal Service* (Baltimore: Johns Hopkins Press, 1966); Hugh Heclo, *A Government of Strangers: Executive Politics in Washington* (Washington, D.C.: Brookings Institution, 1977).

3. William W. Boyer, *Bureaucracy on Trial: Policy Making by Government*

Agencies (Indianapolis: Bobbs-Merrill Co., 1964), 1–7, 39–67. Robert Putnam has articulated a similar theme: "Can there really be any doubt who governs our complex modern societies? Public bureaucracies, staffed largely by permanent civil servants, are responsible for the vast majority of policy initiatives taken by governments. Discretion, not merely for deciding individual cases, but for crafting the content of most legislation, has passed from the legislature to the executive. Bureaucrats, monopolizing as they do much of the available information about the shortcomings of existing policies, as well as much of the technical expertise necessary to design practical alternatives, have gained a predominant influence over the evolution of the agenda for decision. Elected executives everywhere are outnumbered and outlasted by career civil servants. Certainly in a literal sense, the modern political system is essentially 'bureaucratic'— characterized by 'the rule of officials' " (Robert B. Putnam, "The Political Attitudes of Senior Civil Servants in Western Europe: A Preliminary Report," Institute of Public Policies Discussion Paper no. 36 [Ann Arbor: University of Michigan, 1972], 1).

4. William W. Boyer, "Political Science and the Twenty-first Century: From Government to Governance," *PS: Political Science & Politics* (March 1990): 51.

5. Eugene B. McGregor Jr., "Education and Career Mobility among Federal Administrators: Toward the Development of a Comparative Model," Ph.D. dissertation, Syracuse University, 1969, 7, 35.

6. Ibid., 25.

7. Ferrel Heady, "The United States," in Donald C. Rowat, ed., *Public Administration in Developed Democracies: A Comparative Study* (New York: Marcel Dekker, 1988), 405, 408. One might contend that the closest the United States came to experiencing such "a cohesive cadre of high-ranking bureaucrats" was the reinvigorated Bureau of the Budget which became the center of President Franklin Roosevelt's newly institutionalized presidency of 1939. According to Larry Berman, "Budget Bureau veterans, proud of their relatively small staff size and their central role in the resource allocation system of American politics, viewed themselves as the elite of the civil service system" (Larry Berman, *The New American Presidency* [Boston: Little, Brown & Co., 1986], 128, n. 10).

8. Mosher, *Democracy and the Public Service* 138. Mosher discusses distinctions between career and general civil service systems by emphasizing that the latter is an open system in which rank inheres in the job (position

classification is the "pivot"), as well as the other marked differences regarding lateral entry, advancement, and personnel planning (146–50).

9. Harold Seidman and Robert Gilmour, *Politics, Position, and Power: From the Positive to the Regulatory State*, 4th ed. (New York: Oxford University Press, 1986), 174.

10. Golembiewski, "Specialist or Generalist?" 135.

11. R. H. Pear, "United States," in Ridley, *Specialists and Generalists*, 186.

12. Michael Cohen, "The Generalist and Organizational Mobility," *Public Administration Review* 30 (September–October 1970): 544–52.

13. Mosher, *Democracy and the Public Service*, 103, 104.

14. Fred Telford, *The Principles of Public Personnel Administration*, ed. Charles P. Messick and William W. Boyer (Newark: University of Delaware, 1976), 14, 21, 81.

15. Seidman and Gilmour, *Politics, Position, and Power*, 174.

16. O. Glenn Stahl, *Public Personnel Administration*, 5th ed. (New York: Harper & Row, 1962), 137.

17. See, e.g., Louis M. Hacker and Benjamin B. Kendrick, *The United States Since 1865*, 3d ed. (New York: F. S. Crofts & Co., 1947), 97–98.

18. William Harrison Clarke, *The Civil Service Law*, 3d ed. (New York: M. T. Richardson Co., 1897), 17.

19. Heady, "The United States," 406.

20. Van Riper, *History of the U.S. Civil Service*, 84, 85.

21. Hacker and Kendrick, *The United States Since 1865*, 99.

22. Telford, *Principles of Public Personnel Administration*, 14, 22–23, 87–90.

23. Van Riper, *History of the U.S. Civil Service*, 297.

24. Ismar Baruch, *History of Position-Classification and Salary Standardization in the Federal Service, 1789–1941*, 2d ed. (Washington, D.C.: U.S. Civil Service Commission, P.C.D. Manual A-2, 1941), 50–51.

25. Van Riper, *History of the U.S. Civil Service*, 299–300.

26. U.S. Congress, House, *Closing Report of Wage and Salary Survey, Prepared by the Personnel Classification Board*, 71st Congress, 3d Session, H. Doc. 771 (Washington, D.C.: Government Printing Office, 1931), v.

27. Ismar Baruch, *Background of the Supergrade Story, 1923–54, and The Ceiling Rate of the Classification Act of 1949, As Amended*, 4th rev. (Washing-

ton, D.C.: U.S. Civil Service Commission, September 1954), 1–3. All Baruch's studies are in the Ismar Baruch Collection, Pendleton Room, U.S. Office of Personnel Management, Washington, D.C.

28. See Public Law 80-113 (1947); and U.S. Bureau of Executive Manpower, Civil Service Commission, *Administrative History of Federal Executive Manpower Management* (Washington, D.C.: Bureau of Executive Manpower, Civil Service Commission, March 1971), mimeographed, 5, hereafter cited as *Administrative History.*

29. H. Struve Hensel and John D. Millett, *Task Force Report on Departmental Management in Federal Administration, Prepared for the Commission on Organization of the Executive Branch of the Government* (Washington, D.C.: Government Printing Office, 1949), 13.

30. U.S. Commission on Organization of the Executive Branch of the Government, *Personnel Management; A Report to the Congress* (Washington, D.C.: Government Printing Office, February 1949), 12.

31. Public Law 429, 63 Stat. 954 (1949).

32. *Federal Employees Salary Increase Act of 1955*, sect. 12, Public Law 94, 69 Stat. 179 (1955).

33. Donald R. Harvey, *The Civil Service Commission* (New York: Praeger Publishers, 1970), 187.

34. Ismar Baruch, *Background of the Supergrade Story, 1923–54, 7.*

35. Jerry Klutz, "Civil Service Discloses Four Hundred High-Pay Jobs," *Washington Post*, April 26, 1950.

36. For detailed records of these developments, see Ismar Baruch, *Supergrade Story, 1949–1952, bks. 1, 2* (undated).

37. Baruch, *Background of the Supergrade Story, 1923–54,* 11, 29.

38. Harvey, *Civil Service Commission,* 188–89.

39. Baruch, *Supergrade Story, 1949–1952, bk. 2,* p. 153.

40. *Congressional Record,* September 14, 1950, 15036.

41. Ibid., September 21, 1950, 15558.

42. Quoted in Baruch, *Background of the Supergrade Story, 1923–54,* 34.

43. Ibid.

44. Quoted in Heclo, *Government of Strangers,* 71.

45. *Administrative History,* 13.

46. Van Riper, *History of the U.S. Civil Service,* 207n; Van Riper discusses the technical distinctions between schedules A, B, and C, which

together "made it difficult to portray the extent of the Civil Service Commission's jurisdiction."

3. THE SECOND HOOVER COMMISSION'S PROPOSAL

1. Analysis in this chapter is based in part on the work of our former student, Dr. Sung Ho Chung of Seoul, Korea. See his "Politics of Civil Service Reform: The First Attempt to Establish a Higher Civil Service in the Eisenhower Administration," Ph. D. dissertation, University of Delaware, December 1985.

2. "Eisenhower vs. Stevenson: The Major Issues," *New York Times*, November 2, 1952. See also Congressional Quarterly Service, *Congress and Nation, 1945–1964: A Review of Government and Politics in the Postwar Years* (Washington, D.C.: Congressional Quarterly Service, 1965), 5.

3. Dwight D. Eisenhower, "Annual Message to the Congress on the State of the Union, Jan. 7, 1954," *Public Papers of the Presidents of the United States, Dwight D. Eisenhower, 1954* (Washington, D.C.: Government Printing Office, 1960), 7.

4. Dwight D. Eisenhower, "Radio and Television Address to the American People on the Achievements of the 83rd Congress, Aug. 23, 1954," ibid., 749.

5. Herman M. Somers, "The Federal Bureaucracy and the Change of Administration," *American Political Science Review* 43 (March 1954): 146, 147. See, also Herbert Emmerich and G. Lyle Belsley, "The Federal Career Service—What Next?" *Public Administration Review* 14 (Winter 1954): 3.

6. Van Riper, *History of the U.S. Civil Service*, 503.

7. For Executive Order 10452, see *Federal Register*, 18: 2599, May 1, 1953. For reorganization of the commission, see U.S. Civil Service Commission, *Biography of an Ideal: The Diamond Anniversary History of the Federal Civil Service* (Washington, D.C.: Government Printing Office, 1959), 104–105; U.S. Civil Service Commission, *1954 Annual Report: 71st Report, Fiscal Year Ended June 30, 1954* (Washington, D.C.: Government Printing Office, 1955), 1–6. For criticisms of extending presidential control over the Government's personnel machinery, see, e.g., Somers, "Federal Bureaucracy," 135, 139–47.

8. U.S. Civil Service Commission, *Biography of an Ideal*, 105.

9. U.S. Commission on Organization of the Executive Branch of the Government, *Task Force Report on Personnel and Civil Service* (Washington,

D.C.: Government Printing Office, February 1955), 190–91; hereafter cited as *Task Force Report*.

10. U.S. Library of Congress, Congressional Research Service, *History of Civil Service Merit Systems of the United States and Selected Foreign Countries, Together with Executive Reorganization Studies and Personnel Recommendations*, House, 94th Congress, 2d Session, Committee Print 94–29, compiled for the Subcommittee on Manpower and Civil Service of the Committee on Post Office and Civil Service (Washington, D.C.: Government Printing Office, December 31, 1976), 269; hereafter cited as CRS, *History of Civil Service Merit Systems*. See also Van Riper, *History of the U.S. Civil Service*, 246.

11. U.S. Congress, Senate, *Administration of the Civil Service System*, Report to the Committee on Post Office and Civil Service, 85th Congress, 1st Session, Committee Print 2 (Washington, D.C.: Government Printing Office, 1957), 27–40; Part 2 is the so-called Watson Report and is reprinted in CRS, *History of Civil Service Merit Systems*, 290–303, in which this statement appears (292).

12. For detailed discussion of the disclosures of the Willis Plan and the public controversy it engendered, see CRS, *History of Civil Service Merit Systems*, 270–75.

13. *Task Force Report*, 49, 50–51.

14. Ibid., 51–54.

15. Ibid., 54–58.

16. Ibid., 51–52.

17. Ibid., 52, 55.

18. See U.S. Commission on Organization of the Executive Branch of the Government, *Personnel and Civil Service, A Report to the Congress* (Washington, D.C.: Government Printing Office, 1955), 37–44; hereafter cited as *Second Hoover Commission Report*.

19. *Federal Employees' News Digest* (Washington, D.C.: February 28, 1955).

20. *Second Hoover Commission Report*, 89–90.

21. For the contents of the bill, see U.S. Library of Congress, Legislative Reference Service, *Digest of Public General Bills* (Washington, D.C.: Government Printing Office, 1957), E466.

22. William Pincus, "The Opposition to the Senior Civil Service," *Public Administration Review* 18 (Autumn 1958): 326–27.

23. Paul P. Van Riper, "The Senior Civil Service and the Career System," *Public Administration Review* 18 (Summer 1958): 192.

24. For analysis of these agency responses, see Chung, "Politics of Civil Service Reform," ch. 4, esp. pp. 140–60.

25. Herman M. Somers, "Some Reservations about the Senior Civil Service," *Personnel Administration* 19 (January–February 1956): 15–17.

26. Van Riper, "Senior Civil Service," 196–97.

27. Van Riper, *History of the U.S. Civil Service*, 552.

28. Ibid., 553–54.

29. See David and Pollock, *Executives for Government* esp. 76, 88, 108–10; Everett Reimer, "The Case against the Senior Civil Service," *Personnel Administration* 19 (March–April 1956): 31–40. For still other criticism of the SCS proposal, see Stephen K. Bailey, "The President and His Political Executives," *Annals* 307 (September 1956): 33; Harlan Cleveland, "The Executive and the Public Interest," Ibid., 33–54; Richard M. Paget, "Strengthening the Federal Career Executive," *Public Administration Review* 17 (Spring 1957): 91–96.

30. For commentaries favorable to the SCS proposal, see, e.g., Leonard D. White, "The Senior Civil Service," *Public Administration Review* 15 (Autumn 1955): 237–43; Leonard D. White, "The Case for the Senior Civil Service," *Personnel Administration* 19 (January–February 1956): 4–9; Pincus, "Opposition to the Senior Civil Service," 324–31; George A. Graham, *America's Capacity to Govern: Some Preliminary Thoughts for Prospective Administrators* (University: University of Alabama Press, 1960), esp. 85–96.

31. Van Riper, *History of the U.S. Civil Service*, 509.

32. See Edith B. Kidney, *Fringe Benefits for Salaried Employees in Government and Industry*, Personnel Report 542 (Chicago: Civil Service Assembly, 1954).

33. Neil MacNeil and Harold W. Metz, *The Hoover Report: 1953–1955* (New York: Macmillan Co., 1956), 29.

34. "A Letter to Philip Young from President Eisenhower," (January 26, 1956), in U.S. Civil Service Commission, *Senior Civil Service: Chronological Summary of Internal Activities, Memoranda, Conferences, Notes, and Personal Data, March 1955–November 1957*, Archives Collection 1964, vol. 2; hereafter cited as CSC, *SCS, Chronological Summary*. This collection is now in the Office of Personnel Management; for 1955, see vol. 1; for 1956, vol. 2; for 1957, vol. 3.

35. "A Memorandum to the Chairman from O. Glenn Stahl: Recommendations for a Pilot Civil Service Program," (February 6, 1956), in U.S. Civil Service Commission, *Senior Civil Service: Officials Documents and Background Papers, 1957–1958*, Archives Collection 1964, vol. 2; hereafter cited as CSC, *SCS: Official Documents*.

36. See Chung, "Politics of Civil Service Reform," 178–81.

37. U.S. Bureau of the Budget, "The Senior Civil Service: Compilation of Background Material for a Conference Held in Bethesda, Md., December 5, 1956," November 21, 1956, Office of Management and Budget.

38. Meyer Kestnbaum, "Career Administrators in Government Service," *Good Government* 74 (May–June 1957): 30.

39. CSC, *SCS, Official Documents*, 114–18.

40. "The Career Executive Program: A Draft for Discussion," and "Executive Order Authorizing the Establishment and Development of the Career Executive Program," (January 3, 1957), ibid.

41. Heclo, *Government of Strangers*, 25.

42. The occasion for Young's removal was the passage without hearings by the Democratic Congress of Public Law 854 of 1957, which established six-year overlapping terms for the three commissioners, who theretofore had served indefinitely at the president's pleasure. Whereas Ellsworth succeeded Young, Eisenhower replaced George M. Moore with Christopher H. Philips, who was also inexperienced. Minority Commissioner Frederick Lawton remained on the commission for a six-year term. Ellsworth was appointed as chairman for a two-year term, and Philips was appointed for a four-year term.

43. U.S. Bureau of the Budget, "Executive Order: Providing for the Establishment of a Career Executive Board," CSC, *SCS, Chronological Summary*, vol. 3.

44. "A Memorandum for the File: Senior Civil Service—Career Executive Program, Report on Discussion at Interagency Advisory Group on April 18, 1957," ibid.

45. "Bureaucratic imperialism seems pre-eminently a matter of interagency conflict in which two or more agencies try to assert permanent control over the same jurisdiction, or in which one agency actually seeks to take over another agency as well as the jurisdiction of that agency" (Matthew Holden Jr., " 'Imperialism' in Bureaucracy," *American Political Science Review* 60 [December 1966]: 943).

46. "A Letter by Harris Ellsworth to Roger W. Jones," (May 10, 1957, CSC, *SCS, Official Documents.*

47. "Draft of Executive Order Establishing a Career Executive Committee," (July 11, 1957), CSC, *SCS, Chronological Summary,* vol. 3.

48. "A Memorandum to Ross Pollock from Ray Randall: Executive Order, Career Executive Program," (July 16, 1957), ibid.

49. U.S. Office of Federal Register, Section 2, Title 3—The President, 1954–1958 Compilation, *Code of Federal Regulations* (Washington, D.C.: Government Printing Office, 1961), 385.

50. *Administrative History,* 9.

51. Ibid., 10. See also *Code of Federal Regulations,* 407–09.

52. Van Riper, *History of the U.S. Civil Service,* 523.

4. CIRCUMVENTING CONGRESS

1. See, e.g., James Madison [Publius, pseud.], "The Federalist No. 47, *The Federalist* (New York: Modern Library, 1937), 312–26, esp. his comment that "the fundamental principles of a free constitution are subverted" where the power of one department is exercised "by the same hands" that possess the power of another department (314–15).

2. See, e.g., Herber Agar, *The Price of Union* (Boston: Houghton Mifflin Co., 1950).

3. Louis W. Koenig, *The Chief Executive* (New York: Harcourt, Brace & World, 1964), ch. 6.

4. United States Constitution, article II, section 3.

5. According to the Pendleton Act, the rule-making authority of the CSC was to be exercised "to aid the President, as he may request" [Sec. 2, 22 U.S. Stat. 403 (1883)]. Although the president had authority under the act to appoint and to remove without restriction the three commissioners (sec. 1), staggered six-year terms of the commissioners were established by a rider of the Executive Pay Act, approved July 31, 1956.

6. U.S. Congress, House, Committee on Post Office and Civil Service, Subcommittee on Manpower Utilization, hearings, *Manpower Utilization in the Federal Government (Career Executive Program),* 85th Congress, 2d Session, April 30, May 6, 7, 8, 13 and 14, 1958 (Washington, D.C.: Government Printing Office, 1958), 7–8; hereafter cited as Hearings, *Manpower Utilization.* For press accounts, see, e.g., Joseph Young, "Career Executive Plan Drawing Fire," *Washington Evening Star,* May 1, 1958.

7. Hearings, *Manpower Utilization,* 92–94.

8. Ibid., 36, 79.

9. Ibid., 119.

10. Executive Order 10859, February 5, 1960, U.S. Office of Federal Register, 1960 Supplement to Title 3 — The President, *Code of Federal Regulations* (Washington, D.C.: Government Printing Office, 1961), 57. See also *Administrative History*, 11. The demise of the Career Executive Program is recounted in Graham, *America's Capacity to Govern.*

11. *Administrative History*, 11–12.

12. Career Executive Board, "A Report to the President: Report of Activities, March 4, 1958–June 30, 1959," in U.S. Civil Service Commission, *Career Executive Board Records*, Archives Collection, 1960, vol. 5, Office of Personnel Management.

13. James M. Landis, *Report on Regulatory Agencies to the President-Elect*, 89th Congress, 2d Session, U.S. Congress, Senate, Committee on the Judiciary, Subcommittee on Administrative Practice and Procedure (Washington, D.C.: Government Printing Office, December 1960), 11.

14. *Administrative History*, 13.

15. Ibid., 15.

16. Ibid., 16. "PL 313" positions were established to facilitate recruitment, by a limited number of federal agencies, of individuals with special scientific or technical skills.

17. Boyer, *Bureaucracy on Trial*, 44. See also, e.g., J. Leiper Freeman, *The Political Process: Executive Bureau–Legislative Committee Relations* (Garden City, N.Y.: Doubleday & Co., 1955).

18. *Administrative History*, 16.

19. Ibid., 17.

20. Mel H. Bolster, *Federal Career Executives, Three Years' Experience with the Career Executive Roster*, multilithed, April 1964, 13, Library of the Office of Personnel Management.

21. U.S. Bureau of Executive Manpower, Civil Service Commission, *History of the Executive Assignment System*, multilithed, undated, 24, Office of Personnel Management.

22. U.S. Bureau of Executive Manpower, Civil Service Commission, Notes on Meeting of February 15, 1964, on the Upper Career Service, dittoed, 1–17, Office of Personnel Management.

23. U.S. Bureau of Executive Manpower, Civil Service Commission, *Staffing for GS-13 thru 18*, memorandum from Nicholas J. Oganovic

through Warren B. Irons to the Commission, March 31, 1964, Office of Personnel Management.

24. U.S. Bureau of Executive Manpower, Civil Service Commission, *Draft Proposal for an Executive Order to Establish Executive Assignments,* multilithed, August 19, 1964. sec. 9.42, Office of Personnel Management.

25. U.S. Bureau of Executive Manpower, Civil Service Commission, "Considerations in Implementing Proposed Rule IX, A Preliminary Appraisal," typescript, August 28, 1964, Office of Personnel Management.

26. Committee for Economic Development, *Improving Executive Management in the Federal Government* (New York: CED, July 1964). The committee arranged for the publication of its Supplementary Paper no. 20 as Corson and Paul, *Men Near the Top.*

27. *Presidential Documents,* January 10–July 4, 1966 (Washington, D.C.: Government Printing Office, 1966), 2:28.

28. U.S. Bureau of Executive Manpower, Civil Service Commission, "Draft of Form Letter to Heads of Agencies from John W. Macy, Jr., Chairman, Civil Service Commission," June 1, 1966, Office of Personnel Management.

29. Office of the White House Secretary, Copy of Press Release, November 17, 1966, in the files of the Office of Personnel Management. See also *Administrative History,* 28.

30. *U.S. Federal Personnel Manual,* ch. 305, subchs. 1–2 and 1–3. See also *Administrative History,* 29–31; John W. Macy Jr., *Public Service: The Human Side of Government* (New York: Harper & Row, 1971), 217–20.

31. Initially, the inventory included about 25,000 persons. In June 1971 there were 41,367 persons in the inventory including current, retired, and resigned employees, but there were complete records for only about 35,000 then current employees including about 7,000 supergrades (GS-16–GS-18). There were also about 4,600 other federal positions at equivalent grade levels which in mid-1971 were excluded from the Executive Assignment System, including the positions of hearing examiner, executive positions in other branches of the government, those under other pay systems, those which had special statutory requirements, and those filled by presidential appointment.

32. U.S. Bureau of Executive Manpower, Civil Service Commission, "Executive Inventory Record, The Executive Assignment System," Standard Form 161-102, November 1967, *Federal Personnel Manual,* ch. 305.

33. See U.S. Bureau of Executive Manpower, Civil Service Commis-

sion, *The Executive Inventory, Questions and Answers for Executives,* May 1967, 9–10.

34. Nicholas J. Oganovic, executive director, Civil Service Commission, "Basic Changes in the Executive Inventory Search and Referral Process Under the Executive Assignment System," *Federal Personnel Manual System Letter* (FPM LTR. No. 3005-9), to Heads of Departments and Independent Establishments, published in advance of incorporation in FPM ch. 305, Washington, D.C., March 5, 1971, 1–2. The commission experienced other problems with use of the inventory, especially with use of coding information for research purposes concerning the designation of occupation, agency, and job function.

35. For "suggested guidelines" for agencies, see ibid., 3–4.

36. Warner, Van Riper, Martin, and Collins, *American Federal Executive.*

37. U.S. Bureau of Executive Manpower, Civil Service Commission, *Characteristics of the Federal Executive* (Washington, D.C.: Government Printing Office, November 1969).

38. Ibid.

39. U.S. Bureau of Executive Manpower, Civil Service Commission, *The Supergrade Scientist,* draft study, December 15, 1970, Office of Personnel Management.

40. *Administrative History,* 24.

41. U.S. Bureau of Executive Manpower, Civil Service Commission, *Career/Non-Career Executives,* draft study, February 1, 1971, Office of Personnel Management. In 1977 it was claimed that about two-thirds of supergrades (GS-16–GS-18) were career civil service positions and one-third were noncareer (Heclo, *Government of Strangers,* 39).

42. Heclo, *Government of Strangers,* 39–40.

43. U.S. Bureau of Executive Manpower, Civil Service Commission, *Impact of Change of Administration on Non-Career Executives and Positions, 1968–1969,* draft study, January 1971, Office of Personnel Management. The study did not include executives in schedules A and B.

44. U.S. Bureau of Executive Manpower, Civil Service Commission, *Rate of Advancement,* draft study, June 8, 1971, 16–17, Office of Personnel Management. "The difference in typical age of reaching GS-15 for these generation groups results in part from a progressive elevation in starting grade (49% of those entering before World War II entered below GS-5;

31% of those entering during the War did so; and only 4% of those entering after World War II). There has also been an accelerating rate of promotion" (2).

45. U.S. Bureau of Executive Manpower, Civil Service Commission, *Inter-Agency Mobility among Federal Executives*, draft study, March 1971, 1; see also *Extra-Governmental Mobility and Career Patterns of Federal Executives*, June 1, 1971; draft studies, both in the Office of Personnel Management. For other inventory-based mobility studies of this period, see Michael Cohen, "The Generalist and Organizational Mobility," *Public Administration Review* 30 (September–October 1970): 544–52; A. J. Mackelprang, *Executive Mobility in the Federal Service: A Policy Analysis*, paper presented at the Annual Meeting of the American Society for Public Administration, New York, March 22–24, 1972.

5. NIXON'S PROPOSAL FOR A FEDERAL EXECUTIVE SERVICE

1. For Macy's role with the White House during the 1960s, see his *Public Service*; Macy, Adams, and Walter, *America's Unelected Government*.

2. Executive Order of the President 11541, July 1, 1970.

3. U.S. Bureau of Executive Manpower, Civil Service Commission, *History of the Executive Assignment System*, 63.

4. For California's Career Executive Assignments system, see John Birkenstock, Ronald Kurtz, and Steven Phillips, "Career Executive Assignments—Report on a California Innovation," *Public Personnel Management* 4 (May–June 1975): 151–55; Lloyd D. Musolf, "Separate Career Executive Systems: Egalitarianism and Neutrality," *Public Administration Review* 31 (July–August 1971): 409–19.

5. U.S. Congress, House, Committee on Post Office and Civil Service, Subcommittee on Manpower and Civil Service, hearings, *Request for Supergrade Positions*, 92d Congress, 2d Session, March 7, 1972 (Washington, D.C.: Government Printing Office, 1972), 1–2.

6. See CRS, *History of Civil Service Merit Systems*, 306, table 1.

7. Section 5108, Title 5, U.S. Code.

8. Public Law 91-187, January 2, 1970.

9. Robert E. Hampton, chairman, *Memorandum for Heads of Executive Departments and Agencies* (Washington, D.C.: Office of the Chairman, Civil Service Commission, January 7, 1970), 1–2.

10. *History of the Executive Assignment System*, 19.

11. Discussion in this section of the commission's report of its study is

based on: U.S. Civil Service Commission, *The Federal Executive Service: A Proposal for Improving Federal Executive Manpower Management* (Washington, D.C.: Civil Service Commission, February 1971), hereafter cited as: CSC, *FES Proposal*. See also: *Administrative History*, 47–48.

12. But having broached this problem, the commission backed away: "While on the one hand these pressures influence staffing so that programs will be conducted in ways that agree with the desire of the groups exercising the pressures, on the other hand, the success of the programs frequently depends upon the support of the pressure groups" (CSC, *FES Proposal*, 3[4]).

13. Ibid., sec. 3. This report of the commission's study is reprinted in U.S. Congress, House, *The Federal Executive Service: Recommendations of the President of the United States*, For Use of the Committee on Post Office and Civil Service, 92d Congress, 1st Session, Committee Print No. 3, February 3, 1971 (Washington, D.C.: Government Printing Office, 1971), 67–108 (hereafter cited as House, *Federal Executive Service*); and in "Documentation—The Federal Executive Service," *Public Administration Review* 31 (March–April 1971): 235–52.

14. Because of their "unique problems or needs" the proposal excluded the following agencies: General Accounting Office, Peace Corps, Atomic Energy Commission, CIA, Tennessee Valley Authority, National Science Foundation, FBI, Council of Economic Advisors, Federal Deposit Insurance Corporation, Federal Reserve System, Postal Service, Panama Canal Company, Canal Zone Government, VA Department of Medicine and Surgery; and the Office of Comptroller of the Currency and Office of Assistant Secretary (International Affairs) of the Treasury Department. The proposal also excluded these groups of executive branch executives: Executive Levels I-V; Foreign Service; Foreign Information Service; Postal Field Service; hearing examiners; and those excluded by the president "in the interest of national security or foreign relations."

15. In 1969, as we noted in ch. 4, 16 percent of federal executives (GS-15–GS-18 and equivalents) were reported to have been in-and-outers, defined by the CSC as "executives who move from Federal employment to employment outside the Government and back again one or more times" (U.S. Bureau of Executive Manpower, Civil Service Commission, *Characteristics of the Federal Executive*, 10). According to Heclo: "These people are most easily characterized by what they are not: they are not politicians, and they are usually not bureaucrats in any conventional sense of that term. . . . The in-and-outers are a technocratic group called upon to fill

jobs . . . as policy managers and administrative leaders. Their previous involvement in policy matters is often substantial, but their attachments to government or politics as organizational enterprises are always transient." Hugh Heclo, "The In-and-Outer System: A Critical Assessment," in Mackenzie, *In-and-Outers*, 195, 196–97.

16. In 1971 the ratio of career to noncareer executives in the General Schedule was approximately 76 percent to 24 percent.

17. Seymour Berlin, "The Federal Executive Service," *Civil Service Journal*, April–June 1971, 10.

18. Ibid.

19. Ibid., 11. Other FES features concerned mandatory agency training and development opportunities for FES executives, rights of appeal for career executives, transition to the new system, and the effective date (no later than one year after enactment of legislation).

20. H. Doc. 92-41, February 2, 1971; reprinted in U.S. Congress, House, *Federal Executive Service*, 1–3.

21. U.S. Civil Service Commission news release for February 3, 1971; reprinted in ibid., 5.

22. U.S. Congress, Senate, Committee on Post Office and Civil Service on S. 1682, hearing, *Federal Executive Service*, 92d Congress, 1st Session, May 10, 1971 (Washington, D.C.: Government Printing Office, 1972), 38–40; hereafter cited as Senate, *1971 FES Hearing*.

23. "The Senate group appeared strongly in favor of giving a tax break to federal executives" (Joseph Young, "Tax Break Eyed for Top Grades," *Washington Evening Star*, May 11, 1971).

24. Mike Causey, "FES Plan Gains Favor in Congress," *Washington Post*, May 20, 1971. See also his column: "Opposition Slight to Executive Plan," ibid., May 11, 1971.

25. McGee to Hampton, June 28, 1971, Senate, *1971 FES Hearing*, 68–71.

26. Hampton to McGee, July 15, 1971, ibid., 72–84.

27. U.S. Congress, Senate, Report on the Committee on Post Office and Civil Service, *Federal Executive Service*, 92d Congress, 1st Session, Senate Rep. 92-864, June 15, 1972 (Washington, D.C.: Government Printing Office, 1972), 9–13.

28. U.S. Congress, House, Committee on Post Office and Civil Service, Subcommittee on Manpower and Civil Service, hearings on H.R.

3807, *Federal Executive Service*, 92d Congress, 2d Session, April 18, 21, 25, 1972 (Washington, D.C.: Government Printing Office, 1972), 217.

29. Mike Causey, "GAO Criticizes Bill on Supergrades," *Washington Post*, April 19, 1972; Causey, "Panel May Kill Plan for Supergrades." ibid., May 3, 1972.

30. George A. Graham, "On the Federal Executive Service Proposal: The FES Package Won't Do," *Public Administration Review* 31 (July–August 1971), 451, 452.

31. Ibid., 452–53.

32. Roger W. Jones, "What the FES Package Will Do," *Public Administration Review* 31 (July–August 1971): 453–54.

33. Ibid.

34. Mike Causey, "House Panel Mulls Supergrade Bill," *Washington Post*, May 17, 1972.

35. Causey reported that top CSC staffers were polishing a revised FES in September 1973 but that there was absolutely no congressional interest in any such revision. See Causey, *Washington Post*, September 18, 1972.

36. Seidman and Gilmour, *Politics, Position, and Power*, 99, 100.

6. The Making of the Senior Executive Service

1. It is important to note that at the time a similar theme figured prominently in Ronald Reagan's unsuccessful challenge to Gerald Ford in the campaign for the Republican nomination.

2. Jimmy Carter, presidential campaign literature, January 26, 1976. Cited in James McGrath, *Federal Civil Service Reform. The Federal Personnel Management Project (FPMP) and Proposed Changes in the Federal Civil Service System: A Report*, Congressional Research Service Report, Library of Congress, March 30, 1978.

3. Testimony of Alan K. Campbell, in U.S. Congress, House, Committee on Post Office and Civil Service, hearings on H.R. 11280, March 14, 1978, *Civil Service Reform* (Washington, D.C.: Government Printing Office, 1978), 21.

4. The other members of Task Force #2 were Jeffrey Caplan (Department of Commerce), Faye Harler (Civil Service Commission), and Cecil Uyehara (Agency for International Development).

5. Jule Sugarman, quoted in Felix A. Nigro, "The Politics of Civil Service Reform," paper delivered at the annual meeting of the American Politi-

cal Science Association, Washington, D.C., August 31–September 3, 1979, 10.

6. U.S. Federal Personnel Management Projects, *Appendices to the Final Staff Report* (Washington, D.C.: Civil Service Commission, July 1977–February 1978), vol. 2, app. 2, pp. 1–2.

7. Ibid., 11.

8. The task force argued that while a system of more limited scope would arouse less opposition from agencies and Congress, comprehensive presidential and congressional oversight would be best served by a single, integrated personnel structure. See ibid., 4.

9. The option paper defines a limited term appointee as an individual appointed for a maximum of three years to a managerial position in the sciences or professions, the duties of which are expected to expire during that time span. See ibid., app. B, p. 1.

10. Ibid.

11. Ibid., app. D, p. 1.

12. See McGrath, *Federal Civil Service Reform*, CRS-42.

13. The Carter administration would wait until May 1978 to send to Congress its Reorganization Plan no. 2, which provided for the creation of the Office of Personnel Management and the Merit Systems Protection Board and the elimination of the Civil Service Commission, although drafts of this plan were made available to legislators concurrent with their considerations of the Civil Service Reform Act.

14. See U.S. Congress, House, Committee on Post Office and Civil Service, *Civil Service Reform*; U.S. Congress, Senate, Committee on Governmental Affairs, hearings on S. 2640, S. 2707, and S. 2830, *Civil Service Reform Act of 1978 and Reorganization Plan No. 2 of 1978* (Washington, D.C.: Government Printing Office, 1978).

15. See, for instance, the testimony of Ralph Nader and of officials of the National Treasury Employees Union, the National Federation of Professional Organizations, the National Association of Supervisors, and the National Federation of Federal Employees in U.S. Congress, House, Committee on Post Office and Civil Service, *Hearings on Civil Service Reform*, 95th Congress, 2d Session, 173, 218, 237, 282–83, 343. In ch. 8 we analyze in detail some of these concerns, as well as the arguments of SES supporters.

16. SES bonus provisions have been changed several times since the 1978 legislation, both by act of Congress and by Office of Personnel Management fiat. What is described here are the original terms of Public Law 95-454. Subsequent changes are described in ch. 7.

17. As with bonuses, implementation of rank awards has over time shifted from the original language of the Civil Service Reform Act. See ch. 7 for an analysis.

18. See ch. 8 for an extensive elaboration of this argument.

7. REFORM IN ACTION: THE SENIOR EXECUTIVE SERVICE, 1979–1994

1. This chapter draws in part on the substance of Mark W. Huddleston, "The Senior Executive Service: Problems and Proposals for Reform," in C. Ban and N. Riccucci, eds., *Public Personnel Management: Current Concerns—Future Challenges* (New York: Longmans, 1991).

2. U.S. General Accounting Office, *Senior Executive Service: Executive's Perspectives on Their Federal Service* (GAO/GGD-88-109FS, 1988), 20.

3. U.S. General Accounting Office, *Senior Executive Service: Reasons Why Career Members Left in Fiscal Year 1985* (GAO/GGD-87-106FS, 1987), 23.

4. Patricia W. Ingraham, "The Reform Game," in Patricia W. Ingraham and David H. Rosenbloom, eds., *The Promise and Paradox of Civil Service Reform* (Pittsburgh: University of Pittsburgh Press, 1992), 12.

5. Larry M. Lane, "The Office of Personnel Management," in ibid., 109.

6. Ronald Brownstein and Nina Easton, *Reagan's Ruling Class: Portraits of the President's Top One Hundred Officials* (New York: Pantheon Books, 1983), 708, 709.

7. Charles H. Levine, "The Federal Government in the Year 2000: Administrative Legacies of the Reagan Years," *Public Administration Review* (May–June 1986): 201; reprinted in Patricia W. Ingraham and Donald F. Kettl, eds., *Agenda for Excellence: Public Service in America* (Chatham, N.J.: Chatham House Publishers, 1992), ch. 8.

8. Bernard Rosen, "Crises in the U.S. Civil Service," *Public Administration Review* 46 (May–June 1986): 209. Rosen analyzes Devine's partisan political activities, which figured in his failure to be reconfirmed for a second four-year term even by the Republican-controlled Senate.

9. This was nominally legal—that is, it did not officially violate the law that no more than 10 percent of SES positions be filled by noncareer appointees—because the Reagan administration used *authorized positions*, filled and unfilled, as the basis for its calculations. If, for example, there were at any given time 8,000 SES positions authorized, 800 of them, by

this logic, could be noncareer, even though perhaps only 7,000 of those 8,000 were actually staffed.

10. Edie N. Goldenberg, "The Permanent Government in an Era of Retrenchment and Redirection," in Lester M. Salamon and Michael S. Lund, eds., *The Reagan Presidency and the Governing of America* (Washington, D.C.: Urban Institute Press, 1985), 394–98. Lamenting the "brain drain" from the SES, Howard Rosen reported that, between July 13, 1979, and July 13, 1983, a total of 3,486 senior executives left the government (Howard Rosen, *Servants of the People: The Uncertain Future of the Federal Civil Service* [Salt Lake City: Olympus Publishing Co., 1985], 76).

11. U.S. Commission on Executive, Legislative, and Judicial Salaries, *The Quiet Crisis: Report of the 1984–85 Commission on Executive, Legislative, and Judicial Salaries* (Washington, D.C., July 29, 1985), 1.

12. U.S. General Accounting Office, *Senior Executive Service: Answers to Selected Salary-Related Questions* (GAO/GGD-87-36FS, 1987), 2.

13. National Academy of Public Administration, *The Senior Executive Service: An Interim Report of the Panel of the National Academy of Public Administration on the Public Service* (Washington, D.C.: National Academy of Public Administration, 1981), 42.

14. President's Commission on Compensation of Career Federal Executives, *Report* (Washington, D.C.: Government Printing Office, February 1988), 15.

15. Background paper by Mark W. Huddleston, in *The Government's Managers: Report of the Twentieth Century Fund Task Force on the Senior Executive Service* (New York: Priority Press, 1987), 65.

16. President's Commission on Compensation of Career Federal Executives, *Report*, 18.

17. Moreover, because of the structure of the performance awards covering GS-13–GS-15 versus the structure for the SES, the odds of receiving substantial cash bonuses were greater for the non-SESer. Any GS-13, -14 or -15 rated "outstanding" received a guaranteed merit increase plus a cash award of 2–10 percent of pay; no such automatic increases were awarded to SESers. As the report of the president's commission pointed out, any GS-15 invited to join the SES—because he or she was probably an "outstanding" employee—was likely to suffer a cut in income. See ibid., 20.

18. U.S. General Accounting Office, *Senior Executive Service: Reasons*

Why Career Members Left in Fiscal Year 1985 (GAO/GGD-87-106FS, 1987).

19. See, e.g., Charles H. Levine, "The Federal Government in the Year 2000," 201–02.

20. Patricia A. Wilson, "Power, Politics, and Other Reasons Why Senior Executives Leave the Federal Government," *Public Administration Review* 54 (January–February 1994): 12–19.

21. U.S. Office of Personnel Management, *The Status of the Senior Executive Service 1991* (Washington, D.C.: Office of Personnel Management, 1992), 27.

22. For good general discussions of the roles of civil servants and political appointees in national bureaucracies, see Mattei Dogan, ed., *The Mandarins of Western Europe: The Political Role of Top Civil Servants* (New York: John Wiley, 1975); Bruce L. R. Smith, ed., *The Higher Civil Service in Europe and Canada: Lessons for the United States* (Washington, D.C.: Brookings Institution, 1984); Suleiman, *Bureaucrats and Policy-Making*. We return to this theme in ch. 9.

23. "There is no reason . . . why many of the billets occupied by lower-level quasi-political appointees—schedule C's—should not be converted to slots for career members of the senior executive service. The total number of federal political appointees, some 3,000 including senior schedule C's, eliminates advancement opportunities for the very best careerists, often encouraging them to leave government just as they reach the top of their abilities" (John J. Di Iulio Jr., Gerard Garvey, and Donald F. Kettl, *Improving Government Performance: An Owner's Manual* [Washington, D.C.: Brookings Institution, 1993], 57).

24. Not including White House staff, U.S. attorneys, and several other categories, PAS appointments increased from 425 in 1979 to 508 in 1991; noncareer SES appointments from 489 to 722; and Schedule C from 1,543 to 1,832. The overall number of SES positions filled increased from 6,836 in 1979 to 8,012 in 1991 (U.S. Office of Personnel Management, *Status of the Senior Executive Service 1991*, 25, 27, 39).

25. See U.S. General Accounting Office, *Evaluation of Proposals to Alter the Structure of the Senior Executive Service* (GAO/GGD-86-14, 1985), 12; *The Government's Managers*, 7–8.

26. See, e.g., John B. Clinton and Arthur S. Newburg, *The Senior Executive Service: A Five-Year Retrospective of Its Operating and Conceptual Problems* (Washington, D.C.: Senior Executives Association, 1984); Bernard Rosen, "Uncertainty in the Senior Executive Service," *Public Administra-*

tion Review 41 (March–April 1981): 203–07; Bernard Rosen, "Effective Continuity of U.S. Government Operations in Jeopardy," *Public Administration Review* 43 (September–October 1983): 383–92; Patricia Ingraham, "Building Bridges or Burning Them? The President, the Appointees, and Bureaucracy," *Public Administration Review* 47 (September–October, 1987): 425–35.

27. Alan K. Campbell, "Testimony on Civil Service Reform and Organization (Testimony before the Committee on Post Office and Civil Service, U.S. House of Representatives, March 14, 1978)." Reprinted in Frank J. Thompson, ed., *Classics of Public Personnel Policy*, 2d ed. (Oak Park, Ill.: Moore Publishing Co., 1991), 95.

28. Public Law 95-454, Title IV, Section 3396.

29. U.S. Office of Personnel Management, *Status of the Senior Executive Service 1991*, 39.

30. U.S. Office of Personnel Management, *Annual Report on the Status of the Senior Executive Service* (Washington, D.C.: Office of Executive Personnel, 1988), 11.

31. U.S. Office of Personnel Management, *Status of the Senior Executive Service 1991*, 40; see also U.S. General Accounting Office, *Senior Executive Service: The Extent to Which SES Members Have Used the Sabbatical Program* (GAO/GGD-88-90, 1988), 3.

32. U.S. General Accounting Office, *Senior Executive Service: Agencies' Use of the Candidate Development Program* (GAO/GGD-86-93, 1986), 12; U.S. Office of Personnel Management, *Status of the Senior Executive Service 1991*, 5. A related problem has to do with the unattractiveness of the SES as currently constituted for officials in the upper ranks of the GS system who consider themselves primarily scientists; many of these people fear, probably correctly, that entry into the SES would mean abandoning the laboratory bench altogether for the bureaucrat's desk. For further discussion of this problem, see Proposal #3, pp. 122–25.

33. U.S. General Accounting Office, *Managing Human Resources: Greater OPM Leadership Needed to Address Critical Challenges* (GAO/GGD-89-19), 3.

34. President's Private Sector Survey on Cost Control, *Report of the Task Force on Personnel Management* (Washington, D.C.: Government Printing Office, 1983).

35. Edie N. Goldenberg, "The Grace Commission and Civil Service Reform: Seeking a Common Understanding," in Charles H. Levine, ed.,

The Unfinished Agenda for Civil Service Reform: Implications of the Grace Commission Report (Washington, D.C.: Brookings Institution, 1985), 72.

36. U.S. General Accounting Office, *Evaluation of Proposals to Alter the Structure of the Senior Executive Service* (GAO/GGD-86-14, 1985), 16. According to Peters, "the Grace Commission and its recommendations . . . could hardly have come at a more inopportune time for the federal civil service. The report appears to be one more attack on the role of the civil service in American government and . . . is certain to hurt morale, recruitment, and retention" (B. Guy Peters, "Administrative Change and the Grace Commission," in Levine, *Unfinished Agenda*, 38).

37. Clinton and Newberg, *Senior Executive Service.*

38. Ibid., 16.

39. U.S. General Accounting Office, *Evaluation of Proposals*, 12.

40. This section draws in part on the substance of Mark W. Huddleston, "To Track or Not Two Track?" Paper prepared for the SES Advisory Board meeting, Charlottesville, Va., April 1987.

41. U.S. National Institutes of Health, *Report of the Committee on Pay and Personnel Systems on Intramural Research*, May 1983; U.S. Federal Laboratory Review Panel, *Report of the White House Science Council*, May 1983. It should be noted that GS grades 16, 17, and 18 were formally abolished, effective May 1991, and replaced by Senior Level (SL) positions. Employment and pay procedures for so-called SL and scientific and professional (ST) positions, engaged in research and development, were established by regulations issued in April 1991. U.S. Office of Personnel Management, *Status of the Senior Executive Service 1991*, 12.

42. The original proposal by the National Institute of Health was expanded to include the entire Public Health Service (encompassing the institutes; the Food and Drug Administration; the Centers for Disease Control; the Alcohol, Drug Abuse, and Mental Health Administration; the Health Resources and Services Administration; and the Agency for Toxic Substances and Disease Registry).

43. U.S. General Accounting Office, *Evaluation of Proposals*, 27–28.

44. Huddleston, "To Track or Not Two Track?"

45. Ibid.

46. *The Government's Managers*, 14–15, 7–8.

47. Ibid., 8, 10, 13, 11–14.

48. See National Commission on the Public Service, *Leadership for*

America: Rebuilding the Public Service (Washington, D.C.: National Commission on the Public Service, 1989), 1, 13.

49. Ibid., 18, 37.

50. Lane, "Office of Personnel Management," 112. See also Joel D. Aberbach, "The President and the Executive Branch," in Colin Campbell and Bert A. Rockman, eds., *The Bush Presidency First Appraisals* (Chatham, N.J.: Chatham House, 1991), 235-336.

51. U.S. Office of Personnel Management, *Status of the Senior Executive Service 1991*, 12, 45; *Federal Times* 28, no. 12, May 4, 1992.

52. We explore this point in more detail in ch. 9.

53. See, for instance, the dissents that follow the main report of the Twentieth Century Fund task force (*The Government's Managers*, 16-17). There is also debate about whether the comparability principle should be abandoned altogether with respect to senior federal executives, given private sector pay scales.

8. IMAGES OF THE U.S. HIGHER CIVIL SERVICE

1. This chapter draws in part on the substance of Mark W. Huddleston, "America's (Unsuccessful) Search for a Higher Civil Service," in D. Rosenbloom and P. Ingraham, *The Civil Service Reform Act of 1978: Ten Years After* (Pittsburgh: University of Pittsburgh Press, 1992).

2. Byrd is known as something of an historian of Congress and as a particularly dogged—and eloquent—defender of the institution's majesty and traditions. O'Rourke is the author of *Parliament of Whores* (New York: Atlantic Monthly Press, 1991).

3. This is not to suggest that any one ideal-type, however coherent, may not contain potentially conflicting elements, a point Max Weber developed to great advantage in his discussion of bureaucracy.

4. U.S. Federal Personnel Management Project, *Final Report*, app. 2, p. 9 (emphasis added).

5. Ibid., app. 2, D, p. 1 (emphasis added).

6. The task force did urge that the focus of the Executive Service be kept on managers and that those supergrade members who had no supervisory responsibilities be excluded. It also appears that the task force expected far more discriminating self-selection at the time of conversion than actually occurred. By its estimate, "the number of incumbent managers who would elect to enter the service immediately are on the order of 50-70 percent" (ibid., vol. 2, app. 2, A, p. 15). Had the Office of Personnel

Management not induced a conversion rate close to 99 percent, the expectations of the task force for a more managerially oriented Executive Service might have been met. It should be noted, however, that the task force's definition of management was fairly loose: "the first or second in command of a significant organizational segment or of a major project" (ibid., vol. 2, app. 2, A, p. 3). Moreover, even granting its 50–70 percent projection, and absent a more carefully delineated grandfather clause, there was no good reason to believe that it would be supergrade managers rather than supergrade nonmanagers who would choose to convert.

7. On this last point, see recommendation no. 87 in ibid., vol. 1:196–97.

8. Ibid., vol. 2, app. 2, C(1), p. 4.

9. Ibid., vol. 1:198.

10. The chief exceptions to this generalization are to be found in the testimony of administration officials. Virtually all of Carter's cabinet officers were sent up to the Hill at one point or another to speak in favor of the Civil Service Reform Act in general and the SES in particular. To a person, they pursued the strategy of the Federal Personnel Management Project in projecting the SES as a system-for-all-seasons, drawing willy-nilly on all possible images of the higher civil service.

11. See U.S. Congress, House, Committee on Post Office and Civil Service, *Hearings on Civil Service Reform*, 95th Congress, 2d Session, 92–116, 196–99.

12. Ibid., 173, 218, 237, 354, 597.

13. Ibid., 282–83.

14. Ibid., 343.

15. One partial exception was the representatives of the National Academy of Public Administration, who urged some modest changes in the SES proposal in the direction of increasing opportunities for career executives; they also expressed the hope that the ratio of noncareer executives would eventually decline. See U.S. Congress, Senate, Committee on Governmental Affairs, *Hearings on the Civil Service Reform Act of 1978*, 392–401.

9. CONCLUSION: WHITHER THE SENIOR EXECUTIVE SERVICE?

1. For a more detailed discussion of this issue, see Mark W. Huddleston, "The SES: A Higher Civil Service?" *Policy Studies Journal* 17 (Winter 1988–89): 406–19.

2. Milton J. Esman, *Management Dimensions of Development: Perspectives and Strategies* (West Hartford, Conn.: Kumarian Press, 1991), 46.

3. For a broad review of European administrative history, see Ernest Barker, *The Development of Public Services in Western Europe 1600–1930* (London: Oxford University Press, 1944); on Japan see Edwin Dowdy, *Japanese Bureaucracy: Its Development and Modernization* (Melbourne, Australia: Cheshire, 1972). Two works that encompass both Europe and Asia are Gladden, *History of Public Administration*, and Reinhard Bendix, *Kings or People: Power and the Mandate to Rule* (Berkeley and Los Angeles: University of California Press, 1973). Bendix's work, which is the more sophisticated of the two, uses a Weberian framework and places a heavy emphasis on the role of bureaucratic officialdom in the process of historical transformation.

4. A good history of the period may be found in Geoffrey K. Fry, *Statesmen in Disguise: The Changing Role of the Administrative Class of the British Home Civil Service, 1853–1966* (London: Macmillan Co., 1969).

5. The literature on the subject is vast. A few examples include: Ralph Braibanti, ed., *Asian Bureaucratic Systems Emergent from the British Imperial Tradition* (Durham, N.C.: Duke University Press, 1966); Fred Burke, "Public Administration in Africa: The Legacy of Inherited Colonial Institutions," *Journal of Comparative Administration* 1 (November 1969); William Lofstrom, "From Colony to Republic: A Case Study in Bureaucratic Change," *Journal of Latin American Studies* 5 (November 1973); Alan K. Manchester, "The Growth of Bureaucracy in Brazil, 1808–1821," *Journal of Latin American Studies* 4 (May 1972).

6. Alexis de Tocqueville, *Democracy in America* (New York: Vintage, 1990), 72.

7. Samuel P. Huntington, *Political Order in Changing Societies* (New Haven: Yale University Press, 1968).

8. See Armstrong, *European Administrative Elite*.

9. A classic demonstration of this proposition came at the end of World War II when the Labour party gained power in Great Britain. Despite the fears and predictions of many on the left (e.g., Harold J. Laski, *Parliamentary Government in England* [New York: Viking Press, 1938]), the British higher civil service turned its talents toward implementing the program of the new regime with great professionalism. For a thorough review of the "representative bureaucracy" literature, which treats this and similar cases at length, see Krislov, *Representative Bureaucracy*.

10. Tocqueville, *Democracy in America*, 92.

11. From President Andrew Jackson's first address to Congress, December 8, 1829, quoted in Leonard D. White, *The Jacksonians: A Study in Administrative History, 1829–1861* (New York: Macmillan Co., 1954), 318. See also Arthur M. Schlesinger Jr., *The Age of Jackson* (Boston: Little, Brown & Co., 1945), 46–48, esp. 46.

12. Leonard D. White, *The Federalists: A Study in Administrative History* (New York: Macmillan Co., 1948), 303.

13. Ibid., 211–12, 293.

14. See Leonard D. White, *The Jeffersonians: A Study in Administrative History, 1801–1829* (New York: Macmillan Co., 1951), 352–54. White notes, in Jefferson's defense, that our third president forswore *removing* officers for political reasons. It is interesting to speculate in this vein what might have happened had the Federalists held the presidency for another term or had Jefferson been less inclined to bow to partisan pressure in making appointments. Certainly the Federalist legacy in administration was extraordinary: moral and intellectual standards were higher than the nation would see again for generations; assuming good performance, continuity in office was assured. In these circumstances, it is plausible that we would have seen a career service much earlier than the 1880s. An even more intriguing "What if?" is to ponder the effects of a Hamilton presidency—or even a continued Hamiltonian influence on the course of administrative development. Alexander Hamilton was arguably the country's greatest public administrator and institution builder. He not only created and ran the Treasury Department, which at the time exercised nearly all the domestic functions of government, but he also took a leading role in every other area of federal affairs as well—much to Jefferson's dismay at the State Department, one might add. Hamilton's early departure from government (he left Washington's second administration in January 1795 to pursue business interests in New York, though he continued to advise and dabble behind the scenes) and his untimely demise by the pistol of Aaron Burr were tragic for the course of U.S. public administration. For a classic and still fascinating consideration of Hamilton's impact on public administration, see Lynton K. Caldwell, *The Administrative Theories of Hamilton and Jefferson: Their Contributions to Thought and Public Administration*, 2d ed. (New York: Holmes & Meier, 1988).

15. See White, *Jacksonians*, esp. chs. 8, 16–18, and 21.

16. For a classic work on this period, see Richard Hofstadter, *The Age of Reform* (New York: Vintage, 1955).

17. Woodrow Wilson, "The Study of Administration," *Political Science Quarterly* 2 (June 1887).

18. For an elaboration of this argument, see Mark W. Huddleston, "The Carter Civil Service Reforms: Some Implications for Political Theory and Public Administration," *Political Science Quarterly* 96 (Winter 1981–82): 607–21.

19. U.S. Office of Personnel Management, *Status of the Senior Executive Service 1991*, 27. These figures are designated as noncareer appointees with this explanation: "Of over three million Federal employees, about 3,000 are noncareer appointees. About 500 of these are Presidential appointments, which are generally executive level positions such as department and agency heads, assistant secretaries, etc. They exclude White House staff, Chiefs of Mission in the State Department, U.S. Attorneys, U.S. Marshals, and most part-time and temporary positions. Schedule C positions are primarily GS-15 and below, including 100 positions authorized by Executive orders." As we have suggested in previous chapters, it is difficult to extract reliable up-to-date data on numbers of political appointees from the federal government. The figure of about three thousand political appointees is consistent with most contemporary estimates, including that in the final report of the Volcker Commission. See National Commission on the Public Service, *Leadership for America*, 17.

20. Consider classic works in organization theory, such as Alvin Gouldner, *Patterns of Industrial Bureaucracy* (Glencoe, Ill.: Free Press, 1954); or Philip Selznick, *TVA and the Grass Roots* (Berkeley and Los Angeles: University of California Press, 1949).

21. Seidman and Gilmour, *Politics, Position and Power*, esp. ch. 11.

22. Among those making a similar argument is James Pfiffner, who has written: "The argument here is not to discard the in-and-outer system that has served government well. The argument is that the capacity of the White House is being strained and the effectiveness of the government is being undermined by the present trend toward increasing numbers of political appointees. Reversing this direction would increase the capacity of the government to function efficiently and effectively without sacrificing political accountability or responsiveness" (James P. Pfiffner, "Political Appointees and Career Executives: The Democracy-Bureaucracy Nexus," in Ingraham and Kettl, *Agenda for Excellence*, 62).

23. See, e.g., White, *Jeffersonians*, ch. 9.

24. Curiously, Ralph Nader was one of the loudest critics of the SES, on the grounds that it would *inhibit* the use of political appointees.

25. For a general review of the postmodern and deconstructionist turn in social science analysis, with some attention to public administration in particular, see Pauline Marie Rosenau, *Post-Modernism and the Social Sciences* (Princeton, N.J.: Princeton University Press, 1992).

26. Armstrong, *European Administrative Elite*, 17–18. Though he does develop the general model, Armstrong does not apply it to the U.S. case. The other theoretical types of recruitment he identifies are "maximum ascriptive" and "progressive equal attrition." In the former, elite administrators are to all intents and purposes identified at birth. In the latter, regular choices are made from among age cohorts throughout the years prior to entry into the service.

27. Both the Federal Employees Training Act of 1958 and the Intergovernmental Personnel Act of 1970 provided for such assignments to foster mobility.

28. See, for instance, Senior Executives Association, "Proposal for a National Civil Service Academy," mimeographed document, October 21, 1985.

29. Our various university-affiliated schools of public administration may raise objections, of course, fearing a usurpation of their functions. But by restricting such an academy to postgraduate or even post-postgraduate education, on the model perhaps of the French École Nationale d'Administration, such anxieties might be eased.

30. See, for instance, Frederick F. Ridley, *Specialists and Generalists: A Comparative Study of the Professional Civil Servant at Home and Abroad* (London: George Allen & Unwin, 1968).

31. This proposal is elaborated in Huddleston, "To Track or Not Two Track."

32. See Huddleston, "Carter Civil Service Reforms" for an elaboration of this argument.

33. Hugh Heclo, "A Comment on the Future of the U.S. Civil Service," in Bruce L. R. Smith, ed., *The Higher Civil Service in Europe and Canada: Lessons for the United States* (Washington, D.C.: Brookings Institution, 1984), 105–06.

34. See John Rohr, *To Run a Constitution: The Legitimacy of the Administrative State* (Lawrence: University of Kansas Press, 1986), 1.

35. Ibid., esp. chs. 2–4.

36. White, *Federalists*, 314.

37. Carl J. Friedrich, "Public Policy and the Nature of Administrative Responsibility," in Carl J. Friedrich and Edward S. Mason, eds., *Public Policy: A Yearbook of the Graduate School of Public Administration, Harvard University* (Cambridge: Harvard University Press, 1940), 19.

38. George Will, *Restoration: Congress, Term Limits, and the Recovery of Deliberative Democracy* (New York: Free Press, 1992), 3. Will was actually referring to Congress alone here, but we suspect he wouldn't disagree with the spirit of our emendation. The actual quotation is: "By the beginning of the 1990s it was beginning to seem that Congress was not just going through another of its bad patches. Rather, Congress seemed to have settled into a deep trough, and it lacked the strength to lift itself out."

39. Executive Order 12389, February 10, 1993, sec. 1.

40. President Bill Clinton, Address to Joint Session of Congress, February 17, 1993.

41. See Press release, "A Revolution in Government," Office of Domestic Policy, White House, March 3, 1993; Vice President Al Gore, *Creating a Government That Works Better and Costs Less: Report of the National Performance Review* (Washington, D.C.: Government Printing Office, September 7, 1993). Though no reference is made in the text of the Gore Report to improving the SES, buried in its appendix C without elaboration is this recommendation (HRM11): "Create and reinforce a corporate perspective within the Senior Executive Service that supports governmentwide culture change. Promote a corporate succession planning model to use to select and develop senior staff. Enhance voluntary mobility within and between agencies for top senior executive positions in government" (163). The practice of the Office of Personnel Management under the Bush administration of issuing annual reports on the status of the SES was not continued under the Clinton administration. On Clinton's first year, the *Economist* (January 15, 1994, 24) commented, "Often—as with the programme to 'reinvent government'—the fanfare is not matched by the follow-up."

42. See Ronald C. Moe, "The 'Reinventing Government' Exercise: Misinterpreting the Problem, Misjudging the Consequences," *Public Administration Review* 54 (March–April 1994): 116; Roger Garcia, "Growth in Number of Political Appointee Positions as Ratio of Total Full-Time Federal Employees," Congressional Research Service Report, September 1993.

43. *Aeschylus*, vol. 2, trans. Herbert Wier Smyth (Cambridge: Harvard University Press, 1926), 149, l. 1668.

44. Oliver Goldsmith, "The Captivity, an Oratorio," in *Oliver Goldsmith*, ed. Ernest Rhys (London: J. M. Dent, 1910), 94.

Bibliography

Aberbach, Joel D. "The President and the Executive Branch." In *The Bush Presidency First Appraisals*, edited by Colin Campbell and Bert A. Rockman. Chatham, N.J.: Chatham House Publishers, 1991.

Aberbach, Joel D., Robert D. Putnam, and Bert A. Rockman. *Bureaucrats and Politicians in Western Democracies*. Cambridge: Harvard University Press, 1981.

Aeschylus. *Aeschylus*. Vol. 2. Translated by Herbert Wier Smith. Cambridge: Harvard University Press, 1926.

Agar, Herbert. *The Price of Union*. Boston: Houghton Mifflin Co., 1950.

Armstrong, John A. *The European Administrative Elite*. Princeton, N.J.: Princeton University Press, 1973.

Bailey, Stephen K. "The President and His Political Executives." *Annals of the American Academy of Political and Social Sciences* 307 (September 1956): 24–36.

Barker, Ernest. *The Development of Public Services in Western Europe, 1600–1930*. London: Oxford University Press, 1944.

Barnett, A. Doak, and Ezra Vogel. *Cadres, Bureaucracy, and Political Power in Communist China*. New York: Columbia University Press, 1967.

Baruch, Ismar. *Background of the Supergrade Story, 1923–54, and the Ceiling Rate of the Classification Act of 1949, as Amended*. 4th revision. Washington, D.C.: U.S. Civil Service Commission, September 1954.

———. *History of Position-Classification and Salary Standardization in the Federal Service, 1789–1941*. 2d ed. Washington, D.C.: U.S. Civil Service Commission, P.C.D. Manual A-2, 1941.

———. *Supergrade Story, 1949–1952*. Bks. 1 and 2. Ismar Baruch Collection, Pendleton Room, Office of Personnel Management Library, Washington, D.C.

Bendix, Reinhard. *Higher Civil Servants in American Society: A Study of the Social Origins, the Careers, and the Power-Position of Higher Federal Administrators.* Boulder: University of Colorado Press, 1949. Reprint, Westport Conn: Greenwood Press, 1974.

———. *Kings or People: Power and the Mandate to Rule.* Berkeley and Los Angeles: University of California Press, 1973.

Bent, Frederick T. "The Civil Servant: Gentleman or Professional?" *Public Administration Review* 31 (September–October 1971): 577–81.

Berlin, Seymour. "The Federal Executive Service." *Civil Service Journal,* April–June 1971, 7–13.

Berman, Larry. *The New American Presidency.* Boston: Little, Brown & Co., 1986.

———. *The Office of Management and Budget and the Presidency, 1921–1979.* Princeton, N.J.: Princeton University Press, 1979.

Bernstein, Marver H. *The Job of the Federal Executive.* Washington, D.C.: Brookings Institution, 1958.

Birkenstock, John, Ronald Kurtz, and Steven Phillips. "Career Executive Assignments—Report on a California Innovation." *Public Personnel Management* 4 (May–June 1975): 151–155.

Bolster, Mel H. *Federal Career Executives, Three Years' Experience with the Career Executive Roster.* Multilithed. April 1964. Library of the Office of Personnel Management, Washington, D.C.

Boyer, William W. *Bureaucracy on Trial: Policy Making by Government Agencies.* Indianapolis: Bobbs-Merrill Co., 1964.

———. "Political Science and the Twenty-first Century: From Government to Governance." *PS: Political Science & Politics* 23 (March 1990): 50–54.

Boyer, William W., and Earle P. Shoub. "Promoting the Federal Service in Higher Education." *Personnel Administration* 22 (November–December 1959): 31–43.

Braibanti, Ralph, ed. *Asian Bureaucratic Systems Emergent from the British Imperial Tradition.* Durham, N.C.: Duke University Press, 1966.

Brown, R.G.S. *The Administrative Process in Britain.* London: Methuen & Co., 1971.

Brownstein, Ronald, and Nina Easton. *Reagan's Ruling Class: Portraits of the President's Top One Hundred Officials.* New York: Pantheon Books, 1983.

Burke, Fred. "Public Administration in Africa: The Legacy of Inherited Colonial Institutions." *Journal of Comparative Administration* 1 (November 1969): 345–78.

Caldwell, Lynton K. *The Administrative Theories of Hamilton and Jefferson: Their Contributions to Thought and Public Administration.* 2d ed. New York: Holmes & Meier, 1988.

Campbell, G.A. *The Civil Services in Britain.* London: Whitefriars Press, 1955.

Chang, Y.Z. "China and English Civil Service Reform." *American Historical Review* 42 (April 1942): 539–44.

Chapman, Brian. *The Profession of Government: The Public Service in Europe.* London: Unwin University Books, 1959.

Chapman, Richard A. *The Higher Civil Service in Britain.* London: Constable & Co., 1970.

Chiang, Chung-kuang. "The Politics of Revolutionary Higher Education in the People's Republic of China with Emphasis on Beijing University." Ph.D. dissertation, University of Delaware, 1985.

Cho, Suk-choon. "The Bureaucracy." In *Korean Politics in Transition,* edited by Edward Reynolds Wright. Seattle: University of Washington Press, 1975.

Chung, Sung Ho. "Politics of Civil Service Reform: The First Attempt to Establish a Higher Civil Service in the Eisenhower Administration." Ph.D. dissertation, University of Delaware, 1985.

Clarke, William Harrison. *The Civil Service Law.* 3d ed. New York: M.T. Richardson Co. 1897.

Cleveland, Harlan. "The Executive and the Public Interest." *Annals* 307 (September 1956): 33–54.

Clinton, John B., and Arthur S. Newburg. *The Senior Executive Service: A Five-Year Retrospective of Its Operating and Conceptual Problems.* Washington, D.C.: Senior Executives Association, 1984.

Cohen, Michael. "The Generalist and Organizational Mobility." *Public Administration Review* 30 (September–October 1970): 544–52.

Committee for Economic Development. *Improving Executive Management in the Federal Government.* New York: Committee for Economic Development, 1964.

Congressional Quarterly Service. *Congress and Nation, 1949–1964: A Re-*

view of Government and Politics in the Postwar Years. Washington, D.C.: Congressional Quarterly Service, 1965.

Corson, John J. *Executives for the Federal Service: A Program for Action in Time of Crisis.* New York: Columbia University Press, 1952.

Corson, John J., and R. Shale Paul. *Men Near the Top: Filling Key Posts in the Federal Service.* Baltimore: Johns Hopkins Press, 1966.

Creel, H.G. "The Beginnings of Bureaucracy in China: The Origin of the *Hsien.*" *Journal of Asian Studies* 23 (1964): 155–85.

David, Paul T., and Ross Pollock. *Executives for Government.* Washington, D.C.: Brookings Institution, 1957.

DiIulio, John J., Jr., Gerard Garvey, and Donald F. Kettl. *Improving Government Performance: An Owner's Manual.* Washington, D.C.: Brookings Institution, 1993.

"Documentation—The Federal Executive Service." *Public Administration Review* 31 (March–April 1971): 235–52.

Dogan, Mattei, ed. *The Mandarins of Western Europe: The Political Role of Top Civil Servants.* New York: John Wiley & Sons, 1975.

Dowdy, Edwin. *Japanese Bureaucracy: Its Development and Modernization.* Melbourne, Australia: Cheshire, 1972.

Eisenhower, Dwight D. "Annual Message to the Congress on the State of the Union, Jan. 7, 1954." *Public Papers of the Presidents of the United States, Dwight D. Eisenhower.* Washington, D.C.: Government Printing Office, 1960.

————. "Radio and Television Address to the American People on the Achievement of the 83rd Congress, Aug. 23, 1954." *Public Papers of the Presidents of the United States, Dwight D. Eisenhower.* Washington, D.C.: Government Printing Office, 1960.

Emmerich, Herbert, and G. Lyle Belsley. "The Federal Career Service— What Next?" *Public Administration Review* 14 (Winter 1954): 1–12.

Esman, Milton J. *Management Dimensions of Development: Perspectives and Strategies.* West Hartford, Conn.: Kumarian Press, 1991.

Fairbank, John K., Edwin O. Reischauer, and Albert N. Craig. *East Asia: Tradition and Transformation.* Boston: Houghton Mifflin Co., 1973.

Farazmand, Ali, ed. *Handbook of Comparative and Development Public Administration.* New York: Marcel Dekker, 1991.

Federal Employees' News Digest. Washington, D.C.

Federal Times. Washington, D.C.

Fesler, James W. "The Political Role of Field Administration." In *Papers in Comparative Public Administration,* edited by Ferrel Heady and Sybil L. Stokes. Ann Arbor: Institute of Public Administration, University of Michigan, 1962.

Franke, Wolfgang. *The Reform and Abolition of the Traditional Chinese Examination System.* Cambridge: Harvard University Press, 1960.

Freeman, J. Leiper. *The Political Process: Executive Bureau–Legislative Committee Relations.* Garden City, N.J.: Doubleday & Co., 1955.

Friedman, Anne, and Mary Chan Morgan. "Controlling Bureaucracy in Communist China (1949–1980)." In *Administrative Systems Abroad,* edited by Krishna K. Tummala. Lanham, Md.: University Press of America, 1982.

Friedrich, Carl J. "Public Policy and the Nature of Administrative Responsibility." In *Public Policy: A Yearbook of the Graduate School of Public Administration, Harvard University,* edited by Carl J. Friedrich and Edward S. Mason. Cambridge: Harvard University Press, 1940.

Fry, Geoffrey K. *Statesmen in Disguise: The Changing Role of the Administrative Class of the British Home Civil Service, 1853–1966.* London: Macmillan Co., 1969.

Fulton, Lord. Chairman. *The Civil Service, Report of the Committee, 1966–68.* London: Her Majesty's Stationery Office, 1970.

Garcia, Roger. "Growth in Number of Political Appointee Positions as Ratio of Total Full-Time Federal Employees." Washington, D.C.: Congressional Research Service Report, September 1993.

Gladden, E. N. *Civil Services of the United Kingdom, 1855–1970.* London: Frank Cass & Co., 1976.

———. *A History of Public Administration.* 2 vols. London: Frank Cass & Co., 1972.

Goldenberg, Edie N. "The Grace Commission and Civil Service Reform: Seeking a Common Understanding." In *The Unfinished Agenda for Civil Service Reform: Implications of the Grace Commission Report,* edited by Charles H. Levine. Washington, D.C.: Brookings Institution, 1985.

———. "The Permanent Government in an Era of Retrenchment and Redirection." In *The Reagan Presidency and the Governing of America,* edited by Lester M. Salamon and Michael S. Lund. Washington, D.C.: Urban Institute Press, 1985.

Goldsmith, Oliver. "The Captivity, an Oratorio." In *Oliver Goldsmith*, edited by Ernest Rhys. London: J.M. Dent, 1910.

Golembiewski, Robert T. "Specialist or Generalist? Structure as a Crucial Factor." *Public Administration Review* 25 (June 1965): 135–41.

Gore, Al. *Creating a Government That Works Better and Costs Less: Report of the National Performance Review*. Washington, D.C.: Government Printing Office, September 7, 1993.

Gouldner, Alvin. *Patterns of Industrial Bureaucracy*. Glencoe, Ill.: Free Press, 1954.

Graham, George A. *America's Capacity to Govern: Some Preliminary Thoughts for Prospective Administrators*. University: University of Alabama Press, 1960.

———. "On the Federal Executive Service Proposal: The FES Package Won't Do." *Public Administration Review* 31 (July–August 1971): 451–53.

Hacker, Louis M., and Benjamin B. Kendrick. *The United States Since 1865*. 3d ed. New York: F.S. Crofts & Co., 1947.

Hampton, Robert E. *Memorandum for Heads of Executive Departments and Agencies*. Washington, D.C.: Office of the Chairman, Civil Service Commission, January 7, 1970.

Harvey, Donald R. *The Civil Service Commission*. New York: Praeger Publishers, 1970.

Heady, Ferrel. *Public Administration: A Comparative Perspective*. 4th ed. New York: Marcel Dekker, 1991.

———. "The United States." In *Public Administration in Developed Democracies: A Comparative Study*, edited by Donald C. Rowat. New York: Marcel Dekker, 1988.

Heclo, Hugh. "A Comment on the Future of the U.S. Civil Service." In *The Higher Civil Service in Europe and Canada: Lessons for the United States*, edited by Bruce L.R. Smith. Washington, D.C.: Brookings Institution, 1984.

———. *A Government of Strangers: Executive Politics in Washington*. Washington, D.C.: Brookings Institution, 1977.

Hensel, H. Struve, and John D. Millett. *Task Force Report on Departmental Management in Federal Administration, Prepared for the Commission on Organization of the Executive Branch of the Government*. Washington, D.C.: Government Printing Office, 1949.

Herson, Lawrence J.R. "China's Imperial Bureaucracy: Its Direction and Control." *Public Administration Review* 17 (Winter 1957): 44–53.

Hofstadter, Richard. *The Age of Reform.* New York: Vintage, 1955.

Holden, Matthew, Jr. " 'Imperialism' in Bureaucracy." *American Political Science Review* 60 (December 1966): 943–51.

Huddleston, Mark W. "America's (Unsuccessful) Search for a Higher Civil Service." In *The Promise and Paradox of Civil Service Reform*, edited by P. Ingraham and D. Rosenbloom. Pittsburgh: University of Pittsburgh Press, 1992.

———. Background Paper. In *The Government's Managers: Report of the Twentieth Century Fund Task Force on the Senior Executive Service.* New York: Priority Press Publications, 1987.

———. "The Carter Civil Service Reforms: Some Implications for Political Theory and Public Administration." *Political Science Quarterly* 96 (Winter 1981–82): 607–21.

———. "The SES: A Higher Civil Service?" *Policy Studies Journal* 17 (Winter 1988–89): 406–19.

———. "The Senior Executive Service: Problems and Proposals for Reform." In *Public Personnel Management: Current Concerns—Future Challenges*, edited by C. Ban and N. Riccucci. New York: Longmans, 1991.

———. "To the Threshold of Reform: The Senior Executive Service and America's Search for a Higher Civil Service." In *The Promise and Paradox of Civil Service Reform*, edited by P. Ingraham and D. Rosenbloom. Pittsburgh: University of Pittsburgh Press, 1992.

———. "To Track or Not Two Track?" Paper prepared for the meeting of the SES Advisory Board, under the auspices of the U.S. Office of Personnel Management, Charlottesville, Virginia, April 1987.

Huntington, Samuel P. *Political Order in Changing Societies.* New Haven: Yale University Press, 1968.

Ingles, R. "Manner in Which the Literary Examinations Are Conducted." *Chinese Repository* 4 (July 1835): 118–28.

Ingraham, Patricia W. "Building Bridges or Burning Them? The President, the Appointees, and Bureaucracy." *Public Administration Review* 47 (September–October 1987): 425–35.

Ingraham, Patricia W., and Donald F. Kettl, eds. *Agenda for Excellence: Public Service in America.* Chatham, N.J.: Chatham House Publishers, 1992.

Ingraham, Patricia W., and David H. Rosenbloom, eds. *The Promise and Paradox of Civil Service Reform*. Pittsburgh: University of Pittsburgh Press, 1992.

Jones, Roger W. "What the FES Package Will Do." *Public Administration Review* 31 (July–August 1971): 453–54.

Kestnbaum, Meyer. "Career Administrators in Government Service." *Good Government* 74 (May–June 1957): 27–28.

Kidney, Edith B. *Fringe Benefits for Salaried Employees in Government and Industry*. Personnel Report 542. Chicago: Civil Service Assembly, 1954.

Kilpatrick, Franklin F., Milton C. Cummings, Jr., and M. Kent Jennings. *The Image of the Federal Service*. Washington, D.C.: Brookings Institution, 1964.

———. *Source Book of a Study of Occupational Values and the Image of the Federal Service*. Washington, D.C.: Brookings Institution, 1964.

Koenig, Louis W. *The Chief Executive*. New York: Harcourt, Brace & World, 1964.

Kracke, E.A., Jr. *Civil Service in Early Sung China*. Cambridge: Harvard University Press, 1953.

Krantz, Harry. *The Participatory Bureaucracy: Women and Minorities in a More Representative Public Service*. Lexington, Mass.: D.C. Heath & Co., 1976.

Krislov, Samuel. *Representative Bureaucracy*. Englewood Cliffs, N.J.: Prentice-Hall, 1974.

Kubota, Akira. *Higher Civil Servants in Postwar Japan: Their Social Origins, Educational Backgrounds, and Career Patterns*. Princeton, N.J.: Princeton University Press, 1969.

Lach, Donald F. *Asia in the Making of Europe*. Chicago: University of Chicago Press, 1965.

Landis, James M. *Report on Regulatory Agencies to the President-Elect*. 89th Congress, 2d Session. U.S. Congress, Senate. Committee on the Judiciary. Subcommittee on Administrative Practice and Procedure. December 1960.

Lane, Larry M. "The Office of Personnel Management: Values, Policies, and Consequences." In *The Promise and Paradox of Civil Service Reform*, edited by P. Ingraham and D. Rosenbloom. Pittsburgh: University of Pittsburgh Press, 1992.

LaPalombara, Joseph. "Values and Ideologies in the Administrative Evolution of Western Constitutional Systems." In *Political and Administrative Development*, edited by Ralph Braibanti. Durham, N.C.: Duke University Press, 1969.

Laski, Harold J. *Parliamentary Government in England*. New York: Viking Press, 1938.

Lee, Hahn-Been. *Korea: Time, Change, and Administration*. Honolulu: East-West Center Press, University of Hawaii, 1968.

Legge, James. *The Chinese Classics: With a Translation, Critical and Exegetical Notes, Prolegomena, and Copious Indexes*. Hong Kong: Hong Kong University Press, 1960.

Levine, Charles H. "The Federal Government in the Year 2000: Administrative Legacies of the Reagan Years." *Public Administration Review* 46 (May–June 1986): 195–206.

———, ed. *The Unfinished Agenda for Civil Service Reform: Implications of the Grace Commission Report*. Washington, D.C.: Brookings Institution, 1985.

Levinson, Joseph R. *Confucian China and Its Modern Fate*. Berkeley and Los Angeles: University of California Press, 1968.

Liu, James T. C. "Eleventh-Century Chinese Bureaucrats: Some Historical Classifications and Behavioral Types." *Administrative Science Quarterly* 4 (September 1959): 207–35.

Lofstrom, William. "From Colony to Republic: A Case Study in Bureaucratic Change." *Journal of Latin American Studies* 5 (November 1973): 177–97.

Mackelprang, A.J. "Executive Mobility in the Federal Service: A Policy Analysis." Paper presented at the annual meeting of the American Society for Public Administration, New York, March 22–24, 1972.

Mackenzie, G. Calvin, ed. *The In-and-Outers: Presidential Appointees and Transient Government in Washington*. Baltimore: Johns Hopkins University Press, 1987.

Macmahon, Arthur W., and John D. Millet. *Federal Administrators: A Biographical Approach to the Problem of Departmental Management*. New York: Columbia University Press, 1939.

MacNeil, Neil, and Harold W. Metz. *The Hoover Report: 1953–1955*. New York: Macmillan Co., 1956.

Macy, John W., Jr. *Public Service: The Human Side of Government*. New York: Harper & Row, 1971.

Macy, John W., Jr., Bruce Adams, and J. Jackson Walter. *America's Unelected Government: Appointing the President's Team.* Cambridge: Ballinger Publishing Co., 1983.

Madison, James [Publius, pseudo]. "The Federalist No. 47." *The Federalist.* New York: Modern Library, 1937.

Maley, Patricia A. "Comparative Administrative Personnel Practices in Commonwealth Higher Civil Services: A Study of Systemic Emulation over Time." M.A. thesis, University of Delaware, 1981.

Manchester, Alan K. "The Growth of Bureaucracy in Brazil, 1808–1821." *Journal of Latin American Studies* 4 (May 1972): 77–83.

Mann, Dean E. *The Assistant Secretaries: Problems and Processes of Appointment.* Washington, D.C.: Brookings Institution, 1965.

McGrath, James. *Federal Civil Service Reform. The Federal Personnel Management Project (FPMP) and Proposed Changes in the Federal Civil Service System: A Report.* Congressional Research Service Report. Library of Congress, March 30, 1978.

McGregor, Eugene B., Jr. "Education and Career Mobility among Federal Administrators: Toward the Development of a Comparative Model." Ph.D. dissertation, Syracuse University, 1969.

Meadows, Thomas Taylor. *The Chinese and Their Rebellions.* Stanford, Calif.: Academic Reprints, 1856.

———. *Desultory Notes on the Government and People of China and on the Chinese Language.* London: William H. Allen and Co., 1847.

Miyazaki, Ichisada. *China's Examination Hell: The Civil Service Examinations of Imperial China.* New York: Weatherhill, 1976.

Moe, Ronald C. "The 'Reinventing Government' Exercise: Misinterpreting the Problem, Misjudging the Consequences." *Public Administration Review* 54 (March–April 1994): 111–22.

Mosher, Frederick C. *Democracy and the Public Service.* New York: Oxford University Press, 1968.

Musolf, Lloyd D. "Separate Career Executive Systems: Egalitarianism and Neutrality." *Public Administration Review* 31 (July–August 1971): 409–19.

National Academy of Public Administration. *The Senior Executive Service: An Interim Report of the Panel of the National Academy of Public Administration on the Public Service.* Washington, D.C.: National Academy of Public Administration, 1981.

212

National Commission on the Public Service. *Leadership for America: Rebuilding the Public Service.* Washington, D.C.: National Commission on the Public Service, 1989.

New York Times.

Nigro, Felix A. "The Politics of Civil Service Reform." Paper presented at the annual meeting of the American Political Science Association, Washington, D.C.: August 31–September 3, 1979.

Oganovic, Nicholas J. "Basic Changes in the Executive Inventory Search and Referral Process under the Executive Assignment System." Federal Personnel Manual System Letter (FPM LTR No. 3005-9). In *Federal Personnel Manual*, ch. 305, March 5, 1971.

O'Rourke, P.J. *Parliament of Whores.* New York: Atlantic Monthly Press, 1991.

Paget, Richard M. "Strengthening the Federal Career Executive." *Public Administration Review* 17 (Spring 1957): 91–96.

Paik, Wan Ki. "The Formation of the Governing Elites in Korean Society." In *A Dragon's Progress: Development Administration in Korea*, edited by Gerald E. Caiden and Bun Woong Kim. West Hartford, Conn.: Kumarian Press, 1991.

Pear, R.H. "United States." In *Specialists and Generalists*, edited by F.F. Ridley. New York: Barnes & Noble, 1968.

Peters, B. Guy. "Administrative Change and the Grace Commission." In *The Unfinished Agenda for Civil Service Reform: Implications of the Grace Commission Report*, edited by Charles H. Levine. Washington, D.C.: Brookings Institution, 1985.

Pfiffner, James P. "Political Appointees and Career Executives: The Democracy-Bureaucracy Nexus." In *Agenda for Execellence: Public Service in America*, edited by Patricia W. Ingraham and Donald F. Kettl. Chatham, N.J.: Chatham House Publishers, 1992.

Pincus, William. "The Opposition to the Senior Civil Service." *Public Administration Review* 18 (Autumn 1958): 324–31.

Pollock, Ross. *Executives for Government: Central Issues of Federal Personnel Administration.* Washington, D.C.: Brookings Institution, 1957.

Presidential Documents. Washington, D.C.: Government Printing Office.

President's Commission on Compensation of Career Federal Executives. *Report.* Washington, D.C.: Government Printing Office, February 1988.

President's Private Sector Survey on Cost Control. *Report of the Task Force on Personnel Management.* Washington, D.C.: Government Printing Office, 1983.

Presthus, Robert. "Decline of the Generalist Myth." *Public Administration Review* 24 (December 1964): 211–16.

Putnam, Robert B. "The Political Attitudes of Senior Civil Servants in Western Europe: A Preliminary Report." Ann Arbor: Institute of Public Policies Discussion Paper 36, University of Michigan, 1972.

Reimer, Everett. "The Case against the Senior Civil Service." *Personnel Administration* 19 (March–April 1956): 31–40.

Ridley, Frederick F., ed. *Specialists and Generalists.* New York: Barnes & Noble, 1968.

Riggs, Fred W. "Bureaucratic Links between Administration and Politics." In *Handbook of Comparative and Development Public Administration,* edited by Ali Farazmand. New York: Marcel Dekker, 1991.

———. "Why Has Bureaucracy Not Smothered Democracy in America?" Occasional Paper series. Section on International and Comparative Administration, American Society of Public Administration, October 12, 1992.

Rohr, John. *To Run a Constitution: The Legitimacy of the Administrative State.* Lawrence: University of Kansas Press, 1986.

Rosen, Bernard. "Crises in the U.S. Civil Service." *Public Administration Review* 46 (May–June 1986): 207–14.

———. "Effective Continuity of U.S. Government Operations in Jeopardy." *Public Administration Review* 43 (September–October 1983): 383–92.

———. "Uncertainty in the Senior Executive Service." *Public Administration Review* 41 (March–April 1981): 203–11.

Rosen, Howard. *Servants of the People: The Uncertain Future of the Federal Civil Service.* Salt Lake City: Olympus Publishing Co., 1985.

Rosenau, Pauline Marie. *Post-Modernism and the Social Sciences.* Princeton, N.J.: Princeton University Press, 1992.

Rothman, Stanley, Howard Scarrow, and Martin Schain. *European Society and Politics.* St. Paul, Minn.: West Publishing Co., 1976.

Schlesinger, Arthur M., Jr. *The Age of Jackson.* Boston: Little, Brown & Co., 1946.

Seidman, Harold, and Robert Gilmour. *Politics, Position, and Power: From the Positive to the Regulatory State.* 4th ed. New York: Oxford University Press, 1986.

Selznick, Philip. *TVA and the Grass Roots: A Study in the Sociology of Formal Organizations.* Berkeley and Los Angeles: University of California Press, 1949.

Senior Executives Association. *Proposal for a National Civil Service Academy.* Mimeographed. Washington, D.C.: Senior Executives Association, October 21, 1985.

Smith, Brian. "The United Kingdom." In *Public Administration in Developed Democracies: A Comparative Study,* edited by Donald C. Rowat. New York: Marcel Dekker, 1988.

Smith, Bruce L.R., ed. *The Higher Civil Service in Europe and Canada: Lessons for the United States.* Washington, D.C.: Brookings Institution, 1984.

Somers, Herman M. "The Federal Bureaucracy and the Change of Administration." *American Political Science Review* 48 (March 1954): 131–51.

———. "Some Reservations about the Senior Civil Service." *Personnel Administration* 19 (January–February 1956): 10–18.

Stahl, O. Glenn. *Public Personnel Administration.* 5th ed. New York: Harper & Row, 1962.

Stanley, David T. *The Higher Civil Service: An Evaluation of Federal Personnel Practices.* Washington, D.C.: Brookings Institution, 1964.

Stanley, David T., Dean E. Mann, and James W. Doig. *Men Who Govern: A Biographical Profile of Federal Political Executives.* Washington, D.C.: Brookings Institution, 1967.

Steinberg, David I. *The Republic of Korea: Economic Transformation and Social Change.* Boulder, Colo.: Westview Press, 1989.

Subramanian, V. "A Socio-Historical Overview." In *Public Administration in Developed Democracies: A Comparative Study,* edited by Donald C. Rowat. New York: Marcel Dekker, 1988.

Suleiman, Ezra N. "From Right to Left: Bureaucracy and Politics in France." In *Bureaucrats and Policy Making: A Comparative Overview,* edited by Ezra N. Suleiman. New York: Holmes & Meier, 1984.

———. *Politics, Power, and Bureaucracy in France: The Administrative Elite.* Princeton, N.J.: Princeton University Press, 1974.

Sun, Yat-sen. *Sun Yat-sen: His Political and Social Ideals,* translated by Leonard S. Hsu. University Park, Los Angeles: University of Southern California Press, 1933.

Suttmeier, Richard P. "The *Gikan* Question in Japanese Government: Bureaucratic Curiosity or Institutional Failure." *Asian Survey* 18 (October 1978): 1046–66.

Tashiro, Ku. "Japan." *In Public Administration in Developed Democracies: A Comparative Study*, edited by Donald C. Rowat. New York: Marcel Dekker, 1988.

Telford, Fred. *Principles of Public Personnel Administration*, edited by Charles P. Messick and William W. Boyer. Newark: University of Delaware, 1976.

Teng, Ssu-yu. "Chinese Influence on the Western Examination System." *Harvard Journal of Asiatic Studies* 7 (1943): 267–312.

Thompson, Frank J., ed. *Classics of Public Personnel Policy*. 2d ed. Oak Park, Ill.: Moore Publishing Co., 1991.

Tocqueville, Alexis de. *Democracy in America*. New York: Vintage, 1990.

U.S. Bureau of Executive Manpower, Civil Service Commission. *Administrative History of Federal Executive Manpower Management*. Mimeographed. Washington, D.C.: Bureau of Executive Manpower, Civil Service Commission, March 1971.

———. *Career/Non-Career Executives*. Draft study. February 1, 1971. Office of Personnel Management, Washington, D.C.

———. *Characteristics of the Federal Executive*. Washington, D.C.: Government Printing Office, November 1969.

———. "Considerations in Implementing Proposed Rule IX, a Preliminary Appraisal." Typescript. August 28, 1964. Office of Personnel Management, Washington, D.C.

———. "Draft of Form Letter to Heads of Agencies from John W. Macy, Jr., Chairman, Civil Service Commission." June 1, 1966. Office of Personnel Management, Washington, D.C.

———. *Draft Proposal for an Executive Order to Establish Executive Assignments*. Multilithed. August 19, 1964. Office of Personnel Management, Washington, D.C.

———. *The Executive Inventory, Questions and Answers for Executives*. May 1967. Office of Personnel Management, Washington, D.C.

———. *Extra-Governmental Mobility and Career Patterns of Federal Execu-*

tives. Draft study. June 1, 1971. Office of Personnel Management, Washington, D.C.

———. *History of the Executive Assignment System.* Miltilithed. Undated. Office of Personnel Management, Washington, D.C.

———. *Impact of Change of Administration on Non-Career Executives and Positions, 1968–1969.* Draft study. January 1971. Office of Personnel Management, Washington, D.C.

———. *Inter-Agency Mobility among Federal Executives.* Draft study. March 17, 1971. Office of Personnel Management, Washington, D.C.

———. *Staffing for GS-13 thru 18.* Memorandum from Nicholas J. Oganovic through Warren B. Irons to the Commission, March 31, 1964. Office of Personnel Management, Washington, D.C.

———. "Notes on Meeting of February 15, 1964, on the Upper Career Service." Dittoed. Office of Personnel Management, Washington, D.C.

———. *Rate of Advancement.* Draft study. June 8, 1971. Office of Personnel Management, Washington, D.C.

———. *The Supergrade Scientist.* Draft study. December 15, 1970. Office of Personnel Management, Washington, D.C.

U.S. Bureau of Executive Personnel, Civil Service Commission. *Executive Personnel in the Federal Service.* Washington, D.C.: Government Printing Office, 1977.

U.S. Bureau of the Budget. "The Senior Civil Service: Compilation of Background Material for a Conference Held in Bethesda, Md., December 5, 1956." November 21, 1956. Office of Management and Budget, Washington, D.C.

U.S. Civil Service Commission. *1954 Annual Report: 71st Report, Fiscal Year Ended June 30, 1954.* Washington, D.C.: Government Printing Office, 1955.

———. *Biography of an Ideal: The Diamond Anniversary History of the Federal Civil Service.* Washington, D.C.: Government Printing Office, 1959.

———. *Career Executive Board Records.* Archives Collection, Office of Personnel Management, Washington, D.C.

———. *The Federal Executive Service: A Proposal for Improving Federal Executive Manpower Management.* Washington, D.C.: Civil Service Commission, February 1971.

———. *Senior Civil Service: Official Documents and Background Papers,*

1957–1958. Vol. 2. Archives Collection, Office of Personnel Management, Washington, D.C.

U.S. Code.

U.S. Code of Federal Regulations.

U.S. Commission on Executive, Legislative, and Judicial Salaries. *The Quiet Crisis: Report of the 1984–85 Commission on Executive, Legislative, and Judicial Salaries.* Washington, D.C., July 29, 1985.

U.S. Commission on Organization of the Executive Branch of the Government. *Personnel and Civil Service, A Report to the Congress.* Washington, D.C.: Government Printing Office, 1955.

———. *Personnel Management: A Report to the Congress.* Washington, D.C.: Government Printing Office, February 1949.

———. *Task Force Report on Personnel and Civil Service.* Washington, D.C.: Government Printing Office, February 1955.

U.S. Congress. House. *Closing Report of Wage and Salary Survey, prepared by the Personnel Classification Board.* 71st Congress, 3d Session. H. Doc. 771. Washington, D.C.: Government Printing Office, 1931.

———. *The Federal Executive Service: Recommendations of the President of the United States.* For Use of the Committee on Post Office and Civil Service. 92d Congress, 1st Session. Committee Print 3. February 3, 1971. Washington, D.C.: Government Printing Office, 1971.

———. *Report of the Civil Service Commission to the President.* 43rd Congress, 1st Session. Exec. Doc. 221. April 15, 1874. Washington, D.C.: Government Printing Office, 1874.

———. Committee on Post Office and Civil Service. Hearings on H.R. 11280. *Civil Service Reform.* 95th Congress, 2d Session. March 14, 21; April 4, 5, 6, 11, 12, 28; May 8, 12, 15, 22, and 23, 1978. Washington, D.C.: Government Printing Office, 1978.

———. Subcommittee on Manpower and Civil Service. Hearings on H.R. 3807. *Federal Executive Service.* 92d Congress, 2d Session. April 18, 21, 25, 1972. Washington, D.C.: Government Printing Office, 1972.

———. Hearings. *Request for Supergrade Positions.* 92d Congress, 2d Session. March 7, 1972. Washington, D.C.: Government Printing Office, 1972.

———. Subcommittee on Manpower Utilization. *Manpower Utilization in the Federal Government (Career Executive Program).* 85th Congress, 2d

Session. April 30, May 6, 7, 8, 13 and 14, 1958. Washington, D.C.: Government Printing Office, 1958.

———. Joint Select Committee on Retrenchment. *Report: Civil Service of the United States.* 40th Congress, 2d Session. H. Rept. 47. May 25, 1868. Washington, D.C.: Government Printing Office, 1868.

U.S. Congress. Senate. *Administration of the Civil Service System.* Report to the Committee on Post Office and Civil Service. 85th Congress, 1st Session. Committee Print 2. Washington, D.C.: Government Printing Office, 1957.

———. Committee on Governmental Affairs. Hearings on S. 2640, S. 2707, and S. 2830. *Civil Service Reform Act of 1978 and Reorganization Plan No. 2 of 1978.* 95th Congress, 2d Session. April 6, 7, 10, 12, 13, 19, 20, 27; May 3, 4, 5, and 9, 1978. Washington, D.C.: Government Printing Office, 1978.

———. Committee on Post Office and Civil Service. Hearing. *Federal Executive Service.* 92d Congress, 1st Session. May 10, 1971. Washington, D.C.: Government Printing Office, 1972.

———. Committee on Post Office and Civil Service. *Federal Executive Service.* 92d Congress, 1st Session. Rep. 92-864. June 15, 1972. Washington, D.C.: Government Printing Office, 1972.

U.S. Congressional Record.

U.S. Federal Laboratory Review Panel. *Report of the White House Science Council.* Washington, D.C.: Government Printing Office, May 1983.

U.S. Federal Personnel Management Project. *Final Staff Report, Final Report,* and *Appendices.* Washington, D.C.: Civil Service Commission, July 1977–February 1978.

U.S. Federal Personnel Manual. Washington, D.C.: Government Printing Office.

U.S. Federal Register. Washington, D.C.: Government Printing Office.

U.S. General Accounting Office. *Evaluation of Proposals to Alter the Structure of the Senior Executive Service.* (GAO/GGD-86-14, 1985).

———. *Managing Human Resources: Greater OPM Leadership Needed to Address Critical Challenges.* (GAO/GGD-89-1989).

———. *Senior Executive Service: Agencies' Use of the Candidate Development Program.* (GAO/GGD-86-93, 1986).

———. *Senior Executive Service: Answers to Selected Salary-Related Questions.* (GAO/GGD-87-36FS, 1987).

———. *Senior Executive Service: Executives' Perspectives on Their Federal Service.* (GAO/GGD-88-109FS, 1988).

———. *Senior Executive Service: The Extent to Which SES Members Have Used the Sabbatical Program.* (GAO/GGD-88-90, 1988).

———. *Senior Executive Service: Reasons Why Career Members Left in Fiscal Year 1985.* (GAO/GGD-87-106FS, 1987).

U.S. Library of Congress. Congressional Research Service. *History of Civil Service Merit Systems of the United States and Selected Foreign Countries, Together with Executive Reorganization Studies and Personnel Recommendations.* 94th Congress, 2d Session. Committee Print 94-29, compiled for the Subcommittee on Manpower and Civil Service of the House Committee on Post Office and Civil Service. Washington, D.C.: Government Printing Office, December 31, 1976.

———. Legislative Reference Service. *Digest of Public General Bills.* Washington, D.C.: Government Printing Office, 1957.

U.S. National Institutes of Health. *Report of the Committee on Pay and Personnel Systems on Intramural Research.* Washington, D.C.: National Institutes of Health, May 1983.

U.S. Office of Personnel Management. *Annual Report on the Status of the Senior Executive Service.* Washington, D.C.: Office of Executive Personnel, 1988.

———. *The Status of the Senior Executive Service 1990.* Washington, D.C.: Office of Personnel Management, 1991.

———. *The Status of the Senior Executive Service 1991.* Washington, D.C.: Office of Personnel Management, 1992.

Van Riper, Paul P. *History of the United States Civil Service.* Evanston, Ill.: Row, Peterson & Co. 1958.

———. "The Senior Civil Service and the Career System." *Public Administration Review* 18 (Summer 1958): 189–200.

Waldo, Dwight. *The Enterprise of Public Administration.* Novato, Calif.: Chandler & Sharp Publishers, 1980.

Warner, W. Lloyd, Paul P. Van Riper, Norman H. Martin, and Orvis F. Collins. *The American Federal Executive: A Study of the Social and Personal Characteristics of the Civilian and Military Leaders of the United States Federal Government.* New Haven, Conn.: Yale University Press, 1963.

Washington Post.

Weber, Max. *From Max Weber: Essays in Sociology.* Translated by H.H. Gerth and C. Wright Mills. New York: Oxford University Press, 1946.

White, Leonard D. "The Case for the Senior Civil Service." *Personnel Administration* 19 (January-February 1956): 4–9.

————. *The Federalists: A Study in Administrative History, 1789–1801.* New York: Macmillan Co., 1948.

————. *The Jacksonians: A Study in Administrative History, 1829–1861.* New York: Macmillan Co., 1954.

————. *The Jeffersonians: A Study in Administrative History, 1801–1829.* New York: Macmillan Co., 1951.

————. *The Republican Era: A Study in Administrative History, 1869–1901.* New York: Macmillan Co., 1958.

————. "The Senior Civil Service." *Public Administration Review* 15 (Autumn 1955): 237–43.

Wilkinson, Rupert. *Gentlemanly Power, British Leadership and the Public School Tradition: A Comparative Study in the Making of Rulers.* London: Oxford University Press, 1964.

Will, George. *Restoration: Congress, Term Limits, and the Recovery of Deliberative Democracy.* New York: Free Press, 1992.

Wilson, Patricia A. "Power, Politics, and Other Reasons Why Senior Executives Leave the Federal Government." *Public Administration Review* 54 (January-February, 1994): 12–19.

Wilson, Woodrow. "The Stuy of Administration." *Political Science Quarterly* 2 (June 1887): 197–222.

Woodruff, Philip. *The Men Who Ruled India.* 2 vols. New York: Shocken Books, 1953.

Young, Joseph. "Career Executive Plan Drawing Fire." *Washington Evening Star,* May 1, 1958.

————. "Tax Break Eyed for Top Grades." *Washington Evening Star,* May 11, 1971.

Zhang, Cheng F. "Public Administration in China." In *Public Administration in China,* edited by Miriam K. Mills and Stuart S. Nagel. Westport, Conn.: Greenwood Press, 1993.

Index

142, 145; Senior Executive Service developed by, xi, 101, 103
Causey, Mike, 88–89, 91
Central Intelligence Agency (CIA), 98
Chang, Y. Z., 8–9
Chapman, Brian, 6
Chen Committee (National Institutes of Health), 122
China, People's Republic of, 13–14
Chinese civil service: ancient, 6–11, 17, 20; modern, 13–14
civil servants: as career employees, 22–24, 39, 66–69, 133; characteristics of, 21–26, 66–67, 71–72; classification of, 22, 25–26; executive development programs for, 105, 110, 116–19, 155–57; flexibility of job assignments for, 39, 105; as immobile specialists, 22, 24–25, 34; impact of administration transitions on, 69–70; influence on policy, 22–23, 34, 114–16; morale during Eisenhower administration, 35–38, 43, 49, 55–56; morale in Senior Executive Service, 109–10, 113; performance appraisals for, 105; performance awards and bonuses for, 105, 112–13, 136, 145; productivity of, 136; rate of advancement of, 70; recruitment of, 29, 33–34, 40–41, 43, 124, 132, 155–57; retirement of, 40, 109, 112; rights under Career Executive Program proposals, 48–49; sabbaticals for, 117–18; salary of, 27–34, 39–40, 85, 88, 98–99, 106, 110, 112–14, 119, 127–28, 132, 162; status of, 125
civil service: career versus general systems of, 68–69, 173n8; origin of the term, 9. See also British civil service; Chinese civil service; French civil service; higher civil service; United States civil service
civil service, elite. See higher civil service
Civil Service Commission (CSC); administration of Career Executive Program by, 45–49, 52–53; authority of, 27, 30–32, 45, 51, 56–57, 63, 73–74, 77–79, 139; Bureau of Executive Manpower, 56, 62, 65–69, 73, 76–77, 79; chair as liaison with president, 36; criticisms of, 131, 133; Departmental Circular no. 620, 31; development of Executive Assignment System by, 59–62; Eisenhower's control of, 36, 45; established by Grant (1871), 17; executive director of, 36; Federal Executive Service proposed by, 83–91; Interagency Advisory

Group, 42, 46; pilot program for Senior Civil Service proposed by, 44; presidential control of, 36; study of civil service requested by Nixon, 79–83; supervision of Federal Personnel Management Project by, 94
Civil Service Reform Act (CSRA) of 1978: congressional debate on, 101–03, 117; documentation on, 138; passage of, 5, 21, 103, 106–08
Classification Act of 1949, 30–32. See also Position
Classification Act of 1923; 1955 amendment to, 30
class specifications, 28
Clerical, Administrative, and Fiscal Service, 27
Clerical-Mechanical Service, 27
Cleveland, Grover, 26
Clinton, Bill, 3–4, 127, 161–62
Cohen, Michael, 25
Colbert, Jean-Baptiste, 147
Collins, Orvis F., 65
Commerce Department, U.S., 33
Commission on Organization of the Executive Branch of the Government (Second Hoover Commission); Senior Civil Service proposed by, 38–50, 53, 60, 71–72, 74; Task Force on Personnel and Civil Service, 38, 41
Committee for Economic Development, 60, 140
Communist party, Chinese, 13
compensation (salary), 27–34, 39–40, 85, 88, 98–99, 106, 110, 112–14, 119, 127–28, 132, 162
Confucius, 17
Congress, U.S., 51–53. See also House of Representatives, U.S.; Senate, U.S.
Congressional Budget Reform and Impoundment Control Act, 93
Conley, William D., 95 (table)
Constitution, U.S., 158
Continental model (of higher civil service), 18, 100, 130, 132–34, 139, 143, 148
Conway, James R. V., 96 (table)
Cooke, David O., 96 (table)
Coolidge, Calvin, 26
corporate perspective, 135–37, 139–40
Coupal, Joseph R., Jr., 95 (table)
CSC. See Civil Service Commission (CSC)
Cultural Revolution, Chinese, 13
Custodial Service, 27